FORTUNE AND FOLLY

FORTUNE & FOLLY

THE WEIRD AND WONDERFUL LIFE OF THE SOUTH'S MOST ECCENTRIC MILLIONAIRE

⇻ SARA A. H. BUTLER

Published in Association with Georgia Humanities

The University of Georgia Press   *Athens, Georgia*

Published by the University of Georgia Press
Athens, Georgia 30602
www.ugapress.org
© 2023 by Sara A. H. Butler
All rights reserved
Designed by Erin Kirk
Set in Minion Pro and Brighton Spring
Printed and bound by Sherdian Books, Inc.
The paper in this book meets the guidelines for permanence
and durability of the Committee on Production Guidelines for
Book Longevity of the Council on Library Resources.

Most University of Georgia Press titles are
available from popular e-book vendors.

Printed in the United States of America
23   24   25   26   27   P   5   4   3   2   1

Library of Congress Cataloging-in-Publication Data

Names: Butler, Sara A. H., author.
Title: Fortune and folly : the weird and wonderful life of the South's
    most eccentric millionaire / Sara A. H. Butler.
Other titles: Weird and wonderful life of the South's most eccentric
    millionaire
Description: Athens, Georgia : The University of Georgia Press,
    [2023]
Identifiers: LCCN 2023031440 (print) | LCCN 2023031441 (ebook) |
    ISBN 9780820365237 (paperback) | ISBN 9780820365251 (epub)
    | ISBN 9780820365244 (pdf)
Subjects: LCSH: Candler, Asa, Jr., 1880–1953 | Candler, Asa,
    Jr., 1880–1953—Homes and haunts. | Businessmen—
    Georgia—Atlanta—Biography. | Briarcliff Mansion (Atlanta,
    Ga.) | Chandler family. | Atlanta Ga.)—Biography. |
    Millionaires—Georgia—Atlanta—Biography.
Classification: LCC F294.A853 C434 2023 (PRINT) | LCC F294.A853
    (EBOOK) | DDC 975.8/042092 [B]—dc23/eng/20230801
LC record available at https://lccn.loc.gov/2023031440
LC ebook record available at https://lccn.loc.gov/2023031441

To Jason, Jacob, and Owen for giving me room to explore,

to Alicia and Victoria for adventuring with me into the past,

and to everyone else who endured endless anecdotes

all along my journey.

But most of all, to Buddie.

Contents

Foreword

Just outside of downtown Atlanta, about five miles east on Ponce de Leon Avenue, hugging the line between Fulton and DeKalb counties, sits the neighborhood of Druid Hills. Home to Emory University, Druid Hills was once a planned community for the wealthy elite and is now an active, vibrant, affluent neighborhood.

Near the western edge of Druid Hills runs a busy two-lane street called Briarcliff Road. It starts in the northeast at an intersection with La Vista Road and ends just south of Ponce, where it turns into Moreland Avenue.

If you drive south on Briarcliff Road, you might notice the large, century-old houses on either side, interspersed with smaller bungalows and ranch homes, evidence of the evolution that the Atlanta suburbs have undergone over the years. You'll pass Briarcliff Apartments, Briarcliff Frame Shop, Briarcliff Paint, and Briarcliff Dentistry. In fact, the name Briarcliff appears on signs throughout the area.

Continuing south, just past a small side street named Briardale Lane, the view opens to the west. A long, rambling stone wall lines the sidewalk. Beyond the wall you may catch a glimpse of a towering, windowless industrial building and recognize it from the first season of *Stranger Things*, where a character named Sheriff Hopper found a girl floating in an isolation tank.

If you look quickly as you pass the main gate, you may see a house on a rise at the end of the meandering driveway. Not just a house, this is a mansion, a vast expanse of tan brick and white columns overlooking an extensive lawn dotted with magnolia trees.

Briarcliff Mansion as seen from the front lawn, circa 2021. Photo by the author.

The windows are boarded up. The walls rise from a gnarled sea of overgrown grass and weeds. A rusting dumpster in the cracked parking lot out front obstructs the view of a trellis on the side lawn.

This is Briarcliff Mansion, infamous among local urban explorers and aficionados of abandoned architecture. Now owned by Emory University and used mostly as a filming location for major movies like *First Man* and the TV series *The Vampire Diaries* and *Doom Patrol*, Briarcliff Mansion is the epicenter of a swirl of rumors, misinformation, and mythology about the man who built it, the second son and namesake of Coca-Cola founder and mega-millionaire Asa Griggs Candler.

Trying to untangle the history of Asa Candler Jr. requires sifting through myths that have persisted throughout the decades. In order for his history to be complete, cohesive, and accurate, the anecdotal stories must be scrutinized and disassembled. If one assumes truth in the mythology that was left in his wake, his humanity is lost. Teasing out truth from tall tales is critical in order to understand who he was.

DISCOVERING THE WRONG ASA

In 2015, I visited that abandoned mansion on Emory University's satellite campus. I knew very little about its history, just the few details that have remained in circulation. From a quick browse of the Internet, I learned the following:

1. There once was a good and decent businessman named Asa Griggs Candler who started Coca-Cola.
2. He had an eccentric, alcoholic son who built a mansion, squandered his money, and sold the house to the state before he died.
3. Briarcliff Mansion became a mental health and addiction treatment facility that remained active for thirty years before shutting down in the 1990s.
4. And by the way, there may be elephants buried on the property.

I decided to visit the mansion to see it for myself and was instantly captivated. Briarcliff is an idiosyncratic enigma. It's self-consciously grandiose, built to present maximum grandeur to the neighboring properties. Even now, it towers over the landscape, set far back from the road behind a filled-in, overgrown pool. The face of the structure is stitched together where a music hall was added to the main house and the bricks don't quite match up. The addition created odd turns to the perimeter, and a pair of strange courtyards can be seen only from above. Greenhouses around the back remain standing, beautiful glass structures that still contain fixtures that once nurtured a botanical garden's worth of exotic plants. A multicar garage stretches along the rear driveway, and dormer windows dotting the roof reveal that the mansion's top floor was once a ballroom. What on earth was this decaying estate doing smack in the middle of Druid Hills, which, as an outsider, I perceived as simply a residential suburb of average homes?

It turns out that Briarcliff is just one of several mansions left behind by the Coca-Cola clan. As I read about the other Candler homes, I uncovered more questions than answers. The most pressing, or so I thought at the time, was why the property was called Briarcliff. Which came first, Briarcliff Mansion or Briarcliff Road and neighborhood? What about the Briarcliff Apartments at the intersection of North Highland and Ponce de Leon avenues? What about all the other businesses, housing units, and side streets bearing the name Briarcliff?

The life and homes of Asa Candler Sr. are well documented, so the world isn't hurting for insights into his legacy. His oldest son, Charles Howard, the second president of Coca-Cola, left a mansion and a legacy too. Their homes also have names, and the origins of those names are known. Asa Sr.'s younger three children, Lucy, Walter, and William, all had mansions in the area with well-documented property names. But why is Briarcliff named Briarcliff?

I got my answer, but it turns out that to understand the mansion, I had to understand the man. Virtually all the documentation about the life of Asa Candler was about the senior Asa, the "right" Asa. The existing documentation of the junior Asa's life often viewed him through the lens of the elder Asa's story, or as a sidenote, or even as a punch line. Over the decades, Asa Jr. and Briarcliff had become exaggerated, cartoonish caricatures of themselves, and those caricatures were all you'd find if you went looking. I decided to dig into Briarcliff's history out of sheer frustration when I kept finding the same recycled anecdotes repeated in every contemporary resource. I wanted to understand Asa Jr.'s story through his own lens, not through his father's, and not blurred by myth and mystery.

I now have a deeper understanding of who the "wrong" Asa Candler was, where his story has been lost or twisted, what's true in the tales that circulate today, and the areas where Atlanta's history deserves an update.

Allow me to introduce you to the real Asa Griggs Candler Jr.

→ PART 1

THE EARLY YEARS

*I am tired of boarding houses having lived
at them ever since I was eight years old.*[1]

CHAPTER 1

A Boy Named Buddie

Asa Candler Jr.'s story starts before the existence of most of the luxuries we enjoy today. It starts before modern transportation like automobiles, bicycles, and airplanes, although they'll each play a role before we're through. It starts just four years after Alexander Graham Bell invented the telephone. It starts only slightly after toilets moved from the outside to the inside of middle-class homes, and just after the first incandescent lightbulb was invented. The 1870s was a busy decade for new technologies.

During the Gilded Age, fresh ideas and inventions fueled a growing economy, and men with names like Carnegie, Rockefeller, and Vanderbilt made inconceivable fortunes from railroads, steel, oil, and banking. "Robber barons," their critics said. But to starry-eyed small-town entrepreneurs who were looking to claw their way out of poverty, this was an era of endless opportunity.

The story starts with Asa Jr.'s father, Asa Griggs Candler (1851–1929), the eighth of eleven children born in the small town of Villa Rica, Georgia, about thirty miles west of Atlanta. His father, Samuel Charles Candler (1809–1873), was a former Georgia state legislator and a successful merchant before the Civil War swept through the South. His mother was Martha Bernetta Beall Candler (1819–1897). As a result of the economic downturn following the war, Asa and his siblings had few advantages growing up. But they learned the necessity of hard work and were motivated to make successes of themselves.

Asa's brother Milton Anthony Candler (1837–1909) became a U.S. representative for the state of Georgia. Florence Julia Candler (Harris) (1842–1926) was a teacher who ran her own school. William Beall Candler (1847–1928) served as mayor of Villa Rica. Warren Akin Candler (1857–1941) became a Methodist bishop and served as president of Emory College. John Slaughter Candler (1861–1941) became the chief justice of the Georgia Supreme Court. The other siblings were Ezekiel Samuel Candler (1838–1915), Noble Daniel Candler (1841–1887), Sarah Justina Candler (Willard) (1845–1921), Elizabeth Frances Candler (Dobbs) (1849–1922), and Samuel Charles Candler Jr. (1855–1911). The Candlers had the privilege of extended family and social connections in the right places, as well as ambition, a powerful work ethic, and the backing of a societal structure that was designed to put success within reach for folks like them.

Given his family's successes later in life, if you trace Asa's path from the time he left home at fifteen to the launch of the Coca-Cola empire thirty-six years later, it looks as straight and true as an arrow. But fortune didn't simply lay itself at his feet. He took opportunities as they arose, and his shrewd instinct for wise investments served him well. He didn't stumble into success. He learned the value of establishing relationships with other business owners, and the importance of innovation if one wants to build a fortune from a kernel of an idea. He was intelligent, ambitious, and creative, a powerful combination that led to financial bounty.

In the early years Asa labored, networked, and landed a job in the lucrative pharmacy trade. He diligently studied as a shop assistant, always with an eye on creating something for himself, all on his own. And in those days, the biggest opportunity for an aspiring pharmacist was in the patent medicine game.

"Patent medicine" was a blanket term for proprietary concoctions that were bottled by pharmacies and sold as cure-alls. For independent pharmacists, the exclusive sale of a popular patent medicine could be like striking gold. With mixtures often made primarily of alcohol and occasionally incorporating narcotics, like cocaine and heroin, and peddling unsubstantiated claims about poorly understood ailments, pharmacists flimflammed their customers by selling dubious blends of herbal ingredients. Patent medicines were touted as magnificent medicinal marvels that could cure everything from catarrh to "dispepsia," from tetter to chilblains, and from rheumatism to "female troubles." If you're ever rummaging around in an antiques shop and find an old glass bottle with a faded paper label listing suspicious ingredients, you're in the presence of patent medicine. It was all the rage in the late 1800s and early 1900s, a time when practitioners based their decisions on the Hippocratic theory of the four humors. If something ailed you, it was attributed to black bile, yellow bile, blood, or phlegm. Patent medicine often claimed to treat ailments by addressing an imbalance in one of the four humors. But really, it got you drunk.

This bears mentioning because inevitably any conversation about Coca-Cola's history raises one universal question: didn't it originally contain cocaine? Yes it did, because it started out as a patent medicine, and cocaine was considered OK at the time. But Coca-Cola didn't include alcohol. Asa Candler couldn't abide drinking, so that was where he drew the line.

After he settled in Atlanta, then a growing commercial center built around a railroad hub, Asa took a job at a pharmacy owned by a druggist named George Jefferson Howard, the father of his future wife, Lucy Elizabeth Howard (1859–1919). Her mother was Maria Louisa Goldsmith Howard. Asa worked his way up the trade until he could open his own shop. But to be clear, he wasn't a chemist, a doctor, or a healer. He was a businessman. He didn't invent patent medicines; he purchased them and put his marketing talent to work. Before discovering Coca-Cola, he bought the rights to Bucklen's Arnica Salve, King's New Discovery, De-Lec-Ta-Lave, Everlasting Cologne, and Electric Bitters.

Meanwhile he was also creating a life for himself and his young family. Asa and Lucy Elizabeth's first child was Charles Howard (1878–1957), named in honor of Lucy Elizabeth's father. Asa Griggs Jr. (1880–1953) came along next, followed by Lucy Beall (1883–1962), Walter Turner (1885–1967), and William Beall (1890–1936).

When Asa Jr. arrived in 1880, Asa Sr. wasn't a big man yet. He was a twenty-nine-year-old working father who had big dreams and a growing family. He now had two sons to leave a legacy for, and he was driven to build something that would create advantages for them that he'd missed out on as a child.

Asa Sr. poured himself into everything he did as an entrepreneur, a man of faith, a son, a brother, a husband, and a father. Of all the demands placed on him during that period, none had stakes higher than the pressures he applied to himself. He worked long hours at the pharmacy and came home to whatever his children had been up to and to the joys and stresses of Lucy Elizabeth's day as she ran a busy household on what was essentially a mini-farm.

Letters on file at Emory University's Stuart A. Rose Manuscript, Archives and Rare Book Library reveal that Asa Sr. was a worrier, anxious about the health of his family, and his writing reveals introspective moodiness during which he brooded about the potentially bleak outcomes of the stressors in his life. We look back on Asa Candler Sr. as a confident, skilled businessman who built a capitalist legacy that still captivates historians to this day. But in the 1880s, that success was not inevitable.

In 1886, Asa Sr. sampled a fizzy drink concocted from a syrup that was invented by a fellow Georgia native, Dr. John Pemberton. Touted as an alcohol-free brain tonic and headache cure during the early years of Georgia's temperance movement, Coca-Cola appealed to Asa Candler, a staunch teetotaler who suffered from chronic headaches. As a syrup, it was like any other bottled medicine. Combined with carbonated water, it came to life as a delicious and refreshing fountain drink. In discovering this new, unmarketed product, Asa had struck gold, although he had a long way to go to prove it.

He invested in Coca-Cola alongside several other men, and sales of the promising product started to take off. In 1888, Dr. Pemberton and his son sought to sell off the formula and cash out, and Asa moved quickly to obtain a controlling interest in both the recipe and the branding. By the end of August, the transaction was complete. Coca-Cola was his.

Asa Sr. knew from the start that he'd found something unique in Coca-Cola, a product with a huge potential market that could grow and flourish if he tended to it and nurtured it during its fledgling years. Doing so would require all of his attention. But Coca-Cola had competition for his attention: his eight-year-old namesake, who was known to family and friends as Buddie.

Buddie was into everything, causing trouble around the house and at school. Unlike his more reserved and compliant older brother, Howard, he felt no compulsion to obey, and he wasn't motivated to live up to anyone's expectations but his own. Family stories claim that his mother had her hands full managing a busy household while Asa Sr.'s attention was more and more occupied by his burgeoning business. By this time Lucy Elizabeth had a ten-year-old, an eight-year-old, a six-year-old, and a three-year-old. She also had her mother-in-law and a developmentally disabled brother-in-law to care for—and none of the modern conveniences we take for granted to lighten the load. Even with domestic help, she was stretched thin.

A high-spirited rascal of a son like Buddie would be a handful for any parent. But as he grew old enough to enter school, he became too much of a handful to manage on top of everything else, and too much of a drain on the family's energy. Asa Sr., who was now nearing forty, needed every ounce of his mental abilities focused on creating the juggernaut that he believed

Candler family portrait, circa 1895. *Left to right*: William, Asa Sr., Charles Howard, Walter, Lucy, Asa Jr., Lucy Elizabeth. Courtesy of Vanishing Georgia, Georgia Archives, University System of Georgia.

Coca-Cola could be, if he could only dedicate his attention to its growth over the crucial coming months.

On August 30, 1888—three days after Buddie's eighth birthday—Asa Sr. bought out his partners and took ownership of all Coca-Cola stock. His next order of business was to put little Buddie on a train bound for Cartersville, Georgia, a small town about forty miles northwest of Atlanta. Buddie had to go to make room for what history could consider another child of Asa Sr.: the Coca-Cola Company.

However, Buddie wasn't sent off into the wilderness to fend for himself. Cartersville was home to Florence Harris, née Candler, Asa Sr.'s older sister, who was called Sissie by the family. Back in 1870, when Asa Sr. had left his childhood home in Villa Rica to seek his fortune, he hadn't headed to Atlanta right away. Instead, he had relocated to Cartersville to live with Sissie and her husband, retired Colonel James Harris, and sought opportunities that Villa Rica couldn't offer. It was during his time with Sissie that he found a job at one of the local pharmacies, and there he learned the pharmacist's trade and built the foundation of his keen business sense. Sissie provided shelter and comfort during Asa Sr.'s formative years, and they remained close throughout their lives.

With a population of approximately three thousand residents, Cartersville was about one-twentieth the size of Atlanta in 1890.[2] Like many small southern towns, Cartersville grew up alongside the railroad tracks that connected it to larger markets. It had one main street that sprouted businesses a few blocks to the west and a mere block or two to the north and south. When Buddie joined them, Sissie and James lived a third of a mile west of the depot on Bartow Street with a young servant named Richard Turnipseed.[3]

An educator by trade, Sissie ran a private school on her property, which seemed like a perfect fit for her unruly nephew. Asa Sr. could trust her to provide both the discipline and the education his young son needed without having to seek help outside the family. But there was one hitch: the school was an all-girls academy, the West End Institute for Females. No matter, Aunt Sissie was willing to take on her nephew and flex the enrollment to include one male.

And so Buddie stayed there while all his other siblings remained at home—except for Lucy who, according to school transcripts, attended West End in Cartersville for one year.[4] The *Report of the Commissioner of Education* in 1891 shows that the school added a male teacher and began accepting additional boys in 1889. Boys were one-third of the total roster that year. But of 137 students, only 10 were on a college track.[5] Asa Sr. ensured that his son was one of them.

Although stories claim that Aunt Sissie's husband was a no-nonsense man, he made special exceptions for Buddie's unique brand of nonsense. Neither James nor Sissie was hard on Buddie, although they did expect him to perform well in classes and send home good marks. But he continued to find trouble. Family lore says he was a class clown who shot dice with boys in town and that Uncle James taught him to smoke to pass the time quietly. However, that didn't stop Buddie from leaving the property and doing what he pleased.[6] Years later, he would say that his youth was spent in boarding houses.[7] Sure, he stayed with family, but it wasn't home.

Whether the stories of Buddie's troublemaking are all true or whether they're exaggerated to explain his later eccentricities is up to each researcher to decide, since little correspondence exists from that period to document his behavior. However, one family story claims he put his brother down a well at the family's Atlanta home.[8] Based on age and therefore size differences, this was likely William when he was very little, estimated between

1891 and 1895, which would suggest that Buddie continued to make trouble during his visits home between terms. Previous historians have reached a strong consensus that the broader oral history is true, and circumstantial evidence suggests that his parents treated him as someone with unique needs.[9] Certainly, he was enough of a handful to warrant sending him away, unlike their other children.

One can speculate about how Buddie felt about that arrangement, and later correspondence with his family provides evidence that he harbored some resentment toward his parents and perhaps even his siblings. Maybe that resentment would have faded away if he had been permitted to move home permanently after his time in Cartersville. In 1895, however, Buddie left the West End Institute and returned to Atlanta but was only allowed to stay for a few weeks before starting his journey in higher education. He was quickly sent away again, reinforcing the message that he was different from the others.

For my own son who bears my name & for whom I labor & work
& pray to deliberately disgrace me is more than I can bear.[1]

CHAPTER 2

In the Heart of Dear Old Emory

In the summer of 1895, Buddie bid the West End Institute farewell and moved home to Atlanta. It was a short stay. On August 27, he turned fifteen, and in early September he and Howard boarded a commuter train out of Union Station. They took a forty-mile, ninety-minute ride east around the base of Stone Mountain to Covington, Georgia. From there, they hopped aboard a horsecar into Oxford proper to begin the 1895–1896 school year at Emory College, where Buddie was a freshman and Howard was a sophomore. This sounds young by today's standards, but in those days a boy could enroll at Emory College as a sub-freshman as early as age fourteen.[2]

The train from Atlanta to Covington would have passed through dense Georgia forests, stopping in small towns on its way to the coast. Covington and Oxford shared a long, flared-roof passenger depot on Emory Street, which still stands today. Because the Georgia Railroad would not permit horsecars to cross the tracks, travelers had to step off the train onto the plat-form on the south side of the tracks, cross over, and board the local transport on the north side.[3] From there, the multipassenger horsecar rolled 1.3 miles due north into Oxford on street rails. For five cents a ride—or less with a student discount—one could sit in relative comfort next to mail and freight behind a pair of plodding mules. The shade and a slight breeze would have been a welcome reprieve from the summer heat.

The route took the Candler boys up Emory Street, the main thoroughfare of the tiny town, which existed mostly to support the college.[4] On their left was the campus where they would spend their days. Built around an oval with a tree-shaded lawn in the center, the original buildings included two opposing debate halls, Few Hall and Phi Gamma Hall, as well as the chapel and Language Hall. At the midpoint of the oval's south side, the towering, belfry-capped, redbrick building named Seney Hall was an iconic landmark. There were no dormitories on campus at the time, nor was there cafeteria service. Students looked to the townspeople of Oxford to provide room and board.

As the horsecar entered the stretch of road that served as the main street, the students passed the city hall and the Emmie Stewart Helping Hall, one of many off-campus boarding houses that served as student housing in lieu of dormitories. On the right, they passed D. T. Stone's store, a local hangout where students could buy a Coca-Cola and relax, or get their hair cut out back. Stone's was reportedly the first place in Oxford to have a telephone, so lonesome boys could call home from there. On the left, they passed Branham's store, Henderson's store, and the Yarbrough oak, where students lounged in the branches and studied for their classes. At the next intersection, the horsecar route took a left onto Fletcher Street and ended at the Car Barn on Wesley Street, where fresh mules waited and any remaining passengers climbed down and went on their way by foot.[5]

The intersection included Old Church, which held Methodist services and hosted the collegiate commencement ceremonies. If they turned right, the Candler boys would have walked up "the Hill" one rural block to the President's House on the corner of Wesley and West Soule streets, where their uncle Warren Akin Candler presided over the college. If they turned left, they would have walked south one and a half blocks to the edge of campus.

Emory was a fine Methodist school with a history dating back before the Civil War. Its male-only student body could choose one of three degree options: bachelor of arts (A.B.), bachelor of philosophy (B.Ph.), or bachelor of science (B.S.). Howard chose the A.B. track, which followed a challenging, classical education curriculum, and he delivered grades that pleased his father during his first year. Buddie started out seeking an A.B. but switched to a B.Ph. his sophomore year, which dropped the Greek requirement, and he still barely made it to graduation.

WARREN AKIN CANDLER

➔ Warren Candler (1857–1941) was the second-youngest brother of Asa Sr. Devoutly religious and ambitious, Warren attended Emory College and served the Methodist Episcopal Church, South, as a minister before accepting a position as the tenth president of Emory College. He and Asa Sr. shared a special relationship, and Asa Sr. often looked to his younger brother for spiritual guidance and fellowship.

Warren was a man of small stature and huge personality. He was a gifted orator and a strong-willed, opinionated figure in the church. He was eventually granted the title of bishop, but even before then he was a leader in the Methodist community. Warren was infinitely quotable and appreciated by Emory's student body; his unofficial nickname was "King Shorty" because he ruled over the institution like a monarch.[6] His word was law, and his status towered over all others at the school.

That said, he was no tyrant. Firsthand student accounts from his era as Emory's president paint a picture of a dynamic leader who expected obedience but granted clemency. The student-produced annual yearbook, the *Zodiac*, included many funny stories about the staff and friendly ribbing for the college's president. Memorable King Shorty quotes included:

- If you've got the itch, keep out of the crowd.
- Abomination of desolation standing in the place where it ought not.
- Because calomel is good for a purgative, there's no reason why we should use it as a dessert.
- A higher critic is like a "fice-dog" at the front gate.[7] I say to him: "Now here is a great big fact and if you don't get out of the way I'll knock you down with it." Then he drops his ears and the next thing you know he is in the back yard.[8]

For the first two years of Buddie's college life, he and Howard lived together at the President's House with Uncle Warren, Aunt Nettie, and cousins Anne, John, Warren Jr., and Samuel, but otherwise they lived the normal lives of students.[9] They wore school uniforms, which included a blue four-button coat with breast and hip pockets and a tall, wide-brimmed hat with a creased crown, similar in style to a Gus or a Stetson. All students attended worship at the campus chapel, and their classes included science, math, and Greek.

Students were encouraged to participate in athletics, although President Candler enacted a rule prohibiting intercollegiate sports. He wanted his students to be fit, not distracted by competition. But the most revered student organizations were the debate societies, Few and Phi Gamma, which gathered in the dedicated halls that faced each other across the quad and practiced the art of persuasion throughout the school year. President Candler was a Few man and was one of the faculty sponsors for the Few Society.

Unofficial activities included lounging in the shade of the obelisk at the center of the quad, strolling through the woods that lined the western edge of campus, hopping a horsecar into Covington to chat up the young women on the other side of town, illicitly smoking, and playing pranks. Lots of pranks.

Woe be to the freshman who accepted an invitation to go snipe hunting. Here's how the prank worked: upperclassmen would approach an unsuspecting freshman and ask him to join them for an evening of hunting snipe. Snipes, they would explain, were small, nocturnal, ground-dwelling birds that nested in the woods behind the chapel. The freshman would follow them deep into the forest, where they would build a campfire. The upperclassmen would give him a sack and a stick and then disappear into the trees, ostensibly to beat the bushes and scare the snipes out of hiding. When a snipe ran toward the fire, being naturally attracted to light, the freshman was supposed to club the bird and stuff it into the sack. Of course, there were no snipes, and the freshman would discover that he was abandoned and lost in the dark woods, unable to find his way back to campus until dawn.

But that was perhaps an easier humiliation to bear than the elaborate initiation ritual for the fictitious Zeta Chi fraternity, which was billed as a prestigious, invitation-only club. Upperclassmen would lure a freshman to the science building, where he would be blindfolded, smudged with soot, swabbed with kerosene, and dunked in a bucket of water before his tormentors disappeared, laughing and running off into the night.[10]

In this environment, Buddie's freshman year began with social and academic struggles, to his father's dismay. Howard's satisfactory performance plummeted after Buddie's arrival too, which their father attributed to the distraction of sibling rivalry. In January 1896, Asa Sr. wrote:

> I am real blue about my boys today. Everybody tells me how smart you both are.... Your marks are just as low as they can be to admit of your mischief. Can't you do better? Ain't there some way for you to learn your lessons? . . . Buddie especially ought to get the best marks. Sound body. Strong mind. Been in good schools all his life. Now why can't I see better reports? Write to me why. I am

asking only that you do your best. I can give you nothing but a good education. Won't you take that?[11]

Howard, always susceptible to his father's pressures, pulled his grades up. Buddie did only as much as was necessary to stay enrolled, and he felt no obligation to curtail the mischief that the letter alluded to.

There were lots of problems. Some were the natural consequences of two teenage brothers living and socializing together. It's no revelation that siblings fight. But Howard and Buddie had deeply mismatched personalities, and the school community was too small to give them the space to develop outside of each other's influence. They fought frequently enough to necessitate intervention, but their parents' hands were tied by distance and the demands of the growing Coca-Cola business, which was entering a period of legal struggles that dominated Asa Sr.'s attention.

Buddie arrived at Emory at a social disadvantage too. His brother had already spent a year there, making friends and learning the ways of college life. Howard had joined the Kappa Alpha Order fraternity and the Atlanta Club, spent a year with the Phi Gamma debate society, and was a member of the mandolin and tennis clubs. A timid child at home, he came out of his shell when he moved away, and his gregarious younger brother's arrival was not welcome.[12] Howard griped behind his brother's back and was easily lured into physical fights when Buddie egged him on. They battled each other for their parents' favor, and Howard worked hard to maintain his reputation as the "good" son.

In 1896 Asa Sr. wrote to Howard:

> I received your letter [and] also one from your brother. He presents a very different statement of the troubles with him as it touches you—from what you state. While I know he has done wrong, acted more wickedly, I fear you too are not [doing] right. He is your younger brother. You have never treated him as it is your duty to. You prefer other boys to him, speak disparagingly of him to others and allow others to speak to you evilly of him & tear him down.[13]

Their father's instinct about Howard's willing participation in the brotherly conflict may have been correct. Family anecdotes claim that Howard had Buddie blackballed from Kappa Alpha, an organization that many Candler men had close ties to.[14] While no documentation provides evidence of a KA conflict, three clues support this claim:

1. Buddie never joined any fraternity. Most of his schoolmates joined fraternities and the debate clubs. Buddie was listed in the Atlanta Club for only one year. He also briefly appeared on the Phi Gamma roll, notable because, as mentioned, his uncle Warren was a Few man. Later, he established the Emory Bicycle Club and joined a cryptically named and probably joke organization called the Cat Club as "Pet Swiper."[15] That was it. Many of his classmates appeared in multiple organizations every year, and more boys joined fraternities than abstained. Buddie never participated in Greek life. This makes him an odd man out among his classmates.

2. His family had deep ties to the Kappa Alpha Order. Uncle Warren was a lifelong member and champion of KA. Another uncle, future Georgia Supreme Court justice John Slaughter Candler, was initiated into Kappa Alpha in 1877, elected grand historian in 1881, and served as the tenth KA knight commander from 1881 to 1885.[16] Buddie and Howard's younger brother Walter was a passionate KA member who participated in fraternity alumni activities throughout his adult life. Cousins who attended Emory also pledged, including John Slaughter's son Asa Warren Candler. John Slaughter's son-in-law George Speight Ballard even built the historic Kappa Alpha mansion on Eagle Row at Emory University, which still stands today.[17] It's notable that Buddie wasn't a member.

3. Asa Sr.'s letters on file at Emory University reveal his own keen interest in clubs and perhaps some tension between the brothers over Howard's passion for KA. In November 1895, Asa Sr. wrote:

> I hope for your parents['] sake you do nothing that would be wicked or harmful to us and to you both. I hope you, Asa, are not worrying and teasing Howard about decent society affiliations. Don't do that. Wait till I see you. I want you to make so splendid a record in college both as a gentleman & scholar ... that you will be greatly desired by all good clubs.[18]

So there may be truth in Buddie's claim to his grandchildren that their great-uncle Howard had him blackballed from the only fraternity the Candler men ever cared about. But although that would have caused drama for all involved, there was more to come.

The personal correspondence tells a story of impudence and hubris in Buddie's behavior. He felt that his uncle's status on campus gave him leeway to act up and break rules without any fear of consequences. In 1897, at the end of Buddie's sophomore year, the school built and named Candler Hall in honor of his uncle—supposedly despite Warren's protests. Plus, Buddie's daddy's business was gaining fame and clout. Is it any wonder that his family's status went to his head? When caught in a prank or a rule violation, he would invoke his relationship to King Shorty with the expectation that he would benefit from cronyism, which frustrated his father.

But Buddie's attitude may have been justified. Some of his activities should have been serious offenses, but his parents rose to his defense and talked Warren down each time he threatened retribution. Some of Buddie's infractions reported in family lore and in personal correspondence included:

- Skipping classes and church
- Smoking on and off campus
- Behavior deserving of the yearbook superlative "Class Pugilist"
- Hiding a live goat in the belfry of Seney Hall
- Filling the campus chapel with hay or snow (reports vary)[19]

If that wasn't enough, he was also struggling to keep his grades above failing. The *Zodiac* yearbook often included inside jokes about classmates, lampooning them with ironic stories. In the 1897 *Zodiac*, a brief aside mocked Buddie's math skills, and perhaps his ego, as it alluded to the ongoing struggles with his studies, which nearly cost him his graduation:

> There is in our class a man who expects to make his fortune out of the treatise on Plane Geometry and Trigonometry which he is at present preparing for publication. Its title will be Plane Geometry and Trigonometry Made Easy, by Asa G. Candler. The author is confident that his book will be adopted by the public schools and many of the leading colleges in the south.[20]

In the fall of 1897, Uncle Warren brought the hammer down. He wrote to Asa Sr. that he could no longer provide a home to his nephew. Asa Sr. and Lucy Elizabeth campaigned for forgiveness for their son. But by then Howard had participated in enough of the infractions that Warren decided to kick out both nephews. They were forced to take up residence in one of the helping halls for the rest of their school days. Their parents should have seen this coming. In January 1897, Asa Sr. had privately written to Howard: "My brother says he must be taken from Oxford and that he cannot control him.... I cannot think that Buddie has deliberately made up his mind to kill me with remorse. . . . If I have to return him I don't know what I will do with him."[21] Following their eviction, he wrote to both:

Dear Boys: I enclose to you a letter just received which is of all the incidents that I can now recall the most mortifying to me. Immediately upon its receipt telephoned for you to make a change. I am advised that it is possible that you can't find a place to go to. This is an extremity to which I never dreamed that I would be driven. I must leave the matter with you. If you can find a place, go to it. Notify me upon what terms you are accepted so that I may remit accordingly, as I dare say since you have been turned out of your boarding house, I have neither credit nor standing significant to get you a month's board without paying in advance. Twenty-five years ago I came to Atlanta without knowing anybody and had no trouble in finding a place to lodge where I could get board and pay when I had it. It did not occur to me that I would ever have boys who would be placed as you are and which places me where you have placed me.[22]

And finally, in another private letter to Howard, sent on the same day:

I had no idea whatever that you boys were not behaving. Your views of this situation coincide exactly with mine. I am putting implicit faith in both of you behaving exactly right. It is more than ever necessary that you should be perfect gentlemen. You are going to be watched and closely criticized, this is especially true of Buddie. Upon your good conduct depends not only my peace of mind and your best interests, but the future welfare of your younger brothers. Believe that I am trusting you boys to do right. I hope Buddie will remember his promises as to the use of tobacco. He knows I will not stand that. I believe his uncle is mistaken. I can't think he would violate my laws. See to it also that he is not out of his room at night.[23]

Family lore claims that the final infraction was riding a bicycle on the campus quad, and while that may have contributed, their father also mentioned Buddie's smoking in his letter to Howard.[24] That said, Buddie was indeed a documented bicycle fanatic.

It's a common misconception that bicycles are an age-old means of transportation. In reality, bicycles are contemporary machines, and the familiar "safety bicycle" design that we still use today gained traction in the 1880s, right around the time that automobile prototypes were first hitting roads in the United States and Europe. The invention of this new style of bike, with a chain drive and pneumatic tires, resulted in the 1890s bike boom. Bicycle clubs, bicycle races, cross-country bicycle tours, and even cyclist celebrities were born. But when bicycles first became a fad, only the wealthy could afford them. Brands like Overman Victor were highly desirable and could cost well over a hundred dollars each, more than six months of wages for the average working man.

The year 1896 was the peak of the boom, and everyone wanted a bike. Bicycling premiered as an Olympic sport that year. Then the Panic of 1896 hit, and the economy took a dive, driving mass unemployment and financial instability. Since bikes remained popular through the slump, transport manufacturers shifted resources into bike production and flooded the market with affordable options. By the time Buddie fell in love with bicycling, mass manufacturers like Sears had made prices accessible.

All of this is worth noting because Buddie and Howard didn't live like royalty at college. Sure, they lived with the school president, and their father was selling barrels of syrup across the Southeast, but that didn't mean they had endless means. Asa Sr. expected them to learn financial management and to demonstrate responsibility by living on a budget. They received a wired monthly stipend and were required to keep strict records of their income and expenses in a log that their father reviewed. Howard, dutiful by nature, meticulously tracked his funds as required.[25]

Buddie, on the other hand, did what Buddie always did: exactly what he wanted to do. This certainly is true of his decision to buy a bicycle in 1896. Family lore says his father was opposed to the notion of spending money on such frivolity. Many older people at the time regarded bicycles as dangerous contraptions and wanted nothing to do with them. But Buddie wanted one, the first of many speed machines that he would fixate on throughout his life, and he wasn't about to deny himself what he wanted. So, the story goes, he spent his stipend on a bicycle, which forced Asa Sr. to put all purchase approvals through Howard, further straining their sibling relationship.[26] In 1898, Buddie started a student bike club, a group that appears to have existed for one year only, and the only real club he ever joined at Emory.[27]

King Shorty had decreed that bikes were dangerous devices and banned them from campus after a student crashed his two-wheeler into a carriage. So if Buddie rode his bicycle on campus, it would have been in direct violation of his uncle's rule. If the family lore is true, that was the final straw. Howard and Buddie were forced out of the President's House, and their father bawled them out in a letter so furious that the words still leap from the page more than a century later. The boys found lodging in a helping hall and

Emory College Bicycle Club, 1898. Asa Candler Jr. is fifth from the left.
Courtesy of Oxford College Library Archives and Special Collections, Oxford
College of Emory University.

closed out their education with the cloud of their parents' disappointment
hanging over them.[28]

Howard graduated in June 1898 with honors. Buddie graduated in June
1899 with none. In a letter to Howard, Asa Sr. wondered what to do with
Buddie next, expressed pride that he had made it through to the end, and
asked his oldest son to congratulate his brother: "If you have time to, write
him a letter on Sunday directing it to Oxford encouraging him, calling attention to the fact that though he did not take first honor, that you believe
he has taken a good education, and that he has every equipment necessary
to being successful."[29]

This is one of the most interesting pieces of correspondence in the archive because fifty years later, when Howard donated his papers to Emory,
he felt compelled to comment in the margin: "Could not do this with a clear
conscience."[30]

Buddie left this morning . . . to attend Emory Commencement.
I want to be there when he graduates the 14th. I have not
decided yet what to do with him.[1]

CHAPTER 3

Go West, Young Man

In the summer of 1899, Buddie found himself aboard a departing train once again. This time, he probably expected it. After all, Asa Sr. had recently sent Howard across the southern states to sell Coca-Cola syrup and meet distributors. Although he occasionally grappled with a reluctance to saddle Howard with the family business, the senior Asa saw it as part of his earthly duty to ensure that his kin benefited from its success. At every level of the company, he employed cousins, sons, and nephews. Keeping it in the family was a high priority, and despite Asa Sr.'s occasional superficial protests, Howard and Buddie were part of that plan.

Out on the road, Howard traveled from town to town, writing home regularly and reporting his progress to his father. Conscientiousness continued to dominate his personality as he put duty above personal happiness. He expressed gloomy sentiments of loneliness in letters to his sister, claiming he'd lost all of the friends he'd once known.[2] He felt abandoned and exiled, and this showed in his writing. But rather than rebelling, he pulled the reins in tighter. He became more compliant and tried harder to please, restricting his pursuit of fun and focusing on his responsibilities, and he advised his sister to do the same: "Don't be too impulsive or presumptuous. As I have written you before, nothing is so loathsome to culture as the above traits indulged in to excess."[3]

Flip on its head everything that Howard represented, and you have his brother Asa Jr. Ever the jubilant personality, Buddie embodied impulsiveness and presumptuousness. He followed his heart in all pursuits, regardless of whether his family approved or not, and was easily distracted by new opportunities for fun. Aware of his son's predilections, Asa Sr. chose not to give Buddie a traveling gig like Howard's. Instead, he sent his namesake out to Los Angeles, California, to settle there and help run the newly established West Coast office, in spite of his reservations about sending him so far away.[4]

Buddie took up residence at the Hotel Johnson, a small boarding house near Fourth Street and Main that stood in the shadow of the luxurious Westminster Hotel next door.[5] The Johnson offered some amenities, such as exterior windows and private bathrooms, which were still not a universal offering at the time. It did not yet provide telephones in each room. If one wanted private telephone service, one had to look half a block northwest to the Van Nuys Hotel, which still stands today as the Barclay Hotel. Each day, Buddie would walk two blocks southeast to San Pedro Street and work at the Coca-Cola regional headquarters, where he ostensibly ran the front office.

Buddie's older cousin Samuel was already there, working in sales. As a responsible adult, Samuel could check in when he wasn't on the road selling syrup and could keep an eye on Buddie as he oversaw manufacturing and order fulfillment. But rather than acting as a surrogate father, Samuel welcomed his younger cousin by introducing him to L.A.'s active social scene. They caroused like no one was watching—because no one was—and enjoyed the freedom. In a letter to his parents, Buddie took a swipe at their choices for him, asking why they missed him when he'd hardly ever lived at home: "I don't see why you are so lonesome without me for I have never been with you much in my life. I am not at all lonesome because I found such a hearty welcome for me from Sam."[6]

From a safe distance, Buddie could do what he wanted and report only what he thought his parents should know. Without a strong guiding hand, Buddie fell into the sweet embrace of vice. In a 1951 interview, Buddie recounted, "My story was the old familiar one of falling in with the wrong crowd. The habits of my associates gradually became my habits. At the time, if I experienced qualms of conscience about moral laxity, I stifled them."[7] True to his nature, once something fun had him in its grips, there was no room in his field of vision for anything else. That included reporting home on his status and business needs. As other family members noted, throughout his teens and twenties Buddie wrote infrequently, and the letters he did write focused on why he hadn't written and whether he would write again, rather than discussing real matters. By his own admission, he didn't like to write.[8] So he didn't. Howard noted: "Have you heard from Bud yet? He promised

Asa Candler Jr., circa 1899.
Courtesy of Oxford College Library
Archives and Special Collections,
Oxford College of Emory University.

to write to me as soon as he got to [Los Angeles] but I haven't heard a word from him. Hope he is as well and happy as he was when I left him."[9]

Perhaps Asa Jr. did this deliberately to relieve himself of the obligation to report his transgressions to his family. They couldn't control what they didn't know. When Sam and Buddie visited Colorado for what they called a "business trip," Buddie wrote home that he'd gotten sick from drinking bad water, a claim that some family historians have viewed with skepticism.[10] Perhaps he was already drinking alcohol and denying its ill effects.

Although never explicitly stated, Asa Sr. had his doubts about Buddie's activities, and this became evident in the decisions he made in late 1899 and early 1900. He knew his son, and he knew sales weren't growing as he'd hoped they would. But although he had no compunction about defining the direction of Howard's life, with Buddie he demonstrated helplessness and reluctance, and he pushed Howard to be the bad cop to his good cop. He often directed his criticisms of Buddie to Howard and asked his advice as though he were speaking parent to parent rather than parent to child. As he had done during their college years, Asa Sr. appealed to Howard to manage Buddie's failings in L.A. rather than doing so himself. Howard didn't appreciate being put in the position to parent his own brother and to mentor him in business. His recommendations didn't turn things around, assuming he offered them and assuming Buddie heard them.

In March 1900, Asa Sr. pulled Howard off the road and sent him out to L.A. to look in on things, revealing that money management wasn't going well. He expressed optimism that things would turn around once Howard straightened out the financials.

> It seems that it was well for you to stop at El Paso and Phoenix, as you did business at both places. This encourages us to believe that your trip to California will result in good to that branch.... I wrote Buddie this morning as to money. Of course if he needs any more than he has he will draw on us. Either your draft or his will always be good here.[11]

The progression of letters over the next month reveals the degree to which Asa Sr. understood his second son's struggles to manage the business. He sent Howard to L.A. in March, and by mid-April he was making arrangements to bring both boys home. He made no drama about it, but simply informed his sons that they would be departing by June.

Asa Sr. said more than once that the trip home would be for a one-month stay. This was always the plan, although the reason for the duration has not been captured in the archived correspondence. On April 30, 1900, he wrote to Buddie, urging him to depart as close to the first of June as he could, while also trying to ensure that the business wouldn't slide any further in his absence. Asa Sr. wanted a full transfer of knowledge so the office could operate without Buddie, and he spoke encouragingly from one side of his mouth while exposing his doubt in his son's judgment from the other: "You two make such arrangements as calmly, deliberately [as] should be made in the interest of the company. You will certainly be away a month. Can you protect the office for that long an absence? ... your trade has increased largely this year & I hope will continue to grow. Be good, be careful."[12]

This tone, typical in his letters to and about Buddie, was patronizing in its encouragement. He often used words with Buddie that he didn't use with others. Only Buddie was instructed to be calm and deliberate in his decisions. Only Buddie received pleas to be good, to be careful. Given the timeline, it's likely that Asa Sr. had significant concerns and was already making arrangements to permanently extract his son from the temptations of California without tipping his hand and causing Buddie to take flight.

Buddie returned home in mid-June for his one-month break, which should have had him back on a westbound train by mid- to late July. But he never got on that train. On September 17, 1900, a letter from Buddie to Lucy revealed that he was instead relocated again, this time to a tiny town in northern Georgia called Hartwell. There's no record of how the proposal to move him was received. However, it seems likely that the reason for his relocation was made clear to him, given the contents of his first letter to his sister once he settled into his new home. Buddie revealed that he had fallen in with a bad crowd: "I do not care to meet so many people for I found [out in] California that one that meets too many people without knowing who he is meeting often gets with the wrong ones."[13]

Eight days later, he wrote to Lucy again, this time with gushing praise for their parents that reeked of overcompensation, given his past disobedience, recklessness, and disregard for their rules and expectations. It was also out of keeping with his usual tone, which typically alternated between deflective humor and wounded pride. This wasn't the only time in Buddie's life when simpering deference to parental authority appeared at the intersection between self-indulgence and guilt. But it is the most excessive example on record: "We have such sweet, dear parents. We should always do and be what they would like for we can never pay them back for their kindness to us. One way we can show them our gratitude is to obey them and love one another."[14]

Buddie's time in Los Angeles had been short, and the family was discreet enough to never speak directly about what happened during his West Coast adventure. Many of the conclusions about his time there must be extrapolated from letters. A portrait of the nineteen- and twenty-year-old Buddie emerges, showing a thrill-seeking, easily distracted, and poorly organized young man who was unable to fulfill his father's expectations. Whether Asa Sr.'s expectations were too high, given his son's personality and immaturity, is debatable. Howard certainly did his best to prove that youth was no obstacle, which made it even harder for Buddie to be seen in any light other than failure.

But perhaps we should reflect on the L.A. year more charitably. Personality quirks aside, Asa Jr. was young and inexperienced. He'd had few opportunities to practice business before being deployed to run and grow a regional branch on the opposite side of the country from his family. Support from home in the form of written letters was delayed and asynchronous. His rebellious and selfish personality certainly played a role in his failure to thrive, and he pointed the finger at circumstances that he claimed were the cause of his struggles, but success would have been a long shot for anyone in that situation. Asa Sr. had been thirty-seven when he purchased the Coca-Cola formula. He'd had years of successes and failures under his belt before the brand took off. Sending a freshly graduated nineteen-year-old with a personality like Buddie's to California probably wasn't fair.

When Asa Sr. realized his error, he made an executive decision to correct course. His goal was to save his son from the evils of temptation and place him where distractions were few and distant. It wasn't a discussion, it was a mandate, and Buddie's desires weren't considered. His parents made what they felt was the right decision for him, for better or for worse.

Hartwell, Georgia, was no Los Angeles, and that was precisely its best selling point. Without his input or say-so, Buddie was brought home and sent away again with no notice or fanfare, drawing to a close his only year as an active Coca-Cola employee.

*No one loves their parents any more than I do and
I love them more and more every day I live.*[1]

CHAPTER 4

Mill, Marriage, and Family

In the summer of 1900, Asa Candler Sr. bought controlling interest in a cotton mill in Hartwell, Georgia. Witham Cotton Mill was a sizable operation, owned by and named after family friend William "Billy" Witham, but it was struggling to stay afloat. Asa Sr. saw an opportunity to help a friend and diversify his portfolio. He invested with the intention of turning things around and making a success of the venture, but he needed someone to run its operations on his behalf.

At the same time, he had a son who had spent the previous year mismanaging the West Coast branch of his core business and was falling deeper into vice. He needed to pull Buddie out of the hot fires of temptation and place him somewhere peaceful, somewhere with a strong Methodist community where he could sharpen his business skills and contribute to the family's bottom line. Witham Cotton Mill was the answer.

In the summer of 1900, two things happened: Asa Sr. brought Buddie home for what was billed as a one-month stay in June, and he and Billy Witham completed the mill transaction in late July. On September 3, he put his son on a train and sent him more than one hundred miles northeast to Hartwell, a tiny community near the border of South Carolina. Buddie was quick to acknowledge his drastic change of scenery in a letter to his sister Lucy: "I supposed a letter from your country brother would be welcomed therefore I write you. I am away off here in a little country town."[2]

Asa Sr. installed Buddie as a bookkeeper at the mill and later promoted him to secretary and treasurer. He told Howard that he hoped Buddie would do well enough to be promoted to president of the mill someday. And for once, Buddie seemed invested in making the most of it. In correspondence with Lucy, he spoke highly of himself and his role. He bragged about his status, which would emerge as a theme in his writing throughout his life. When his letters weren't ordering her to stay away from boys or explaining why he hadn't written, that he didn't like to write, and why he might not write more in the future, he painted a portrait of an important businessman: "Since I returned from Atlanta I have had about all I could attend to, for with the ending of March our mill year ends and of course that means extra work for me because the books have to be balanced up and stocks all figured out. So you see I am [keeping] real busy."[3]

A very important businessman. "I thought I would write you to tell you I have been promoted and am now Secretary & Treasurer of the mill. This is a very responsible place I am called upon to fill, handling other people's money and I must be very careful how I do it."[4]

The most important businessman. "I don't have as much time to think about going home as you do. I have too many other things that take my attention elsewhere. Besides, I am here now to stay. There is no way to get me away except for the mill to go to pieces and if it were to do that my reputation would be lost."[5]

While Hartwell was far from a bustling metropolis—its train only ran twice a day to the next town over—its modest size may have made Buddie a big fish in a small pond. Always one to leverage his family's status for an advantage, he held an important position at the largest business in town, and that grew his self-assurance, perhaps making him overly confident.

A look at the turn-of-the-century *Sanborn Fire Insurance Maps* reveals that Hartwell was heavily dependent on cotton and warehousing, with much of the warehouse space utilized for guano storage.[6] Aside from the fertilizer industry, there wasn't much else driving local employment other than the dominant mill operation. The mill even had its own village adjacent to the industrial property, which still stands today. In this small town, cotton was king, which made Asa Sr.'s trajectory for his son a clear path to the crown.

Which isn't to say Buddie was happy. His letters from this time period reveal a bitterness that seeped in at the edges as he lavished his younger sister with affection. He referred to her, just three years his junior, as "little girl" and offered repeatedly to buy her candy. Her whole family infantilized her like this, but Buddie's letters are the most egregious on record. When he wasn't speaking to her like a child or gushing about his career, he was stewing about his isolation. In a letter from March 1901, he brushed off her request for a photo and brooded over the reason that he had none to offer. He revealed his loneliness and his identity as an outsider.

> Mama wrote me you wanted one of my pictures. I must tell you I have not one to my name. I am not so conceited as to have several pictures of myself laying around in my room. Besides, no one ever cared enough for me to want a picture of myself. They only ask for it for politeness. Now I don't say this about you but people in general.[7]

However, he didn't sit around the boarding house as a shut-in. He threw himself into his work and dabbled in an exciting new hobby as one of the first automobile owners in Hartwell, which of course meant parts and maintenance and all kinds of welcome distractions. But work and his loudly declared devotion to his parents could only hold him accountable in his new life for so long, and his commitment to avoiding new friendships didn't stick. He was an extrovert, someone who enjoyed the revelry of company and needed social interaction, in spite of his claims to the contrary. So when he met Helen Magill (1880–1927), she became the center of his world.

Helen was the second child of John Henry Magill, the editor and owner of the *Hartwell Sun* newspaper, and Laura Lepex Eberhardt Magill.[8] John Magill's prominent role with the local paper made him a keystone in the community, and his family's affiliation with the local Methodist church put them in Buddie's social circle. Church is likely where he met Helen, who had earned a reputation as a talented singer. When Buddie fell for her, he fell hard.

Yet there's no mention of Helen in his 1900 letters. No mention in his family members' letters to each other. In early 1901, he tested the waters by making a blasé reference in a note to Lucy. One must conclude that Helen wasn't mentioned over Christmas and that they may not have been dating yet, since his unguarded, candid nature suggests that he would have mentioned her if there had been any relationship to mention. On January 22, 1901, he updated Lucy on his life and included his usual protests about how busy he was. And then, almost as a throwaway, he said: "I have to work at night a great deal and I have to go to see my <u>Girl</u> once a week."[9]

Capitalized and underlined.

The relationship then progressed quickly. By April they were planning to marry, but for unspoken reasons Buddie felt compelled to keep their engagement a secret. He first told Lucy in early May and swore her to secrecy in another passage that exposed his pain over his lifelong separation from his family.

> I will have to make myself a little home up here and I intend to do it just as soon as I can. I am tired of boarding houses having lived at them ever since I was eight years old. And besides you would like to have a sister. I cannot write much but you will take the will for the deed.[10]

Her response is lost to time, since his papers, including letters written to him, were not archived. But his next response suggests that she was dismayed by his plans, and he was hurt by her reaction. Once again, he showed the bitterness of isolation, his hurt at not sharing a home with his family, and his desire to change his situation for the better.

> Am sorry you take the position you do about me. There is no use in it. I will never be able to have a home with you all again, and why not make a home of my own? However, your advice will be of no use to me this time for you are too late in giving it. Everything is near planned and I truly wait for the day. It will be impossible for me to come home when you asked me to come. Now I am not saying this and mean to come, but I cannot come, that is all. I wish I could be with you but I cannot.[11]

There was no swaying him. Buddie always did what he wanted to do, and not even his sister's objection would slow his plans. His emotions were raw and unfiltered, scrawled on the page in long, run-on sentences with spelling and grammar errors not seen in other family members' writings. Again, her reply is not on record, but it's clear from his next letter that she came around, and once she did he decided to go full bore into the announcement of his plans.

> I am going to tell you a secret. You must not tell it to anyone. Don't write it home for I am going down home on the 25th and I will tell it to Mama & Papa. And I want to be the one to tell it & not you. . . .
> You say you will stand by me. Now I am going to hold you to that. I may have to call on you to aid me. I hope not. We have been writing each other about marrying. Well I had long before I wrote you decided to do that thing and only wrote you to see what you would say before you knew I was going to be married. I am to be married on June 12th and would like for you to come up here to see me and be with me when this happy time comes.

I will have to get me some clothes when I go to Atlanta. And you can now first consider yourself as having a sweet little sister that will love you real hard. Keep above to self.[12]

Lucy gave him the support he desperately needed. His relief in his next letter was palpable, as were his excitement to be married and his infatuation with Helen. This letter demonstrated a breathless passion that verged on poetic in a way that no other archived letter does, highlighting the bright, charming, and jovial—when he wanted to be—personality his descendants remembered. Buddie's narcissistic, martyred public persona later in life can sometimes overshadow the more positive aspects of his personality, but this letter gives a glimpse into the man his family loved and his friends found so charismatic.

Your sweet letter received. You cannot imagine how glad I was to receive it. I thought you would be on the other side of the fence but you are not and it gives me great pleasure. I think I have done better than anyone could have wished and I know I have the sweetest & dearest girl in the world.

Our little circle is nearly broken but I am glad to say we will love each other more than ever before for we will appreciate what we are to each other more. Your sister to be is Miss Helen Magill. About your own type. About as tall & large as yourself and for this reason if no other I love her. I know you will love her for she sings divinely and is a very entertaining talker. I will be so glad to have you & Mama come up here June 12th and I am mighty glad to hear you say you would rather come than go to Emory commencement. For by this I know you love me and want to show your love for me by giving me this much pleasure. I will be in Atlanta until May 28 so I will see you then and I will be so glad to see you.[13]

His next step was to tell his parents in person on May 25, giving them just two and a half weeks' notice. His parents convinced him to postpone until July. He agreed to one month, no longer. The wedding was now on for July 16. In addition to the immediate family, they were joined by his uncles and aunts: Bishop Warren Candler with Sarah Antoinette Candler, née Curtright, and Judge John Slaughter Candler with Marguerite Louise Candler, née Garnie. On Helen's side, the attendee list was sparse. She had no wedding party attendants, and neither her parents nor her brother were listed in the announcement. The ceremony took place at her aunt and uncle's house, not her own home. The complete absence of Magills at Buddie and

Asa Candler Jr.'s home (now the Candler-Linder House), Hartwell, Georgia, circa 2015.
Courtesy of the City of Hartwell and Downtown Development Authority.

Helen's wedding suggests that perhaps her parents were reluctant to approve of their union.

The next day, Helen and the Candlers frolicked in the sun at Lake Toccoa on a full-family honeymoon. On the eighteenth they boarded a train for Atlanta, and on July 19 the family threw a grand celebration in honor of the newlyweds at their home on Seaboard Avenue. After the wedding, Asa Sr. bought them a house, which stood on Johnson Street in Hartwell until 2017.

It's interesting that Helen's parents didn't attend any of these events and that her father wasn't swayed by the prominence of the Candler family. By then, Coca-Cola was well known throughout the South, and Warren and John Candler were well-respected community leaders. But Helen's father didn't concede.[14]

THE MIRACULOUS BIRTH OF LUCY III

➔ Asa Jr. and Helen welcomed their first child, Lucy III, into the world on March 21, 1902. Helen endured a hard labor, and possibly due to chronic illness she delivered a small baby (five and a half pounds) who needed extra care. Family lore says Lucy III was born prematurely and that Lucy Elizabeth whisked her first grandchild away to provide special care and ensure her survival. This, the story says, included feeding the baby Coca-Cola syrup from a dropper and keeping her warm in a chicken incubator.[15] It's an incredible story of Lucy Elizabeth's maternal expertise and the restorative properties of the Coca-Cola formula, but it is unlikely to be true.

On March 22, Asa Sr. sent a telegraph to Howard in New York City announcing that his niece had been born. He followed up with a handwritten letter the same day, describing the birth in detail. According to his report, Helen was in intense labor for more than ten hours. The baby presented backward with one leg bent up by her neck. It was a forceful delivery, but there was no tearing or "vaginal rupture," as had happened during Howard's own birth. Asa Sr. noted that Lucy III was very pretty and doing well.[16] He mentioned nothing about prematurity, nothing about frailty or ill health, nothing that suggested a risk to her survival. One would think that a man who was comfortable discussing vaginal rupture in such plain language would have been equally comfortable describing neonatal care for a premature baby.

The timeline also seems a bit off. If Lucy III were conceived on her parents' wedding night, a full-term birth would have arrived sometime around April 21. Lucy III was born almost five weeks earlier than that. Records of survival rate by gestation time in the 1800s and early 1900s do not exist. Regardless, the likelihood of survival of a four- or five-week premature infant in 1902 was extremely low, since intervention techniques for premature births were virtually unknown.[17]

Additionally, while using a chicken incubator wouldn't have required a giant leap of logic, the use of incubators for premature babies was only in its earliest trials when Lucy III arrived. Lucy Elizabeth would have been prescient, on the cutting edge of medical technology, to employ her chicken incubator to save her premature granddaughter's life.[18] Last, sugar-laden Coca-Cola syrup contains no protein, which is critical for a baby's survival, and a premature baby's electrolyte balance can be disrupted if she is given too much water. Not to mention the presence of both caffeine and cocaine. Malnutrition in this scenario would have been highly likely, and survival would have been highly unlikely.

But the enduring story of Lucy Elizabeth's nursing skills is *so* Buddie. His writings from later in life are rife with exaggerations, and he and Howard both recalled their mother as a saint.[19] And although Buddie wasn't directly involved in Coca-Cola, he promoted it his whole life, never missing an opportunity to boost the brand name. Saving a baby's life with its restorative powers would be in keeping with the scale of his tall tales.

The more likely scenario about the child's birth is that Lucy III was conceived out of wedlock, and the story of her prematurity was intended as a cover-up.

Following Lucy III's birth, Helen required extended recovery time. She remained with her in-laws in Atlanta while Buddie returned to work at the cotton mill. Weeks passed. Buddie spent the spring that year traveling back and forth between Hartwell and Atlanta, one hundred miles each way, to visit his young family. Traveling this distance would have been an all-day ordeal. The wood-fired, narrow-gauge Hartwell train engine named the *Nancy Hart* only made the trip to Bowersville twice a day. From there, Buddie had the option to transfer to either the Elberton line or the Athens line, and then transfer again to an Atlanta line.[20]

In April, Asa Sr. wrote to Howard to update him on Helen's recovery. He noted Buddie's impatience to have her home with him. Whatever sentiment Buddie had expressed about the situation was so objectionable that Asa Sr. enclosed it in his letter to Howard so he could read it for himself. Then he took a jab at his second son to his first: "Helen is improving very slowly. Poor Bud, he is getting impatient. . . . He is a child!"[21]

On May 7, Asa Sr. complained about his daughter-in-law to Howard, suggesting that she was "utterly short on maternal wisdom."[22] It was the same old dynamic that had played out in college, where Asa Sr. criticized Buddie's life to Howard as though they were peers.

To distract his frustrated, impatient, exiled namesake, he sent Buddie to New York City to visit Howard and investigate claims that Billy Witham was gambling with cotton mill funds on the Cotton Exchange. This was in response to Buddie's claim that the mill's finances were in shambles due to Witham messing with their money. There may have been some truth to that. Witham wasn't a cotton man. He was in banking, and the cotton mill was nothing more than an investment opportunity. But given Buddie's troubles managing the California Coca-Cola branch and his later business challenges, it's possible that Buddie was at least as much of the problem as Billy Witham was.

Asa Sr. wanted to give Witham the benefit of the doubt. He sent Buddie to investigate a rumored attempt by a group of financiers to purchase the mill, and he looked into the claim that Billy had lost $9,000 after winning $8,000 right before the trip. Asa Sr. considered this kind of speculation to be gambling and didn't approve. On May 10, he wrote to Howard to have him peek in on Billy when Buddie wasn't there: "Did you see Mr. Witham this week? He has spent a week on the N.Y. Cotton Exchange. His results so far [are] a loss of nearly $5,000.00 to Witham Cotton Mill and Buddie is in a big huffy. Says he won't stay up there and work day and night for Mr. Witham to waste."[23]

History isn't black and white. Billy Witham may very well have played too much with the mill's money. And Buddie may very well have struggled to keep things on track. Buddie claimed that Billy was gambling and losing money, but there's no record of Asa Sr. confronting him about it. He described Buddie as a "brave, good boy" in a letter addressed to Howard when the finances looked dire.[24] This thematic choice appeared during Buddie's worst college escapades, during the L.A. office mismanagement, and during the mill's financial struggles. One wonders whether "good boy" was wishful thinking or whether it was coded insincerity to prevent Asa Sr.'s frustration from being spoken plainly.

Regardless, Buddie was clearly distracted from his work, which couldn't have helped the mill's operations. Of course, he sought distractions even in the best of circumstances. With a frustrating job and his wife and baby far away in the big city with the rest of his family, he was isolated and living on the outside once again.

Buddie found reasons to visit Atlanta whenever an opportunity presented itself. In late May 1902, he learned of the crippled younger sister of two mill employees. Their parents were both dead, and the girl had become paralyzed from the waist down. Buddie decided to accompany her to the National Surgical Institute in Atlanta, where the prospects of recovering the use of her legs were good. He left her in the care of the Decatur orphan's home.

He also traveled to Atlanta to pick up parts for his first automobile. During his twenties, the side of his personality that had fallen in love with bicycles reasserted itself, and he fell in love with cars. Automobiles were rich men's toys, and as an important man at an important mill, his status necessitated a toy or two. Presumably, Buddie's burgeoning love of automobiles influenced

Howard's 1902 urge to purchase a car in New York City following one of his brother's visits.[25] Asa Sr. was initially against the idea, seeing it as a waste of company resources. But as he usually did when pressured by his sons, he came around. So then both Buddie and Howard had automobiles to preoccupy them.

Whatever the reasons, all of Buddie's traveling added up to one thing: a lack of focus at the mill while Billy Witham gambled with its finances. The business suffered. It ran in the red year after year and never showed signs of stabilizing. One can only speculate about how long Asa Sr. would have permitted the struggle to continue, but the family wasn't given the chance to see it through. When the great ice storm of 1905 hit, the decision was made for them.

That was a year of winter storms throughout America. In early February 1905, a cold front swept across the southeastern states from Alabama to South Carolina and caused damage as far south as Florida. On the evening of February 4, freezing rain descended over Atlanta, glazing every surface. The ice caught the unprepared population by surprise as it coated the roads and caused accidents throughout the city. Falling tree branches tore down telegraph lines, and all travel, including rail, came to a halt. For a major railroad hub, this was a massive disruption.

Up in the North Georgia foothills, a blizzard hit even harder. Helen had already moved home, and across the northern expanse of the state, all residents were snowed in. The roads were impassable.[26] These were the conditions that Asa Candler Jr. and his young family faced when they woke up on the morning of February 5.

By then, Asa Jr. and Helen had two children. Lucy III was about a month away from turning three, and her baby brother, Asa III, born June 10, 1904, was almost eight months old. As two of the first three grandchildren, little Lucy and Asa were the joys of Asa Sr. and Lucy Elizabeth's life. Buddie and his family visited Atlanta as often as they could, but the all-day journey on three different rail lines and making two transfers was challenging with two young children. When the storm hit, rails throughout Georgia closed down, including the narrow-gauge Hartwell line that was the only ride out of town.

Hunkering down and waiting it out was the best approach for most residents, but as the winter storm continued to snap telecom wires and block roads on February 6 and 7, Asa Jr. and Helen faced a growing crisis: Asa III was sick. Those were the days before antibiotics and other modern medicines we take for granted, so all they could do was soothe him, try to alleviate his discomfort, and pray for the ice to melt enough to grant them passage to the town's doctor.

Although the storm eased up in a few days, the damage was widespread, and temperatures held below freezing.[27] In Atlanta, the storm had caused pandemonium. Some local phone lines worked, as long as the telephone poles held up against the elements, but the city was cut off from the outside world, as were most towns across the state. Some folks ventured out to take in the sights of the frozen city, but mobility was limited to foot traffic. Anything larger slid out of control.[28]

In Hartwell the roads remained impassable. Asa III's illness worsened, and on February 8, he passed away. Asa Jr., Helen, and Lucy III remained isolated in North Georgia, grieving alone, with no way to contact his family and no trains running south. Just like everyone else, they had to wait until cleanup could begin.

Meanwhile, Asa Sr., Lucy Elizabeth, and the rest of the Candler clan were unaware of the tragedy. On the ninth, the sun broke through, and forecasts called for the ice to start melting. With the end in sight, Atlanta celebrated with humor and optimism as linemen went to work fixing the power lines and telecom connections to the surrounding areas.[29]

But even by February 10, there was still no way to wire a message from Hartwell to Atlanta. Trains had started running again, even in the northern reaches of the state. Asa Jr. and Helen faced a decision: should they wait until the lines were back up and send a telegraph, or should they take the first available train and tell their loved ones in person? They chose the latter, and prepared to make their way toward family support. They built a small casket, placed the baby inside, and carried him and Lucy III to the train depot.

Leaving in the morning meant arriving in the evening, and they traveled the whole way with the gravity of their news weighing on them.[30] When Asa Sr. arrived to pick them up at the depot, he finally learned that he'd lost his first grandson and namesake. The telegraph wires were reconnected the very next day.

The funeral was held at the Candlers' home, Callan Castle in Inman Park. Bishop Warren Candler officiated, as he did for every family wedding and funeral. Friends of the extended Candler circle were invited to visit and offer their condolences.[31] After that, life went on, as it must.

Asa Jr. and Helen welcomed their next child, John, on December 16, 1905. In total, they had seven children, six of whom survived. Family lore says Asa Jr. had wanted to give his name to his next son, but Helen wouldn't allow it.[32] The name ended up passing to Walter and his wife, Eugenia Winnie Bigham Candler, who named their second son Asa IV in 1909. Family lore also claims that Buddie and Walter bickered about the rightful lineage of the name, and Buddie won. His first grandson, born to John and his wife, Elizabeth Brandon Candler, was named Asa V, and the name has remained in his lineage ever since.

Asa III's loss was felt deeply by the family. In a photo taken in 1909, Asa Sr. and Lucy Elizabeth are shown with all of their children and grandchildren, and at the center of the photo stands a portrait of their lost grandson, four years after his death.

In the wake of this sorrow, Asa Sr. had made his final executive decision about Asa Jr.'s life. The mill had suffered continual financial losses since he purchased it, and the thought of his son, daughter-in-law, and grandchildren isolated so far away was more than he could bear. He decided to sell the mill at a loss and bring Buddie home. They spent the rest of 1905 wrapping up his duties, and in 1906, Buddie, Helen, Lucy III, and John boarded the Hartwell railway one last time, bound for Atlanta for good.

The mill struggled on for a few more years. In 1910, Asa Sr. flirted with the idea of building a mill closer to Atlanta and transferring the equipment. That idea never became reality. Instead, he sold it.[33]

PART 2

YOUNG PROFESSIONAL

Mr. Candler is of the type that always succeeds. He comes from a family of successful men. His father, Asa G. Candler, is one of the city's leading financiers, bankers and capitalists, and his son inherits all his good qualities.[1]

CHAPTER 5

The People's Buddie

In 1906, Asa Candler Jr. relocated from Hartwell, Georgia, to Atlanta with his wife, Helen, and children, Lucy III and John. They moved temporarily to a house in the Fourth Ward neighborhood at 348 North Jackson Street, between Angier and Pine.[2] The other Candlers had all relocated to the Inman Park neighborhood by that point, and Buddie wasn't going to be left out again. Right away, he secured a lot in Inman Park and began building a home one block up Euclid Avenue from his parents.[3]

The first thing Asa Jr. needed after settling in was income. His father gave him a nominal role as a shipping clerk at Coca-Cola, a tenure so brief that few records exist to prove it happened.[4] Asa Sr. also arranged for him to join the board of directors of the newly formed Southern States Life Insurance Company. A look through the directors list in the Southern States announcement is telling. Every board member was an executive with another existing, profitable venture. Buddie was one of only two board members with no business ties and no pedigree to speak of.[5] So why was he a member? One word: tontine.

In short, a tontine is a financial agreement wherein the last surviving member of the group becomes the sole beneficiary. Tontine life insurance was a popular scheme in the 1800s that enabled wealthy men to contribute money to an initial payout pool and then sell policies that were highly unlikely to be cashed in. Their initial investment was held at minimal risk, and they made good money from the premiums paid by customers who didn't realize the odds were against them ever benefiting. For a young capitalist looking to lay his financial foundation, this was a potential-filled opportunity.

However, the U.S. government began investigating tontine insurance in the early 1900s, and Southern States Life Insurance Company came under scrutiny.[6] After a round of testifying by industry investors before the Armstrong investigation in June 1906, Southern States appears to have lost steam. By 1907, the state of Louisiana had listed Southern States Life Insurance by name in legislation barring tontine insurance.[7] Following the investigation, Buddie left the insurance game as abruptly as he'd entered.

The challenge he faced upon his return to Atlanta was that he was now in his mid-twenties with no established business prospects. He'd moved around so much that he had few existing relationships in the metro area on which to base partnerships and alliances. By contrast, his father was a well-respected businessman who could spin straw into gold and had become a dominant force in the regional business community. How was Buddie to create a name for himself when his father had already taken full ownership of it?

Asa Candler Jr. is often portrayed as the spoiled beneficiary of his father's wealth, a man who inherited a fortune and spent it willy-nilly on extravagances. Some stories include speculation that he squandered his inheritance and died with little left to his name. But this broad portrayal misses the mark. It's not that he wasn't spoiled or that he didn't squander money throughout his life. He was and he did, and both of those qualities would quickly become apparent after he hit it big in 1919. But in the nineteen-aughts, he didn't wait for his father's wealth. One can criticize Asa Jr. for plenty of reasons, but if his history shows us anything, it's that the man hustled. Nowhere is this more apparent than during the decade between his return to Atlanta and his inheritance.

Buddie was keenly interested in establishing himself and stepping out of his father's shadow. He explored various options, trying a diverse set of opportunities before finding his footing. This left him open to suggestions from those who may not have had his best interests in mind. In 1906, for example, he was misled into an opportunity that could have undermined his burgeoning reputation. He almost went into politics.

On Friday, June 22, 1906, Buddie surprised his family by announcing that he intended to run for a seat on the Atlanta City Council, representing the Fourth Ward neighborhood.[8] This was unprecedented. Buddie had never been a joiner, instead always following his own whims for his own enjoyment. The only time he'd ever volunteered for responsibility was when he started the Bicycle Club at Emory College, and that was short-lived. He'd spent his time in California feeding his indulgences, and he hadn't taken on any significant role in Hartwell's civic community. So why was he suddenly interested in politics?

He may not have come up with the idea himself. On that same Friday, a group of citizens claiming to represent the interests of the Fourth Ward had come knocking on his door. They presented a petition that read as follows: "Dear Sir: We the undersigned citizens of the fourth ward, earnestly request of you that you permit the use of your name as a candidate to represent the fourth ward in the city council in the coming primary."[9]

WOODRUFF MEN VERSUS CANDLER MEN

➜ Ernest Woodruff (1863–1944) was a powerful force in the development of Atlanta in the late 1800s and early 1900s. He and his brother-in-law Joel Hurt (1850–1926) invested in steel, railcars, and banking. They financed the development of Inman Park and were the original backers of the Druid Hills land development. They built roads, businesses, and transport. The name Woodruff appears nearly as often as the name Candler in parks and on buildings in the city of Atlanta.

Ernest Woodruff didn't like Asa Candler Sr., and the feeling was mutual. They didn't appreciate each other's business methods, and they competed for dominance in an infrastructural pissing match that benefited the city in spite of its pettiness.[10] One need only look at Asa Sr.'s grand Inman Park mansion, Callan Castle, in relation to Joel Hurt's and Ernest Woodruff's properties to see how the Coca-Cola king thumbed his nose at them.

The Candlers and the Woodruffs bumped heads in business many times, often in financial transactions that were competitive rather than cooperative. Woodruff and Hurt built the original bank-anchored Equitable Building on Edgewood Avenue and Pryor Street in 1892, and took the title of tallest building in Atlanta. In 1904, Asa Sr. broke ground on the much taller Candler Building with a similar triangular shape and more extravagant detailing, and it too had a bank as its anchor business.[11] In 1908, Woodruff and Hurt's Kirkwood Land Company put its languishing Druid Hills development up for sale, and Asa Sr. purchased it and brought the neighborhood to completion.[12] In 1919, when the Candler kids sold Coca-Cola, they chose Ernest Woodruff as the buyer, wounding their father's pride deeply in the process. The deal was negotiated by Samuel Candler Dobbs, who was ostensibly a Candler man, but he demonstrated over the years that he was loyal to the Woodruffs.

The competition between the Candler camp and the Woodruff camp didn't stop with the senior generation. Charles Howard's brothers-in-law, Thomas, Walker, and William Glenn, were all Woodruff men. Glenn family lore claims that Thomas's home, Glenridge Hall in Dunwoody, was designed to outclass Howard's Callanwolde mansion in both style and amenities.[13] The stuff of legends, the family feud between the Candlers and Woodruffs ran deep.

The list of signatories on the petition reveals some clues. While it contained some key, prominent names in the Atlanta business community, those in the Candler inner circle were absent, including his immediate family members. More interesting is that the list was full of Woodruff men, including Ernest Woodruff, Samuel Candler Dobbs, members of Joel Hurt's family, and members of the Glenn family. Eight names can be documented as Woodruff men. Given the competition between the factions, why would Ernest Woodruff seek to advance a Candler's standing in the local government? There are two possibilities:

1. He knew of Asa Jr.'s background, his business follies, and his personality. Urging Asa Sr.'s impetuous and unpolished son into the political spotlight could have been a setup for Buddie to lose. He could be a fall guy who would ensure the Woodruffs' preferred candidate would win the primary, and at the same time scuff some of the shine off the Candler name.
2. Woodruff wanted another Candler in his camp. He already had Samuel Candler Dobbs on his side, and that paid off handsomely years later when Dobbs pulled off what Asa Sr. had resisted, which was a transfer of the Coca-Cola money machine to Woodruff control. One of Asa Sr.'s offspring, especially the one who bore his name, could be an interesting alliance.

The answer is probably the latter rather than the former. In a 1925 deposition in the case *United States v. the Coca-Cola Company*, Ernest Woodruff said: "From time to time I had in mind—probably in 1907, 1908, 1909 and 1910 or along there—getting hold of the [Coca-Cola] company. Circumstances were such that I thought it best to make no direct efforts to do so, but

I talked at various times with various people who were understood to have Mr. Candler's ear."[14]

But Asa Sr. spotted the looming trouble and intervened immediately. Just one week after accepting the nomination, Buddie issued a carefully worded notice of withdrawal that included the phrase "he feels he might embarrass a number of his friends if he remains in the race."[15] Perhaps Asa Sr. should have let Buddie try, but in all likelihood he correctly anticipated a poor fit between public office and his son's proclivities.

Soon after his one-week foray into the local political scene, Buddie accepted a role as the building manager for the newly opened Candler Building and took a basement office on the premises. His and Helen's daughter Laura was born in December 1907, and the family moved into their newly completed home in Inman Park, which they shared with Helen's brother William Magill, a machinist at the Candler Building, and a servant named Landrum Anderson, who had moved from Hartwell with them.[16]

Soon after, Buddie broadened his purview by adding oversight of another of his father's ventures, the Candler Investment Company, which held Asa Sr.'s sizable real estate portfolio. Buddie's duties included collecting rent, leasing offices, and managing maintenance workers, but no strategic business management. It seemed to be a better fit than the higher level of responsibility he'd been saddled with in California and Hartwell, and it gave him valuable experience that would serve him well as he built a real estate empire of his own in the 1920s and '30s. The Candler Building manager position granted him prominence and put him in contact with lessees who ran important, successful businesses. It also gave him access to the spoils of daily operations, including wholesale coal pricing. Starting in June 1907 and throughout 1908, Buddie ran ads for discounted bulk coal for homeowners and businesses, distributing his supply out of a yard on Krog Street.[17]

At the same time, he socialized and participated in events that indulged his interests. In a life filled with passions, cars were his number one fixation for more than a decade, and he threw his energy, money, and professional reputation into promoting driving as a viable sport. He had already been possessed with automobile fever when he moved home from Hartwell. Fortunately, many of the city's wealthy men shared his passion.

In July 1907, Buddie participated in a citywide event that gave more than 350 orphans a day of fun and pleasure. More than a hundred automobiles piloted by wealthy local men, including Buddie, Edward Inman, and A. G.

Candler Building entrance, circa 2019. Photo by the author.

White marble
staircase, Candler
Building lobby,
circa 2019. Photo
by the author.

Rhodes of Rhodes-Haverty, lined up to give the children what was likely their first ride in a motorized vehicle.

104 MACHINES PARADE TODAY

There will be one hundred and four cars in line this afternoon at 2:30 o'clock when the orphan children's great automobile parade starts from Trinity Methodist church, at the corner of Whitehall street and Trinity avenue.

... Each child will be provided with a tin horn and all along the line of march they will make the welkin ring. Ed Inman's big car will lead the procession and Chief Cumming, of the fire department, will furnish a bugler to go with this car. W. O. Jones will be marshal of the day and will direct the formation of the line on Trinity avenue.

Manager Hugh L. Cordoza of the Ponce de Leon park, has tendered free access to all the amusement features of the park.... There will also be a bountiful supply of ice cream and candies, Wiley contributing the former and the Frank E. Block Company and Harry L. Schlesinger the latter. Gershon Brothers donated 500 wooden saucers and Dr. M. Turner as many spoons.

...When the children are put down at the park the automobiles will disperse their several ways and the children will revel in the delights at Ponce de Leon till 6 o'clock, when five electric cars will be in waiting to take the little fellows back home, there being one car for each home, these cars being tendered free by the Georgia Railway and Electric Company.[18]

Automobile fever wasn't limited to Atlanta, of course. Around this time, the annual Vanderbilt Cup races were taking off as a popular sporting event. In upstate New York, the Briarcliff Trophy stock car race drew massive crowds. While managing the mill, Buddie had traveled to New York for business as the Vanderbilt Cup and Briarcliff Trophy races were peaking in popularity. Due to the timing of these events and Buddie's skyrocketing obsession with automobiles, one could speculate that he may have attended one or more of these events in the early 1900s.

In July 1908, Buddie drove with a party of prominent Atlantans to Marietta to nominate Joseph M. Brown for governor.[19] At this time, Buddie reportedly owned a Peerless car, a luxury purchase for the time period. This event was his first public appearance with a fellow automobile enthusiast named Edward Durant. Buddie and Ed soon formed a fast friendship, and they put their heads together to create more automobile events in Atlanta, starting with pathfinder road tours.

ROAD TOURS

➔ When automobiles were new, roads that were smooth enough for motorized traffic were hard to find. Pitted, rutted dirt lanes were fine for wagons and carriages, which traveled at slow speeds relative to what an automobile could do. Even the earliest steamers were capable of traveling a mile a minute, but rough roads limited drivers to lower gears. Cities, which often laid down gravel or macadamized their busiest streets, were congested with pedestrians, horse-drawn carriages, and streetcars. And even if congestion weren't an issue, Atlanta's downtown was paved with Belgian blocks of Stone Mountain and Arabia Mountain granite, which didn't make for the smoothest ride.[20]

Cruising simply wasn't what it is today.

The pathfinder road tour phenomenon gave us the open road concept and birthed the vast network of smooth streets and highways that we drive on today. In 1907, William K. Vanderbilt broke ground on the first commuter road in the United States, the Long Island Motor Parkway, so he could drive his beloved collection of cars in conditions more pleasurable than country roads.[21] But he was part of a family that could afford to lay down roads wherever they pleased. Your average wealthy-but-not-Vanderbilt-wealthy driver had to be more creative.

Driving clubs sprang up and, often in partnership with local newspapers, started sponsoring the pathfinder tours. Participants would compete to find the fastest, smoothest route between two points and map the way while also trying to set timing records. Winning routes were then published for other motorists to enjoy. These tours defined routes that became major roadways that still exist today.

Buddie was eager to join in the pathfinder tour fad. He drove or rode in a number of tours around the state. Then, in November 1908, he joined the newly established Atlanta Automobile Club as a member of the executive committee under club president and founder Ed Inman.[22]

That was when the trouble began.

*No other city in the country twice Atlanta's size has ever
put on anything in the entertainment line half so big
nor nearly so successful as automobile week.*[1]

CHAPTER 6

Gentlemen, Start Your Engines

Just before the turn of the twentieth century, automobiles roared into existence and captured the imaginations of gearheads around the globe. Because
these early machines were handmade, bespoke feats of engineering, their
very nature made them expensive, impractical playthings of the wealthy.
Henry Ford's consumer-friendly Model T didn't come along until 1908.
Before that, your average Joe wasn't in the market for an automobile.

In the earliest days, pitting cars against each other in competition was an
obvious and exciting use for the technology. How else could manufacturers
and wealthy gadabouts prove their superiority over each other? Auto racing,
typically over bumpy rural roads on cross-country courses, gained popularity in Europe first. In 1895 the first true automobile race ran from Paris to
Bordeaux, France. That same year, the United States held its first automobile
race in Chicago, but the European racing community coordinated better and
pulled together many competitions before the United States became a real
contender.

In 1904, William K. Vanderbilt decided the United States was overdue for
a trophy run of its own. He established the Vanderbilt Cup race on Long
Island, New York, which was open to international competitors. American
auto manufacturers jumped at the chance to demonstrate their viability
against their European counterparts. But try as they might, they couldn't
grab a win. In fact, they wouldn't win until 1908, when George Robertson
took the cup in a Locomobile known as Old 16.

The Vanderbilt Cup was a massive sporting event, pulling record attendance numbers and inspiring wealthy men across the country to travel to New York just to watch. In February 1908, a few months prior to Old 16's win, the start of a round-the-world race from New York to Paris captured imaginations and made headlines. Only three of the six participants made the full run, and an American-made Thomas Flyer came in first on July 30. So when George Robertson's Locomobile clinched the Vanderbilt Cup in the autumn of that year, proving America's mechanical might, the victory became a watershed moment for domestic auto racing.

Due to the hazards of driving on country roads, which occasionally resulted in both driver and spectator deaths, the notion of specially designed and dedicated racetracks gained popularity. Controlled conditions, spectator barriers, and consolidated action certainly sounded more appealing than sitting idly on the side of a road, waiting for competitors to roar into view and disappear in a cloud of dust. While many regions kicked off racetrack projects, the most notable for the purpose of this story was Indianapolis, Indiana. Following Old 16's win, planning began for the Indianapolis Motor Speedway, which is known today as the home of the Indy 500 and the U.S. Grand Prix. Construction crews broke ground in March 1909, and the two-mile course opened in June for a balloon race with over forty thousand attendees.[2]

What does this all have to do with Asa Candler Jr.? Here's how the timeline plays out:

- In 1906, Buddie moved back to Atlanta and settled into the city's business community. In July 1907, he participated in the city's largest automobile event to date, which featured 104 cars in a parade supporting local orphanages.
- In July 1908, he attended a political event thrown by a nominee for the governor's office, where he rode in the car of honor with a man named Edward Durant. Also in July 1908, an American-made Thomas Flyer driven by George Schuster took first place in the New York to Paris race.
- In October 1908, George Robertson took the Vanderbilt Cup for the United States, marking America's first stateside win.
- In November 1908, just thirteen days after Old 16's win, Edward Inman established the Atlanta Automobile Club, with Buddie as one of the

founding members. The stated goal of the club was to promote automobile events in the city and build a fancy clubhouse. The group later
changed its name to the Fulton County Automobile Club to avoid sharing initials with the Atlanta Athletic Club.[3]

- In March 1909, Indianapolis broke ground on the Indianapolis Motor
  Speedway, announcing that it would be the world's greatest automobile
  racing track and that Indianapolis would be the undisputed center of
  the automobile industry.
- That same spring, Buddie and Edward Durant stirred up rumors in
  the Atlanta business community when they were spotted in Hapeville,
  Georgia, about seven miles south of downtown Atlanta. Leveraging
  assets available to him as the manager of the Candler Investment
  Company, Buddie bought 290 acres of farmland. He and Durant responded evasively when asked about their intentions, even claiming
  that they were planning to establish a large cemetery.[4] Behind the
  scenes, however, they took a proposal to Asa Sr., who agreed to partially
  fund the construction of their secret project.
- In April 1909, Asa Candler Sr. rallied the business community around
  a proposal to host a national week-long automobile industry event in
  November known as Auto Week.
- On May 23, 1909, Buddie and Durant announced their plans to build a
  $225,000 (well over $6 million in 2020 dollars) world-class racing track
  that would establish Atlanta as the leader in automobile greatness.

The South was already home to other regional tracks, including one in
Savannah, Georgia, and one in Birmingham, Alabama. But in 1909, Indianapolis was the project to beat, and Atlanta was now in the race.

The day after their announcement, Buddie and Durant participated in a
pathfinder tour sponsored by the *Atlanta Constitution*. The purpose of the
tour was to find and map the best, smoothest, fastest roads between Atlanta
and Macon. Buddie convinced Asa Sr. to come along for the ride, and they
started their route down Stewart Avenue (now Metropolitan Parkway), which
was a long stretch of road that ran directly between downtown and Hapeville.[5]
The *Constitution*'s pathfinder tour gave them the opportunity to finalize the
plans for their racetrack, which included identifying how race attendees would
get from the city center to the outskirts where the track would stand.

Through the end of May and into the beginning of June, Buddie and
Durant rallied for subscriptions to fully fund the track's construction. In

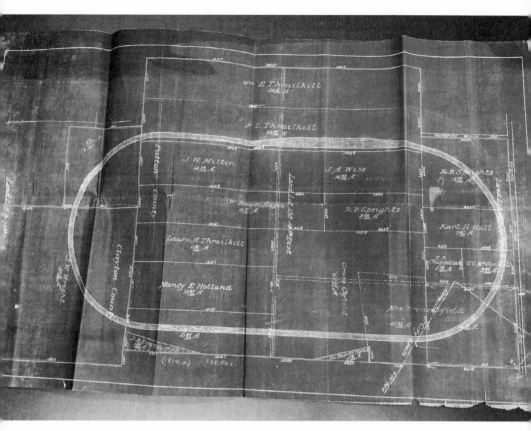

Original blueprint of the Atlanta Speedway, which shows the former farmland property lines. Courtesy of the author.

the meantime, details emerged about the speedway's planned features. With thirty thousand grandstand seats and open-air viewing, the two-mile track would be sixty feet wide on the turns and back stretch, and one hundred feet wide on the home stretch. The banks would rise ten feet to the outer edge at a "scientifically shaped" angle of six degrees. The track bed was built on a red earth base and covered in Augusta chert mixed with a special oil. The elevated grandstands made fences and rails unnecessary to protect the spectators, and a wire suspension bridge above the racing surface would provide safe passage for track officials.

Eleven farmhouses would be removed from the planned center of the oval to make way for a speedway village, providing living and working quarters for racing teams and management. They planned for at least twelve fireproof garages, each accommodating four cars—two in the front, two in the rear—with drivers housed in rooms directly above. Additionally they planned a machine shop with power, a clubhouse, groundskeeper quarters, a complete waterworks and lighting plant, and restaurants beneath the grandstand near the ticket gates.[6]

Of course, these details varied depending on the publication, and not all came to fruition. For example, the garage paddock was reduced by omitting the second-floor apartments. The specs were made public well before the construction crews made any significant progress. This was the PR machine ramping up, building the necessary excitement to drive ticket sales and re-coup the cost of the build.

In June, the two Asas and Ed Durant accepted bids from construction companies that were willing to work within their budget and according to an aggressive timeline. The goal was to build their two-mile track, on par with the Indianapolis plan, in just five months. Must-haves included the state-of-the-art racing surface, the grandstands, the mechanic sheds, the clubhouse, and a deadline of November to coordinate with Auto Week. Of course, since Indianapolis was aiming for its first auto race in August, the Georgia team would have shortened the timeline if they could. But November was their best shot, and even that was asking a lot of their workforce.[7]

By the end of June, they had their construction contract in place. The crew—nearly a thousand laborers—broke ground and began leveling the farmland and routing the drainage of the various waterways that threaded through the landscape.[8] At the same time, Asa Sr. continued to coordinate with the Atlanta business community to ensure the success of Auto Week, which would offer a roster of automobile-themed events throughout down-town Atlanta while the races were running. These included welcoming the arrival of participants in the New York to Atlanta Good Roads Tour, a mas-sive auto show, and parties galore. It would be, Asa Sr. claimed, a huge boon to Atlanta businesses. A surefire moneymaker for all.[9]

Because Asa Sr. was putting so much on the line, he expected to control the decisions about the track's costly construction and operation. However, he didn't want to be personally liable for the potential losses if his son's far-fetched scheme went awry. That meant he needed to form a new business entity through which he could arrange the financing and management of the project. In July 1909, with a combined majority of shares, the two Asas launched the Atlanta Automobile Association, borrowing two-thirds of Ed Inman's original club name.[10]

Naturally, Asa Jr. was appointed president of the AAA. He was the face of the organization and its speedway project, and rightfully the face of its success or failure. The board of directors, all men in Asa Sr.'s inner circle plus Ed Durant, appointed an executive committee with complete authority over all things related to the track. This maneuver gave Asa Sr. absolute control. On the surface, it appeared that Asa Jr. was in charge, and evidence suggests that he was given a long lead to make decisions and guide the project. But at the end of the day it was Asa Sr.'s money, and since he'd been burned by his son's poor business instincts before, he had arranged things so that he would retain oversight. After all, Asa Griggs Candler Sr. didn't get rich by playing fast and loose with investments.

Indianapolis's first official automobile event ran in August 1909, but safety concerns arising about the integrity of the compacted, oiled track surface cut the races short. A few days later, another race there made dramatic headlines when the surface broke up, with debris striking famed driver Louis Chevrolet in the face and killing driver Wilfred Bourque and his "mechanician," Harry Halcomb. On day three of the event, a car careened into the crowd of spectators, killing two attendees and mechanic Claude Kellum. Then, driver Bruce Keen hit a pothole and crashed into a bridge support.[11]

The Atlanta Automobile Association leaped at the opportunity to use Indianapolis's failures to its benefit. The AAA promoted its scientifically designed track surface, safe spectator distance, and banked turns, promising that its first races would be nothing like the disastrous Indy event.[12]

In September, the AAA threw a barbecue at the track and invited five hundred of the wealthiest, most important members of the local community to attend. This wasn't just any barbecue; this was a fundraiser.[13] Word had gotten out that the project was well over budget and needed more funds. Rumors circulated that perhaps the AAA generally, and Buddie specifically, were in over their heads. To push back on this growing public perception, the AAA completed its luxurious clubhouse and invited guests to take the new track, or at least the section that was complete, for a spin. They could tour the grandstands and see the concessions area, which of course served Coca-Cola and absolutely no alcohol. The racetrack offered near-beer only, which one journalist noted was "not too near but near enough."[14] Others noted that the hard stuff wasn't too hard to come by, if one knew whom to ask.

Of critical importance was the solicitation of funds to finish paving Stewart Avenue from the city center all the way out to the track. While the AAA had managed to lay an oiled bitumen surface from the track to the edge of the city, promising a dustless drive, the stretch of road from the city limits into the center of town was still unimproved. The AAA needed to rally support for the route that would reach the track from in-town hotels and rail stations.[15]

Behind the scenes, Asa Sr. was working with the Central of Georgia Railway company to lay down tracks from Terminal Station to the speedway, promising that the investment would pay off nicely during Auto Week. Business correspondence on file at Emory University's archives reveals a tense, dubious relationship between the rail company and the AAA, suggesting that while local businesses got on board with the plans for Auto Week, they weren't all convinced that it would be a success.[16]

In spite of this, Asa Sr. continued to gather as much support as he could, raising donations to build up the city's infrastructure to support the influx of tourists. As an active member of the city's chamber of commerce, the man had a knack for bringing businessmen together and pooling money to make more money. Plenty of Atlantans had profited by going along with the elder Asa in other endeavors, so the city put itself on the line to follow him toward a big tourism payoff.

Asa Sr. had an eye for opportunity. He had established the Candler Warehouse Company in 1908 near the intersection of Marietta Street and Fairlie Street, right by the railroad tracks, and he recognized that it was the perfect place to bring in money during Auto Week by housing the supplies that vendors would transport for the auto-themed expo. As the owner of Central Bank and Trust, he offered lending that permitted warehouse customers to use stored goods as collateral. This offered small businessmen an opportunity to store and distribute goods with low overhead, and gave them access to low-interest lending to keep their businesses growing.[17] As a key revenue generator and portfolio diversifier, the Candler Warehouse Company was a valuable player in the growing Candler empire, and Auto Week would prove that value handily. Even Buddie's younger brother Walter got in on the act. He planned to offer automobile storage for out-of-towners who needed a safe place to leave their valuable vehicles at the Candler Garage on Edgewood, down a block from the Candler Building.[18]

In September, the Vanderbilt Cup race planning went into full swing, and Buddie and Durant traveled to New York to do some networking. They spread the word about the Atlanta Speedway, and they cozied up to famous drivers in the hopes of recruiting the best men for their inaugural race. They also announced that they would offer up to $25,000 in prizes and a trophy worth $10,000. On October 19, 1909, the *Indianapolis News* reported the following, including a misrepresentation of Greek mythology. Note the superlative.

> The $10,000 trophy which will be contested for during the meet . . . is considered by experts and judges of high art to be the most magnificent automobile trophy ever designed. The trophy is six feet high and made of solid silver. It is a representation of the mythological god of speed, Atlanta, running away with the Greek goddess, Atalanta.
>
> Atlanta has outspread wings to assist him in his speed, and the maiden he holds in his arms holds the laurel leaves of victory in one hand and an automobile of gold in the other. Around the base of the trophy is the picture of an automobile race, below which are the seals of Atlanta and the state of Georgia.[19]

While this was going on, newspapers were starting to spread the word that the racetrack project had gone $5,000 over budget (more than $130,000 in 2020 dollars).[20]

Then, more gossip emerged. Rumors spread that Ed Inman's Fulton County Automobile Club and the Atlanta Automobile Association would merge. In fact, the primary rumor was that the AAA had asked the FCAC to absorb it. This was, of course, anathema to Buddie's growing sense of superiority. He insisted that there was no way the two clubs would merge. And besides, he claimed, the FCAC had approached the AAA, not the other way around. Inman gave an evenhanded statement, claiming he didn't care either way, and if the club members voted to merge he would not block the move. Buddie, on the other hand, emphatically insisted that the FCAC had made repeated appeals for the AAA to merge with it, but as a member of both clubs he saw no point in the merger. Finally, establishing a pattern that would play out later in his life, he blamed the premature press for souring the whole deal, which was a bit contradictory.[21] After all, if there were no deal, how could the papers sour it?

On October 23, 1909, the AAA declared the track complete and celebrated with an exhibition race. The group recruited big names to participate, including legendary drivers Barney Oldfield and George Robertson. Ed Durant set the statewide amateur speed record in his Renault, while Buddie's racer was driven by a young man named Florence Michael, who adopted the stage name Louis Cliquot for his racing debut.[22]

On October 30, the Vanderbilt Cup in New York drew big crowds and the biggest names in auto racing. When the race was over, those same big-name racers turned back around and headed south to Atlanta once again. Auto Week was about to begin. On November 5, another exhibition race entertained the early birds who had arrived before the festivities kicked off. The famous driver Joan Cuneo took her car onto the track and handily defeated the competition as she ran the two-mile circuit in one minute, forty-five seconds. On November 6, the first cars in the New York to Atlanta Good Roads Tour arrived and were greeted by an exuberant welcome and a celebration in their honor. The crowd was growing every day, and the stakes were so high that Buddie and Durant took out a $100,000 insurance policy to protect their investment in case of rain.[23]

Finally, on November 9, the official races began. More than 150,000 racing enthusiasts attended the inaugural event, and the auto show in downtown Atlanta went off without a hitch. When the week of festivities wrapped, the *Atlanta Journal* had this to say:

> With the completion of the speedway races in the afternoon and the closing of the automobile show last night, a new page in Atlanta's history was written. The page will stand out in bold relief when the special events it chronicles are compared with others among the many notable achievements of the city.
>
> The success of the whole affair may be summed up in the statement that Atlanta had something to offer, and offered it in the best possible manner. No other city in the country twice Atlanta's size has ever put on anything in the entertainment line half so big nor nearly so successful as automobile week.[24]

With such high praise and massive turnout, it seemed the event was a rousing success. Asa Jr.'s vision had paid off, and Asa Sr.'s investment had been well placed.

Well, not exactly. Trouble loomed, and although on the surface the endeavor was successful, the Atlanta Speedway's failure was inevitable. Despite all of the Candlers' efforts to bury Indianapolis, Indy's track still exists, and Atlanta's track barely survived two seasons. Under scrutiny, the reasons for the failure become quite apparent, and they all lead back to Buddie Candler.

This car goes some.[1]

CHAPTER 7

The Legend of the Merry Widow

By 1909, racing had embraced the concept of the "stock car," which usually stipulated that the entrants had to be models that were for sale to the general public with a minimum number of vehicles already manufactured. The stipulation could vary from race to race, and many races included events for both stock cars and specialized racers.

The list of brand names one encounters when reading about this period in U.S. history contains familiar ones that still exist, like Fiat and Renault, but others, like Christie, Isotta, Stearns, Simplex, Apperson, Matheson, Marmon, and Pope-Toledo, have faded from common memory. During their day, they were hot contenders for racing titles and highly sought after by wealthy car enthusiasts. One particular Pope-Toledo ended up making headlines at Atlanta's inaugural races, but not for its success.

Pope-Toledo started out as the Pope Motor Car Company. It struggled to compete in a hot automobile market and attempted to diversify into a number of lines by acquiring other brands. The company offered the Pope-Hartford, Pope-Robinson, Pope-Tribune, Pope-Waverley, and Pope-Toledo. The latter was the most expensive of its lines and was marketed exclusively to the very wealthy, especially those with a need for speed.

The Pope-Toledo brand was well respected, and the quality of fabrication was undeniable, but there just weren't enough rich playboys to go around. Unable to keep up with the exponentially expanding field of competitors, Albert Pope filed for bankruptcy in 1907. Pope passed away in 1909, and his company limped along for a few more years before closing its doors. It simply wasn't cost-effective to produce cars the way it did when Ford was cranking out mass-marketed affordable models. But the company tried its hardest to make a name, and to this end in 1909 it built a beast of a car that became known as the Merry Widow.

Based on a profile that appeared in the *Atlanta Constitution*, it appears this vehicle was built especially for the Vanderbilt Cup races, but it never appeared in a lineup there.[2] Instead, the Pope Motor Car Company gave the car to Buddie, who was by that time a well-known amateur driver. That was in the same month that Buddie broke ground on his ambitious project to build the Atlanta Speedway and hold record-breaking races by November 1909. This Pope-Toledo, valued between $10,000 and $35,000, was gifted to him as a thank you for his efforts to support American auto racing. Split the difference on that valuation, and in 2020 dollars the car was worth more than $600,000. That's an expensive racer. The Pope company wasn't kidding around; it wanted a win.

At 136 horsepower, the four-cylinder powerhouse was called a "two-mile-a-minute car" by the press. Its tank held thirty-six gallons of gasoline and could go five hundred miles without fueling up—a gas efficiency of about 13.8 miles per gallon. Described as "nearly all engine," it weighed 2,202 pounds; the engine accounted for 1,800 pounds. Painted a color known as "French gray," it was described by a fanciful writer as a "graveyard rabbit," just one of the many grim phrases used to describe the vehicle during its rise to fame. The exhaust pipes that emerged from the side of the hood were described as sounding like a Gatling gun when the car was driven at high speeds. The Merry Widow was guaranteed to reach 125 miles per hour. Pope's test driver clocked in at 127 during its maiden drive and claimed it hadn't topped out yet. As one writer opined, "This car goes some."[3]

The biggest drivers in racing were lined up for the first Atlanta Speedway event in November 1909. They brought their biggest and baddest cars. In reviewing the list of entrants, only three of the competing cars approached the 136-horsepower Pope-Toledo. None exceeded it. Louis Strang's Fiat, Barney Oldfield's Benz, and Walter Christie's Christie were the Merry Widow's closest competitors in terms of horsepower. However, if one reviews the lineups for individual races, the Merry Widow is mentioned nowhere.

The 1909 Atlanta races were open to professional drivers only, with the exception of one amateur event. That meant Buddie couldn't drive his own car in the big races. Although he wasn't averse to driving fast, he likely wouldn't have wanted to drive even if he could. Wealthy men who owned showy race cars liked to hire big names to drive on their behalf. It was what one did when one had the means. That meant the president of the Atlanta Speedway had to find someone to drive his car or he wouldn't be represented at the event.

During the October exhibition race, which was intended to drum up press for the November event, Buddie had asked Louis Cliquot to drive the Merry Widow in a speed trial. Cliquot was a rookie, totally unknown to the racing world. (Only a single record exists of Louis Cliquot competing outside of the 1909 Atlanta event. In 1910, he drove a Knox, led for zero laps, and dropped out due to a broken crankshaft. After that, his racing career was over.)

Buddie hired young Cliquot to drive his most powerful car at the exhibition race. This point is worth emphasizing because the Merry Widow had a fairly unpleasant reputation among sports journalists who covered the auto-racing beat. Driven to purple prose, writers described the car as ornery, temperamental, spiteful, and "of ill-repute and worse manners."[4] Many experienced drivers had passed on the opportunity to drive it, preferring not to run afoul of its fury. But Cliquot was keen to establish his name, and the invincibility of youth probably played a part in his willingness to take on the beast. The October exhibition went off without a hitch, and Cliquot drove the Pope-Toledo without incident, although he kept it well below the two-mile-a-minute mark.

Then Auto Week arrived. On the first day of the five-day event, Cliquot went into the Pope-Toledo's garage to prepare it for the day's races. He hand-cranked the engine, which suddenly backfired and kicked back, wrenching the crank into a reverse rotation and fracturing his arm in three places.[5] Cliquot was out and would not race another time until May 1910, and then never again.

Buddie now had no driver, and this would not stand. He approached Charles L. Basle, one of the two Renault drivers, and asked if he would take on the Merry Widow. Mind you, these were professional drivers, so this request came with a paycheck. Given the last-minute urgency and Buddie's reputation for playing liberally with his money, it was likely an attractive offer. Basle worked on the engine for a day, trying to tune it up to racing condition. In those days, race cars went down in the blink of an eye, setting records one second, rattling to broken bits the next. Frequent tune-ups were part of the game. Basle put some time in but ultimately decided to politely decline.

He passed the opportunity over to Hugh Judson "Juddy" Kilpatrick, who had arrived with a Hotchkiss that he'd driven in the 1908 Vanderbilt Cup race. Unfortunately for Kilpatrick, the Hotchkiss was dead on arrival and

Asa Candler Jr. (*center*) with the Pope-Toledo Merry Widow at the Atlanta Speedway inaugural races, 1909. Courtesy of the National Automotive History Collection, Detroit Public Library.

refused to be resurrected. This left him without a car or a chance at any of the prize money, much less the cup. He was a racer of great skill, having set the straightaway record at Long Island at thirty-seven seconds for a mile, but now he was out of the running. Buddie agreed to let Kilpatrick drive the Pope-Toledo if he was willing to take it on.

Kilpatrick took a look under the hood and tinkered around to see what he could do. Walter Christie dropped by and advised him not to drive it. He said it was too dangerous, that its speed was greater than the cylinders could stand.[6] Christie was an auto manufacturer as well as a racer, so he knew machines. And he knew high-powered machines, having brought one himself to the races. His own racer had been speed tested by Barney Oldfield, who later played up its dangerous performance, dubbing it the Killer Christie. It's telling that Walter Christie was willing to get behind the wheel of the Killer Christie but advised Kilpatrick to give the Merry Widow a pass. Kilpatrick disregarded his warning and agreed to pilot the Pope-Toledo in Thursday's race.

On day four of the five-day event, Kilpatrick got the Pope-Toledo up and running. Before the long day of races began, he requested a chance to take it around the track and get a feel for it before vying for a win in the fifty-mile free-for-all. At two miles per lap, his chosen race would require twenty-five laps without major incident. A test drive was a fair ask. He and his mechanician, Roland B. Church, climbed in and set off on their first circuit.

Kilpatrick quickly got the Merry Widow up over a mile a minute. Walter Christie manned the stopwatch and clocked the car at eighty-five miles per hour as it accelerated into the turn at the south end of the track. That was when something went wrong.

As Kilpatrick and Church flew into the back stretch, the engine blew a piston, and two cylinders ejected through the hood of the car, shooting high into the air and blowing the hood off. Kilpatrick reached for the clutch but found it frozen. The engine ignited in a twenty-foot sheet of flame as the car veered uncontrollably to the outer fence, where the banked track dropped off sharply on the other side. The fence took the blow and redirected the car back onto the track, but the impact bucked Kilpatrick and Church free. Without a safety belt, there was nothing to hold them secure, so they flew an estimated 150 feet over the fence and down into the ditch on the other side, where a pile of brush took the brunt of their fall. The car toppled onto its side and tumbled over and over until it came to rest, "turned turtle," in the middle of the track. Then, as one writer of the day described it, "it exploded out of spite."[7]

The Atlanta Speedway featured a state-of-the-art track surface, a mix of red clay, chert gravel, and a special oil to bind it all together, which the owners advertised in response to an accident at the Indianapolis Speedway. Unfortunately for the Merry Widow, Asa Candler Jr., and the forty thousand race attendees, this special asphalt was flammable. The Merry Widow and the track beneath it burned furiously for over an hour before crews could extinguish the flames and safely remove the car from the track. They hurled the charred hulk of twisted metal over the fence and then moved on with the day's events.

Kilpatrick and Church were surprisingly fine. On-scene emergency crews found Church climbing back up the bank to the track laughing, without a scratch on him. Kilpatrick had a few minor cuts, bruises, and burns on the right side of his face where flames had blown back from the engine. His right eyelid was burned, and due to concern over the possibility of losing his sight, he was rushed to the hospital.

The burning wreckage of the Merry Widow after the crash, 1909. Courtesy of the National Automotive History Collection, Detroit Public Library.

Christie visited him in the hospital later, and Kilpatrick reportedly said to him, "You were right, Walter, I sure was lucky."[8] Juddy Kilpatrick fully recovered from his injuries. The carcass of the Merry Widow was unceremoniously disposed of, and the car was never rebuilt. Out, out, brief candle.

Now that the Merry Widow was dead, Atlanta Speedway president Asa Candler Jr. was left without a car to compete. So he did what any wealthy car enthusiast with more pride and money than sense would do. He approached the driver with the best performance over the previous four days and offered to buy his car. That happened to be George Robertson, the very same driver who had bagged the first American win in Old 16 at the 1908 Vanderbilt Cup.

Robertson had shown up to the Atlanta races with a red ninety-horsepower Fiat—sometimes reported as sixty horsepower but inconsistently so—and set impressive times in event after event. He had the most solidly winning machine on the track at that point. On Friday morning, the last day of the event, Buddie approached Robertson and offered to buy his Fiat right then and there. That would make Robertson his driver and give him the best chance for a win in the hotly anticipated two-hundred-mile race. Robertson accepted, and the lineup was set.

Robertson was the favorite to win, and for 163 miles he held the lead. Then the Fiat's chain gave way, and the car ground to a halt. He did his best to perform a fast repair and get back into the race, but he was unable to regain the lead. Impressively, he came in second in spite of the breakdown, but the win went to Louis Disbrow in his Rainier. In third and fourth place, two Renaults put in solid times, emerging from the five-day event with the best demonstrations of reliability. Ray Harroun in a Marmon was a distant fifth, and he only did that well because every other car dropped out.

Louis Strang's oil pump broke. Louis Chevrolet's Buick suffered a total breakdown of its transmission. Both of the Chalmers-Detroit cars were out at the start. The Apperson threw a spring. In the end, only five cars finished out of the eleven that started.

And where was Barney Oldfield in all of this? It seems his Benz was outclassed from day one. Unable to beat the biggest contenders, he sat out most of the races. Resigned to his fate, Oldfield told reporters that Louis Strang's car had him beat. If only Strang's oil pump hadn't failed in the two hundred.

That was what Barney Oldfield said. But what Barney Oldfield did with his free time during those five days laid the groundwork for the drama that erupted in the months that followed, and ultimately led to the track's demise.

We may soon see a residential park or a cemetery made
of the finest automobile speedway in the world.[1]

CHAPTER 8

Trouble at the Track

The inaugural auto races at the Atlanta Speedway in November 1909 looked like a huge success to any outsider or daily attendee. The biggest names in racing participated, records were set, and exciting crashes created thrilling climaxes on days four and five. Concession stands kept attendees fed, and Coca-Cola flowed like wine. Photos of the week-long event captured grinning, laughing, joyous faces during an era when posed photos were still mostly stoic. One would think that the Atlanta Automobile Association would be thrilled by the end result.

And maybe the AAA would have been, if not for Barney Oldfield.

Oldfield was a madman of a race car driver. He started in bicycle racing, but had only tried one gasoline-powered bike before getting into auto racing in 1902. His debut opportunity came about when Henry Ford attempted to race his now-famous Ford 999. When it failed to start up, he sold the automobile to Barney for $800. Barney learned to drive in Ford's machine and won his first race the very same day. Oldfield went on to become one of the most famous early race car drivers, a record setter, and the first man to ever drive a car over sixty miles per hour. His most famous car was the Blitzen Benz.

Oldfield made a name for himself in and outside of the racing world. He had a big personality, and his jovial, cigar-chomping mug can be spotted in photos throughout racing archives. His manager, Bill Pickens, capitalized on Oldfield's braggadocious reputation by promoting him as a speed demon of the highest caliber. And since Barney spent much of his career banned from official events for "outlaw" racing, Pickens also ensured that Barney could make a living by charging premium fees for participation in speed record challenges and public appearances. Ever the opportunist, Oldfield took a role as himself in a ten-week stint on Broadway in a play titled *The Vanderbilt Cup* and even starred in the 1913 film *Race for a Life*.

So when the AAA recruited racers for the Atlanta Speedway's 1909 races, the members knew they had to have Barney Oldfield. It wouldn't be a top-tier event without him, regardless of his reputation for drama. And boy, did he bring the drama.

Auto Week arrived, and the races were ready to kick off. Oldfield showed up with his Benz and his manager and was all set to go. According to testimonials provided in the aftermath, Oldfield and Pickens arrived on Monday for an exhibition race, for which Oldfield was to be paid his usual rate. But just before the race started, Pickens raised the asking price, and he and Oldfield refused to participate unless paid the higher amount. This wasn't unusual for Oldfield and Pickens. The two had built a reputation of being contentious business partners who often started trouble for anyone who wanted to showcase Barney's skills.

The exhibition race was in question while the fees were renegotiated at the last minute. AAA president Asa Candler Jr., secretary Edward Durant, and general manager Edward Clapp discussed the rate hike and came to a consensus: *no way*. They refused to increase their payment and demanded that Barney race at the originally offered price. Then, to put it mildly, words ensued. Candler, Durant, and Clapp unanimously ordered Pickens off the track and banished him to the grandstands. Durant was appointed to keep an eye on him and have him removed if he attempted to enter the track area again.[2] It's worth noting here that Oldfield was not included in the banishment, just Pickens.

This seems to be the agreed-upon version of the events up to this point. The story was reported nationwide in early 1910 in various racing columns, featuring interviews, anonymous insider stories, and speculation by journalists. While the published details vary somewhat after this, the above version is fairly consistent across most sources. But from here on, the reports vary widely, depending on the interviewee.

All reports agree that at some point during the five-day event, Pickens reentered the track area. Tasked with the job of enforcing the ban, Durant took one of two possible actions:

1. Either Durant sought out a police officer and calmly but firmly requested Pickens's removal.[3]
2. Or Durant confronted Pickens in an ungentlemanly way, forcing Buddie to intervene and break up the confrontation.[4]

But Pickens refused to go, instead informing Durant that Buddie himself had invited him back. Then, depending on who told the story, one of two things happened:

1. Either Durant immediately departed without a fight, fed up with some undocumented preceding behavior that made him cut ties with Buddie on the spot, and peacefully returned to the clubhouse because there was no use in arguing.[5]
2. Or Durant and Buddie had become increasingly frustrated with each other over the course of the track's construction, and the tense friendship snapped when Pickens characteristically acted up. The resulting argument inspired Durant to wash his hands of the whole event, and he stormed off to the clubhouse to stew.[6]

No matter which way it went, the undisputed facts are that Bill Pickens was banned from the track for quarreling about Barney Oldfield's fees, Buddie invited him back without consulting the other AAA officers, and Buddie and Durant split their alliance over the incident. This is significant because Buddie and Ed had been publicly inseparable up to that point. They had become best friends and worked the whole track project together over the course of many months.[7] Buddie had even shared the spotlight with Durant in the press coverage, and Buddie rarely shared the spotlight willingly. The fight must have been a doozy.

When Ed Durant returned to the clubhouse to cool off, Asa Candler Sr. sought him out to try to mend the rift. This is how Durant described the exchange:

> I left, intending to have nothing more to do with the meet. I left the track and went to the club house to await the arrival of a party of friends. My action was noised about and soon Mr. Candler's father came to me and asked that I return. He asked me to overlook Asa's action on the ground of his youth.[8]

Overlook his actions on the ground of his youth? Buddie was almost thirty years old. But Asa Sr. always had a way of making excuses for his namesake. This is just one well-documented episode in a lifetime of shielding his drama-prone son from consequences.

Durant claimed that he agreed to let bygones be bygones and returned to the track to fulfill his duties through the end of the five-day event. The Merry Widow crashed on day four, Buddie bought George Robertson's Fiat on day five, and Barney Oldfield continued to race throughout, in spite of the dustup and drama with his fees and manager. Oldfield ran in the one-mile free-for-all, the two-mile free-for-all, and the ten-mile special. He might have won, if not for Louis Strang, whose 120-horsepower Fiat beat him in all three races.[9] It was this triple upset that inspired Oldfield to tell the press that Strang had the fastest car in the world.

If Oldfield stuck around and continued to race, he must have gotten his pay hike. Contentious personality or not, he knew his celebrity value. It's also noteworthy that although he was part of the brouhaha, his manager was ejected, but he was permitted to stay. The AAA had brought in lots of famous names and hadn't made a big deal in the press about Oldfield's attendance in particular. In the end, the event didn't require his reputation as a headliner to succeed. So why was he permitted to continue racing?

One thing that becomes apparent when one researches the life of Asa Candler Jr. is that he loved celebrities. He wanted to be invited into their inner circles. He took on new hobbies and quickly aligned with whoever was the biggest name in the field, making a show of friendship that went beyond business associates or fellow hobbyists. When he started investing in athletics, for example, he became friends with team managers and big-name ballplayers like Ty Cobb. When he discovered magic, he befriended the Great Blackstone and Dante the Great. He also claimed throughout his life that Harry Houdini was a close friend. When he became a Shriner, he aligned with the highest members in the local and national brotherhood. When he became interested in airplanes, he forged connections with the best-known names in air racing, and attempted to share headlines with Charles Lindbergh. When he became a born-again Christian, he traveled in the inner circle of the top figures in the Methodist and Southern Baptist churches.

During Buddie's auto years, he loved famous drivers. He loved the most famous drivers most of all, and they didn't come bigger than Barney Oldfield. Buddie wanted, perhaps needed, to be Oldfield's friend. Comparing personal photos taken throughout Buddie's life, one may notice a unique approach during this time period where his style of dress and presentation changed. In 1909, he started showing up in racing photos with a stub of a cigar jammed deep in his cheek pocket. Although it's well documented that he'd smoked

C 11,280   2272

Atlanta Speedway and grandstands, circa 1909. Courtesy of the National Automotive History Collection, Detroit Public Library.

tobacco since his school days, prior to 1909 he was never photographed with a cigar. After the 1909 racing drama that split alliances, the tucked-in stub was no longer his style. Later in life, he was photographed occasionally with a cigar, but always in his hand, never in his mouth.

If one compares how Buddie presented in 1909 to similarly dated photos of Barney Oldfield, the resemblance is striking. Oldfield was rarely seen without his chomped-down stogie. It was his signature look. The change in Buddie's style around the time that he started mingling with the top names in racing, combined with his behaviors later in life, reveal that he was something of a hero worshiper. As such, he wanted very much to be Barney Oldfield's friend. And if that meant going back on his agreement with his business partners and granting clemency to Bill Pickens, then he was willing to do it.

The November drama could have been the end of it. In fact, Edward Durant thought that was the end of it. He claimed that he went back to the track to see the event through and make the races a success, and he thought he and Buddie would put the incident behind them. But Buddie wasn't over it. There's no record of whether he and Durant exchanged any more words, and since the Candlers rarely made public statements when embroiled in drama, we only have Durant's testimony and anonymous insider statements from other AAA board members to go on. The following information details Durant's version of events, which is corroborated by the other sources.

In December 1909, about a month after the close of the races, the AAA met to hold an election of its officers. Buddie was reaffirmed as president, which was to be expected. Durant assumed he would retain the role of secretary, but to his surprise he was replaced by Buddie's brother-in-law Bill Owens. Insulted by the ouster, Durant decided to have nothing more to do with the active management of the organization, although he still held a seat on the board of directors and owned $5,000 in AAA stock.[10]

In January, he leveraged his position to arrange another meet at the Atlanta Speedway, this time a matchup between Louis Strang and George Robertson. He made the arrangements with the help of Edward Clapp, and they agreed that as a board director and the general manager they had the right to do so. But this didn't go over well with Asa Jr. He declared that no one had authority to arrange a matchup but the AAA president. He withdrew the offer to Strang and Robertson and struck the meet from the schedule.

When approached for a statement, Clapp told the press, "Since Mr. Candler's repudiation of the match race between Strang and Robertson, my resignation, which was to take effect at the pleasure of the board of directors, becomes effective at once."[11]

Durant told the press, "I was canned from the secretaryship at the last meeting of the directors in December by Mr. Candler and his father."[12]

Asa Candler Jr. said, "There is no trouble whatever in the Atlanta Automobile Association."[13] And when asked about Clapp's resignation, he said, "Ed Clapp had no position to resign; he was simply a hired man and his services had been discontinued."[14] That was a lie, since it was established on record that Clapp was indeed the AAA general manager, not a mere hired man.

The drama made the rest of the board of directors nervous. Speaking anonymously to the *Atlanta Georgian*, one director noted that the total track build had cost $300,000 and that approximately $124,000 worth of stock was sold. More could have been sold, but Asa Candler Sr. chose to keep as much of it to himself as he could, since he was the primary financier. Additionally, Asa Sr. had taken a mortgage out on the property, and the mortgage was scheduled to come due in December 1910. Said the anonymous director:

> I do not think Mr. Candler [Sr.] will ever foreclose as long as the track looks like it will make money, but when such races as arranged by Ed Clapp between Strang and Robertson are turned down because the president was not consulted in the preliminary arrangements, we may soon see a residential park or a cemetery made of the finest automobile speedway in the world.[15]

On January 24, Buddie announced that Edward Clapp's replacement had been found. He had hired a former Secret Service agent by the name of J. M. "Bill" Nye to act as general manager. Durant and another anonymous director said Nye was never approved by the board. Asa Jr. was going rogue.

Nye was originally an assistant superintendent of the Atlanta federal penitentiary and had left prison work to pursue a career with the Secret Service in Washington, D.C. In 1909, he was stationed in San Francisco, appointed to an anti-counterfeiting task force, and very highly regarded in his field. According to a press statement appearing in the *Los Angeles Herald*, he left seventeen years of government work to accept a long-term contract at the Atlanta Speedway that promised a higher salary than that of his current chief.[16]

The press statement pointed out the obvious: managing a racetrack is a far cry from civil service and law enforcement. Nye's work history showed no qualifications other than an affable personality and an appreciation for automobiles. But having reviewed Buddie's full history, it's no stretch to assume he was enchanted by Nye's provenance, and that's all it took for him to hand over the keys to the expensive operation. Starry-eyed as ever over people in romanticized lines of work, Buddie offered Nye the general manager position and a generous paycheck if he would relocate to Atlanta. It is clear that Clapp's resignation, whether self-motivated or imposed upon him, coincided with Nye's appointment. Buddie didn't wait for the ink to dry on the want ad before replacing Clapp with someone new.

At the end of January, Buddie hopped on a train bound for New Orleans for a Mardi Gras party. He joined Bill Pickens and drivers George Robertson and Ralph DePalma to discuss perhaps holding the race that Durant and Clapp had tried to arrange. Ever the pot-stirrer, Pickens announced that he would never have worked with the AAA as long as Durant and Clapp were involved, but with them out of the picture, he was ready to work with Buddie and Bill Nye to make things happen.[17]

But the fight between Ed Durant and Asa Jr. wasn't over. In February, Asa Sr. and Asa Jr. orchestrated a vote among the board of directors to kick out Durant completely. They tried to force him to retract all of his public statements, and made the remaining directors sign a note from the AAA stating that all was harmonious. However, anonymous board members continued to approach the press and suggest that many of the directors felt strong-armed into going along with their president's personal vendetta.[18]

In a scathing tell-all to the *Atlanta Georgian*, Ed Durant spilled details of the inner workings of the AAA, including the dysfunctional power structure that gave the Candlers indisputable control over decision-making.[19] He then made statements to the *Atlanta Constitution*, reaffirming and doubling down on his statements: "The truth is, there was never a moment during my connection with the speedway when the slightest suggestion of Mr. Candler, Sr., was not like the law of the Medes and Persians."[20]

He also repeatedly called out Buddie as a spoiled child.[21] Durant portrayed his former friend as a spiteful, irresponsible young man whose authority only existed due to his powerful father's insistence. He protested the way he was treated as both AAA secretary and director, and he insisted that he had done nothing to deserve the treatment, even going as far as to claim that there was history to the rift and that Buddie had been a problematic friend for months: "Mr. Durant says that the hostility of Asa Candler, Jr., dates back to the time when the speedway was in course of construction and has been increased by a number of differences occurring from time to time."[22]

And, understandably, he wanted receipts to justify the poor treatment he had received. He wanted his reputation restored, and he wanted Buddie to go down for his behavior.

Now, as to my resignation from the board of directors. When I went into the speedway, it was with the understanding that I should be an officer and a director, and as such should have a chance to make my investment good. I was never told that my services were not satisfactory, and I yet believe I could have contributed largely to the ultimate financial success of the undertaking.

But since the directors have first deprived me of the opportunity to make good by relieving me of the office I held, and now ask me to still further surrender my interests by resigning from the board, if they will in justice to me publish all of the facts and give their true reasons for ousting me as secretary and manager, and where they found me when I went into the business with them, I will cheerfully give the desired resignation.

As long as I am one of the six largest stockholders and no charge of incompetency or mismanagement has ever been made against me by the directors, individually or collectively, I cannot exactly see the fairness in throwing up my hand at the caprice of a young man, who is unfortunately in a position where he can make a plaything of a great opportunity, and through the influence of a kind-hearted father have a set of directors, most of whom only have a nominal financial interest at stake, frame the resolutions to suit his whims.[23]

But Durant forgot one thing: the Candler family owned more than just the Atlanta Speedway. They also owned the Candler Building in which his offices were located. His rent was processed through Asa Sr.'s bank, and his lease was under the management and control of Asa Jr., the very man who had turned every ounce of spite he possessed against his ex-friend. Durant forgot that much of his life and livelihood was in Candler hands, but Buddie didn't forget. Buddie's next move was to serve his former friend with an eviction notice and instruct him to vacate his seventh-floor office.[24]

Meanwhile, other cracks were starting to show. While Buddie responded to press inquiries by telling them he had no time to answer questions, another AAA director anonymously suggested that Buddie planned to escape the negative attention by giving up management of the track, canceling his plans to build a $100,000 "palace"—a monstrous price tag for 1910—in his father's new land development in Druid Hills, and moving to New York permanently.[25]

To fight back against the eviction, Durant's lawyer successfully argued that he had a right to a sixty-day notice and did not need to immediately depart. In response, Buddie shut off the radiator in his office and froze him out during the coldest month of the year. In March, Durant gave up his vigil and found new quarters in the Fourth National Bank Building at the corner of Marietta and Peachtree Streets. And he stuck with his insult, calling his former friend a "spoiled child" at every opportunity.[26] All of this played out in the local papers, and sometimes even made news as far away as California.

One might wonder whether this was all a storm in a teacup, a minor drama magnified under the microscope of historical research. However, this matter *was* a big deal to the Candlers at the time of its unfolding. In the Candler Papers collection at the Stuart A. Rose Library at Emory University, there is a box dedicated to Asa Sr.'s paperwork during the Atlanta Speedway era. The papers are mostly contracts, deeds, and business correspondence. But in the middle of the stack, the only example of a preserved newspaper clipping in the collection, is an article from the *Atlanta Georgian* containing Durant's claims against his son.[27] It mattered enough to save.

By April, the drama finally had blown over, and the press refocused attention on the efforts of Buddie and Nye to recruit drivers for the 1910 fall races. But dustups with some of the biggest drivers and chaotic track management hindered their ability to orchestrate an encore performance of the 1909 event. With the initial opening races falling short of recouping the cost of construction, followed by a total breakdown of the Atlanta Automobile Association's management structure, the future of the Atlanta Speedway was teetering on the brink. Buddie's falling-out with Edward Durant was a turning point. From then on, there was no escape from the eventual demise of the Atlanta Speedway.

Foreclosure was an inevitability, and Asa Sr. saw it coming.

CHAPTER 9

The Fall of the Atlanta Speedway

Following the November 1909 inaugural races, all eyes were on the Atlanta Speedway for an encore performance. Internally, the AAA was in turmoil as it grappled with the remaining debt that the ticket sales had failed to recoup. The track was further in the red than planned following Auto Week. Asa Candler Sr. was the majority shareholder and stood to gain the most from its success and lose the most if it failed. By the first week of December 1909, he had an exit strategy planned and drew up a contract that would extract him from the growing quagmire of the speedway's finances.

A contract on file at the Stuart A. Rose Library at Emory University provides a glimpse into how Asa Sr. maneuvered his way out of financial risk in case the Atlanta Speedway was unable to meet its projected potential. It also shows how he placed the success or failure of the endeavor entirely in his son's hands. The contract language can be summarized as follows:

On December 2, 1909, Asa Candler Jr. sold the Atlanta Speedway property to the Atlanta Automobile Association for $57,000. The AAA already owed $73,000 for construction of the track, so to address the total outstanding $130,000 of debt, the contract laid out terms by which it would be repaid. In short, Asa Candler Jr. would lend the AAA money to pay its construction bills, and the $130,000 total would be repaid to Asa Jr. over the following two years. The AAA gave Asa Jr. the title to the property and a lien on future gate receipts until the loan was paid in full. Once the $130,000 debt was paid in full, Asa Jr. would return the property title to the AAA. The agreement was signed by Asa Candler Sr. and Asa Candler Jr. and was witnessed by Atlanta

Speedway general manager Edward Clapp. Asa Sr. was the AAA representative in this agreement.[2]

But why would Asa Sr., the primary financier and true owner of the AAA, structure the agreement as a round robin of money changing hands? It was likely intended to shield him from the financial failure that he could see on the horizon as soon as the November races fell short of the goal. It may have also been intended to motivate Asa Jr. to do everything he could to make the business a success, since his personal wealth was now on the line. And it may have been the action of a father who had been burned before by his son's poor business management in Los Angeles and Hartwell. One can only speculate, but the maneuvering that minimized Asa Sr.'s risk and maximized Asa Jr.'s risk is evident in the document.

By the time the contract was in place and the AAA had agreed to eject Ed Durant and Ed Clapp, Atlanta was well into the winter months. No one wanted to sit outside in the grandstands or race around the oval in low temperatures. So at first, the association's upheaval didn't coincide with any race scheduling and thus didn't impact its revenue projections.

In March, as his drama with Durant came to a close, Buddie ramped up race planning like the conflict had never happened. First things first, he and Nye had to get the speedway bringing in income, so they headed up to New York to recruit drivers for a spring event. Buddie also batted around the idea of including motorcycle races and putting on an "aeroplane" exhibition to show off the latest in daredeviltry and technology.[3] He needed to come up with a gimmick that would bring out attendees in sufficient numbers to offset his mounting debt. Press coverage from the time shows that it was no secret that the speedway was hemorrhaging money.[4]

This might be why in April Buddie made headlines again as one of several people who were called to testify before a grand jury in an investigation into illegal "wirehouse" stock trading.[5] He may have been relying on illegal bucket shop gambling, where betting men wagered on the stock market's performance, rather than purchasing shares, to bring in extra income. After all, the track was far in the red and he'd tied up his personal finances in his collection of expensive cars.

In May, the Atlanta Speedway held its spring races. Although Buddie and Nye were able to secure some big-name drivers, like Ray Harroun, they were unable to bring in enough celebrities to fill out the event. Instead, they padded the lineup with local amateur drivers. Asa Jr. raced his own Fiat with his pals, including William J. Stoddard, the father of modern dry cleaning,

Original Atlanta Automobile Association stock certificate (ten shares).
Courtesy of the author.

who appears to have been one of his closest friends during the aughts, teens, and early twenties.[6] Due to low interest, they failed to turn out a significant enough crowd to turn a profit, and the lackluster coverage reflected the ho-hum response to the event.

In the meantime, Buddie was busy righting his upended public image by securing a full-page puff piece about himself in a weekly publication called the *Greater Atlantan*. Based on the aggrandized claims of his success, as well as grammar errors consistent with his personal correspondence, he appears to have penned the article himself in the hopes of convincing the public that he was not the man the press had made him out to be. Here's a sample:

> Greater Atlanta and her progressive movement among the greater cities of the country could not be better emphasized than in the life of Asa G. Candler, Jr. Wide awake at all times, progressive in everything he undertakes, with an intuition to seize upon things for their true value and a knowledge of business affairs and financial business that is remarkable, Mr. Candler ranks with the best of the business men of Atlanta today.[7]

He also made several boastful statements to the papers in response to the rumors that the AAA and the Atlanta Speedway were struggling to stay afloat. But as he spun yarns and dodged rumors throughout May, he was also busy liquidating assets, which only fueled speculation that he was struggling to stay afloat. He sold his seat on the New York Cotton Exchange, canceled his plans to build a mansion in Druid Hills, and reportedly sold one of his prized racing Fiats.[8] Liquidating assets, stalling his plans to break ground on a house, participating in risky wirehouse gambling—all suggest that he was juggling his finances during a time when he needed to appear successful to the public eye.

Then, the churn of speculation came to a halt when he made an important announcement: he had purchased a Lozier.

Lozier was a luxury automobile brand of the highest order. Intricately engineered and finely finished, Loziers were some of the most expensive cars of their time, five times the price of a high-end Cadillac. This purchase cost Asa Jr. more than $5,000 ($122,000 in 2020 dollars) and was the ultimate status symbol. He badly needed a Lozier so he could thumb his nose at his detractors. Based on timing and his financial activity before and after the purchase, it's likely the aforementioned juggling was done especially for this acquisition, which added to his already notable collection of five other premium automobiles.[9] Buddie's new Lozier was a 1910 four-cylinder, forty-five-horsepower Briarcliff H model with a rear tonneau.

Yes, Briarcliff. Atlanta residents, take note.

The short version of the generally accepted history is that the Lozier company developed this model especially for the famous Briarcliff road race, which ran in Briarcliff Manor, New York, as a companion to the Vanderbilt Cup. It was designed for peak performance in both endurance and speed over long distances on real-world roads. And it was beautiful too.

The Lozier Briarcliff was a superlative car for a man who lived for superlatives, and it was designed to do exactly what he planned to do with it: drive from Atlanta to New York in a road race called the Good Roads Tour.[10] In 1909, the Good Roads Tour had run from New York City to Atlanta and ended with the participants taking a victory lap around the new speedway. In 1910, the tour reversed direction, and the lineup of drivers was a who's who of the Atlanta amateur driving scene, including Edward Inman and Buddie's future brother-in-law Henry Heinz.[11] Notable in the list of entrants was Edward Durant, who chose to make the trip with his wife and children in his personal Pope-Toledo, which was registered in the same class as Buddie's Briarcliff.[12]

The objective of the tour was to demonstrate endurance and speed by making the trip in the shortest amount of time with the fewest mechanical faults. Timers checked speed and odometers and kept a running score for each entrant. They stopped together in various cities along the route, and the huge line of cars caused a stir everywhere they went. Some cars dropped out along the way, unable to handle the mechanical stresses of the trek. Most arrived successfully in New York City and were greeted by Mayor William J. Gaynor at the New York Herald Building. Sixty-two cars started, forty-eight finished, but only seven arrived with a perfect score. Of the seven, three are familiar names by now: Ed Inman in his Pope-Hartford, Ed Durant in his Pope-Toledo, and Asa Candler Jr. in his brand-new Lozier Briarcliff.[13]

The Lozier company was thrilled with the result and asked Buddie to participate in a nationwide advertising campaign to publicize his success. Diamond Tires wanted to advertise his achievement too. Suddenly, after so many bad headlines, Buddie was getting high praise and free press, all thanks to his Briarcliff.

Reputable auto racing reporters noted all seven finishers with perfect scores, including Ed Durant's car. But the Lozier ad said it was "the only car with a perfect score in the Big Car Class in which it competed (except one car which may be given a Perfect Score although admittedly late at one control)."[14] The jab at Durant's shared accomplishment was no accident.

It should be noted here that Asa Jr. didn't drive his own car, at least not for most of the race. He employed a driver named Frank Hardaman McGill Jr., known as Mack. Mack McGill was a registered chauffeur before becoming Buddie's personal driver.[15] He sometimes raced his boss's cars at the track, and he drove most of the route from Atlanta to New York, while Buddie took the headlines and credit as the skilled driver whose amazing automobile had made the journey with a flawless performance.

This was Asa Candler Jr.'s finest hour, his defining moment, his brush with B-list celebrity status. From coast to coast, in virtually every market, the automobile column in the local newspaper mentioned the results of the Good Roads Tour. Buddie was a minor star, if only briefly.

Riding the high of favorable press coverage, Buddie and Nye dove straight into planning the summer races at the Atlanta Speedway, which were scheduled to take place at the end of July. But once again, they had trouble booking the big names in pro racing. Like he did for the spring event, he filled out the roster with local amateurs, including Edward Inman, John Woodside Jr., and William Stoddard, as well as his brother William Candler and their brother-in-law Bill Owens. The lineup looked like a list of Buddie's inner circle of associates.[16]

Asa Jr. entered his Renault and his famous Fiat 90, which he'd purchased from George Robertson in the inaugural races. William entered his SPO, Ed Inman entered a Simplex, and Bill Stoddard entered a National that he raced frequently.[17] All of them had designated drivers to race on their behalf, with Mack McGill driving Buddie's cars.

In a fun exhibition, Buddie and Nye staged a one-on-one race where Buddie proved his big Fiat could circle the track twice in the time Nye took to make one lap in his little Fiat. Buddie wagered thirty-three cents against Nye's sixty-six cents and took a fifteen-second handicap. The big Fiat won, beating the baby Fiat by a nose.[18]

For the rest of the summer races, the lineup was lean. While many events were listed, the same names repeated throughout the roster, making each race similar to the one before. Predictably, the ticket sales weren't great. Worse, the skies opened up on Saturday, July 23, and rained out the event. Rain checks were issued, the roster was juggled around, and employees spent the next week patching up the track and preparing for the following Saturday. To encourage folks to come out, Buddie had an associate over at the *Atlanta Constitution* write a puff piece on his behalf to get potential customers excited.

> Howard Spohn, special representative of The Automobile and Motor Age, a noted automobile expert, visited the track yesterday afternoon as a guest of Asa G. Candler. After looking at the track he said, "There is no hope of making me believe that this is as smooth as Indianapolis."
>
> "You'll eat those words," replied Secretary Nye. Shortly afterwards Mr. Spohn was taken around the track in Asa Candler, Jr.'s prize-winning Lozier, winner in the New York to Atlanta run. The machine hit a 50-mile an hour clip and slipped around the course as smoothly as though running on glass.
>
> "I take it back," was Mr. Spohn's comment before the circuit was finished. "It rides about ten times smoother than it looks and it is certainly better than Indianapolis."
>
> That means, of course, that it is better than anything in all America.[19]

Notice how the story had now evolved to declare Buddie the "winner" of the Good Roads Tour.

The July ticket sales still didn't pull the AAA out of debt. By then, rumors were swirling about the upcoming December deadline when the mortgage, held by Asa Sr., would come due. There weren't enough puff pieces in the world to make Atlantans forget the tenuous path their relatively new speedway was on.

In August, Buddie successfully sued a child for striking a match on his car.[20] This has nothing to do with the speedway; it's simply a delightful example of his occasionally petty personality.

Planning for a smaller September race was under way, as was planning for the November races, which would mark the first anniversary of the track's opening. That needed to be a big event, since it was the last chance to bring in enough money to pay off the speedway's construction and vendor debt and pay down the looming mortgage. The clock was ticking.

Unfortunately, Nye was unable to recruit enough drivers for the September event, and the races were called off. To distract from the embarrassing press, Buddie announced that he would embark on another tour in his winning Lozier. He called it the All 'Round the State Tour and traveled across Georgia in his open-top Briarcliff with friends Frank Weldon, J. S. Cleghorn, and Frank Fleming along for the ride. And of course, Mack McGill shared the load as driver and mechanician.[21]

Buddie hit the press hard. Three articles were published on the same day, hyping his and the track's reputations. One article announced that he would let a well-liked local stage actress, Florence Webber, drive his big, famous Fiat. Another disclosed plans for a spectacular matchup between baseball superstars. The third overflowed with Frank Weldon's admiration for Buddie's 117-mile journey:

Asa G. Candler, Jr., upon his return yesterday, said that the route of the All-Round-the-State tour is fine.

Although he had been through a week's strenuous work, he looked hard as iron, and said that he now felt better. He and all the party were bronzed until their faces and hands matched in color their khaki suits. He loves to drive, and is not averse to some speed, but he is careful and skillful.

Twice he was driving until far into the night, but he was always ready to be up and off by sunrise or before. He is thoroughly game, and was just as anxious to make the circuit in six days as I was.

That he was driving far into the night on two runs was no fault of his or of his car. He was in the seat at the wheel for twenty-two hours on one run, except for the time taken by entertainment and helping another motorist who was in trouble.[22]

Then, the *Wilmington Morning Star* published an article about what makes the best drivers so good and included Buddie in its list of men with the physical prowess to win a race, along with big names like Robertson, Strang, and Oldfield. What made great drivers great? Brute power, said the writer. He declared that all great drivers were "beefy" men. What followed was a thinly veiled advertisement for the Atlanta Speedway. It recapped the heroism of the manliest of manly drivers, noted Buddie's fine physical qualities, and promoted the upcoming November races.

> All these are big men and strong. And their very strength has been a tremendous advantage to them in the racing game. . . . When it comes to rounding turns and dodging in and out among racing cars it takes wonderful muscle and weight as well.
>
> There was an example this summer on the Atlanta Speedway. In the early practice for a local meet F. H. McGill and Asa Candler, Jr., did all the tuning up for Mr. Candler's giant Fiat-60 [sic]. This is a car which is particularly vicious at steering. It yanks and bucks and raises sand, especially on the turns. In every practice spin Mr. Candler could get two or three seconds better time for a round than his driver. Both men are equally fearless and equally skillful. The secret lay in weight and proportionally more strength.[23]

A notable detail in this article is that the writer referred to the other men either by last name or, in Barney Oldfield's case, by first name. Only Asa Jr. was mentioned as the formalized "Mr. Candler." Similar to previous puff pieces, Buddie may have commissioned this article.

Atlanta was abuzz with the preparations for the upcoming November races. Cars were loaded up and shipped from all over; baseball players Ty Cobb and Nap Rucker were scheduled for their big matchup; and Lozier sent a "brigade" of cars to participate. Fifty-three cars were registered, the largest roster yet recruited for a single event at the track. Asa Jr. and Nye even arranged for an airplane demonstration to take place in the center of the racing oval between events. They had spared no expense to make the event successful, including paying the freight fees to bring in competing cars by rail.[24] Sparing no expense was part of the problem, however. As the December financial deadline loomed, Buddie spent more than he could possibly offset with ticket sales even if the event was a smash success.

The press coverage illustrated once again how the event pivoted around Buddie and his inner circle of racing pals. Bill Stoddard drove Buddie's Fiat after the rough steering tore up Mack McGill's hands. The manager for the New Orleans Pelicans baseball team, Charlie Frank, came out for a friendly visit, and Buddie took him on a wild spin around the track for a laugh. It was all fun and games for wealthy auto racing insiders.

On November 3, the three-day race event kicked off. The number of entrants had dropped from fifty-three to forty-six. Ty Cobb had to call off the highly anticipated matchup with Nap Rucker or risk a penalty to his baseball career. Barney Oldfield had been disqualified from all sanctioned auto races and could no longer participate. This didn't bode well.

The grandstands were noticeably emptier than in the previous year. The events also failed to draw as many track-side spectators, who had filled the center of the oval and parked along the inner embankments to watch the action up close in 1909. Even the demonstration of flying by a daring pilot in a fragile contraption failed to bring out sufficient crowds.

On November 5, 1910, the races ended without fanfare. To offset the embarrassment of the track's low attendance, Buddie reran his personal puff piece from the *Greater Atlantan* in the *Atlanta Constitution*, even though it remarked on the "upcoming" November races three weeks after they had run.[25] His reputation as a businessman was under public scrutiny again, and he knew it. The reality was that the AAA didn't pay down its debt, vendors were still waiting for their share, and public interest was waning. The track's struggle to prove its financial viability was widely known. A December issue of *Horseless Age* pondered whether Atlanta could rally enough interest to keep the venture going much longer.[26]

Further, Asa Candler Sr. was running short on patience. One year after he had put the financial burden directly on his son to make the speedway project work, he called in the debt. Together, they faced the harsh reality of closure.

In January 1911, Buddie ran a last-gasp PR effort by shopping around a story about his son John, who he claimed was only four years old and a crack driver. He successfully pitched the tale to several newspapers, and with every publication it evolved and became more outrageous.

Undoubtedly the youngest racing driver in the world is the four-year-old son of Asa G. Candler, Jr., owner of the Atlanta Speedway and himself an amateur driver of ability.

This Lilliputian Knight of the Wheel not only drives his father's 46-horse-power Briarcliff model on the Atlanta Speedway, but is a racing driver of no mean ability. He drove this big powerful Lozier car for one hour, making forty-two miles in that time and carried in the tonneau two newspaper reporters and the senior Candler.

Such a performance would be almost unbelievable were it not for the fact that it is vouched by Howard Spohn, representative of Automobile and Motor Age, Percy Whiting, sporting editor of the Atlanta Constitution, and J. M. Nye, assistant secretary of the speedway in Atlanta, who were all present when this diminutive driver made this really wonderful performance.

Asa Candler, Jr., who sat in the mechanic's seat on one side of the little chap when he was making the run, stated that he would have made a greater mileage in the hour's time had he not been several times cautioned to slow down. At one time, when taking the lower turn of the track at a 50-mile clip, the car swerved slightly. Master Candler was not in the least affected. Looking up out of the corner of his eye at his father, he merely remarked, "she skidded a little that time, dad."[27]

The same story ran verbatim in the *San Francisco Chronicle*, with an added embellishment at the end.

Not long ago he was told by his father in a joking way to go out to the garage and get the Lozier and take the family out for a ride. The young man disappeared and when search was made for him half an hour later he was discovered out in the garage making a desperate effort to start the motor. "What's the matter, dad?" was his comment, as his father appeared. "I would have had her around in a few minutes more if you had not come out."[28]

Clearly, it was meant to be taken in good humor, but the story also reeked of the kind of aggrandizement that Buddie was known for. A collection of photos on file at the Detroit Public Library photo archive from the November 1910 races includes a pair of images showing little John sitting behind the wheel of his daddy's famous Lozier, and those charming photos likely inspired this cockamamie story, which was engineered to create a legend.

After that final effort in January 1911, it was over. The Atlanta Speedway was done. All media coverage of the track ceased, and the next time the track came up was in retrospect after the land transitioned to its new life as an expanse of open field with an indeterminate future. Bill Nye resigned and returned to California, where he went back to his old job in law enforcement.[29]

For Buddie, the fiasco was a public hit to his image. As before, he had to demonstrate that he was bigger and more important than this one small failure. But this time, instead of running puff pieces and making blowhard statements to the press, and instead of purchasing a winning Fiat race car or laying out big cash for a luxury Lozier, he threw a Hail Mary. In February 1911, Asa Candler Jr. went down in flames and then, much like the city he called home, rose from the ashes.

*It will be impossible to replace the Fiat. . . . I do not know
yet what I will do about the purchase of new cars.*[1]

CHAPTER 10

Buddie the Phoenix

The Great Garage Fire of 1911

On the afternoon of February 7, 1911, Buddie went out to his garage to work
on his Renault racer. He lit a blowpipe and started cutting into a clogged
gas line between the fuel tank and the carburetor. The fuel in the blowpipe
exploded, and then the fuel tank of the Renault ruptured and blew, scattering
flames around the garage.[2] Cornered by the rapidly spreading blaze, Asa Jr.
leaped across the burning car but found the garage doors secured shut by
a spring mechanism, trapping him inside. In a frantic bid for survival, he
dashed across a sheet of flame and broke the door down, escaping with only
moments to spare. He was mildly injured, but emerged relatively unscathed,
given the scale of the event.[3]

Fire crews responded and prevented the flames from spreading to the
main house or to neighboring properties, but the garage was destroyed,
along with three of Buddie's five cars. The big red Fiat, a Pope-Toledo seven-
passenger touring car, and his racing Renault were burned beyond repair.
Not included in the inventory of damaged vehicles was his Renault limousine, which was parked up by the house. His famous and beloved Lozier
Briarcliff was unaccounted for. Either the Briarcliff survived or it was no
longer in his collection by then. For all of its celebrity, it's mentioned nowhere in any of the national press coverage of the incident. Although reports
varied slightly across several newspapers, nearly every account included one
consistent detail: the lost property was insured for a total of $20,000, which
adjusts to about $500,000 in 2020 dollars.

Then, sometime between February and June 1911, Asa Jr. found the funds to complete his Druid Hills real estate transaction, and he moved his family to an existing farmhouse on the new property. But it wasn't what he originally wanted.

In 1910, in an effort to control his public reputation while grappling with gossip and what appears to be a deep insecurity about his value, Buddie claimed to be working on a plan to build a $100,000 home in Druid Hills, which was a huge amount for the time. There are no direct quotes from Buddie, so the terms he personally used to describe the project are unknown. But there are reports of his expressed intentions. The *Atlanta Journal* claimed an inside source said that Asa Candler Jr. might abandon his plan to build a $100,000 "palace" due to the speedway uproar.[4] Whether Buddie said "palace," the source said "palace," or the *Journal* chose the word is unknown. But one can infer from its usage that his reputation at that point made the word sound plausible to the paper's readers.

The new house, however, wasn't a palace. It wasn't even new. It didn't match his vision of grandeur, but at least he'd made the move in spite of his financial failure. It was a small victory for his public image, but it was a victory nonetheless.

What had happened in the months after the fire? In March and April, Buddie distracted himself from the speedway's failure by throwing his support behind his father as Coca-Cola faced a serious legal challenge in Chattanooga, Tennessee, in what is known as *United States v. Forty Barrels and Twenty Kegs of Coca-Cola*. He rounded up witnesses to testify on Coca-Cola's behalf and ran them back and forth between Atlanta and Chattanooga, ensuring that his family's business could demonstrate the harmlessness of their product as the government tried to prove otherwise.[5]

In May, Asa Jr. made a lukewarm statement about the AAA trying to arrange a race that didn't seem likely to happen, and indeed it never did. He stated, "There is a possibility that there may be a meet in the fall. It all depends on a lot of things that can't be discussed right now."[6] In June, a man named William Walthall moved his family into the Inman Park house, which was noted as "formerly occupied" by Asa Jr.[7]

In October 1911, citing illness, Buddie issued a last-minute cancellation of his cross-country drive in his Lozier Briarcliff for the Glidden road tour. Either he was unfit for the job, or the Briarcliff was. Either way, the famous Lozier was never mentioned again.

Asa Candler Jr. in driving attire behind the wheel of one of his racers, circa 1909. Courtesy of the National Automotive History Collection, Detroit Public Library

A year later, Buddie started promoting his new property as Briarcliff Farm, Atlanta's finest source for top-quality chickens.[8]

BUDDIE'S SIGNATURE CYCLE

Asa Candler Jr.'s life was an ongoing cycle of soaring highs and crashing lows. Like the mythical phoenix, he occasionally burned his holdings down to ashes—sometimes figuratively, sometimes literally—and emerged flush with cash, ready to start spending again.

His seven-step cycle went as follows:

1. Embark on a grand, publicly visible endeavor.
2. Generate positive press through advertisements and puffery.
3. Build momentum and attention with outlandish features and investments.
4. Make several showy purchases.
5. Flounder, misrepresent, and distract with hyperbole and lies.
6. Liquidate assets in rapid succession and abandon the venture.
7. Lie low for a while.

One can observe a portion of this cycle as it preceded the acquisition of his Lozier Briarcliff. It played out again in the 1920s, 1930s, and 1940s in a clearly defined pattern.

The Atlanta Speedway saga was the first full example of the seven-step cycle. He launched a project, hyped it up, and spent money like price was no object, actions that cover steps 1–4. Asa Sr. put the debt of the Atlanta Speedway in his son's name, the press dragged Asa Jr.'s name and reputation through the mud, and one of the few statements he made in response was to claim he was busy building an impossibly expensive mansion in Druid Hills. Asa Sr. foreclosed on the track in early 1911 when Buddy's real estate deal was still pending, and that foreclosure meant no chance of future racing events to bring in income to offset his debt. These actions correspond with step 5, which was always a doozy.

When he moved his family out to Druid Hills, there was no big mansion waiting for them. In fact, he didn't break ground on his "palace" for another decade. But he did manage to complete a real estate transaction and lie low for a year. That's step 7, with the launch of Briarcliff Farm bringing him back around to step 1. But what about step 6?

In February 1914, Asa Sr. bought back the foreclosed Atlanta Speedway land at a sheriff's auction for $1,000. He also obtained a judgment of $130,000 on his civil lien against the AAA, which, as documented in the contract on file at Emory University, was debt owned solely by Asa Jr. This means the debt was not resolved between the 1911 foreclosure and the 1914 judgment. Additionally, family lore claims that when Asa Sr. and Lucy Elizabeth gave their kids their inheritance in 1916, Asa Sr. balanced his books and deducted any outstanding debt from each child's portion. Famously, Buddie's debt was reported as approximately $100,000.[9] If he was indebted to his father all of that time, where did he get the money to complete his Druid Hills transaction and move his family to the new property? Step 6: liquidate assets.

The track was a failure, and he had no other ventures that were big enough to resolve the debt. It wouldn't help to sell off the track, because any money made from the sale would go to his father. If he wanted to follow through on his claim that he was moving out to Druid Hills, he had to free up funds some other way.

It's possible that his Lozier Briarcliff was sold off as the first casualty of step 6. He had bragged to the press about its performance in January, but in February it appeared nowhere in the coverage of the garage fire. The illness that later forced him to cancel his participation in the Glidden tour may have been a cover story. Perhaps, he couldn't drive his Briarcliff in the Glidden because he didn't own it anymore.

If one scrutinizes the various accounts of the garage fire, some of the details don't add up. Buddie was an early adopter of automobiles. Purchase records demonstrate that he performed his own maintenance on his cars from the beginning.[10] He owned a variety of cars and had transitioned from steam to internal combustion engines as soon as gas-powered cars hit the market. Anyone who raced knew the risk of gasoline igniting. Why would someone so knowledgeable about cars and engine maintenance use a blowpipe to cut a fuel line on a car that still had fuel in the tank? It could have been a lapse of judgment. He could have made an assumption that the clog in the line would prevent the vapors from catching fire. But neither of those options is likely.

A more plausible explanation is that Asa Jr. set the fire and intentionally burned his car collection and garage. After all, with the track going belly up, he had no use for racers anymore. The Atlanta community had turned racing into a humiliation, which made the cars a reputational liability. Selling off the whole collection just when the track was visibly failing would have also been embarrassing, which could be why he kept quiet about the sale of the Lozier. But a fire would turn the cars into cash quickly, without having to expose his financial need to the community.

As mentioned, he started out in tontine insurance, which was a rigged pyramid scheme that made investors rich while policyholders paid into funds that they were unlikely to benefit from. Ed Durant had showed him the ins and outs of property insurance, so Buddie was familiar with the way insurance could be cashed in to offset financial losses. He'd benefited from his policy on the Merry Widow. And insurance fraud by fire was commonplace. It's no difficult task to find scholarly articles studying the increase of insurance fraud due to arson during recessions.[11] In fact, it's such a long-standing practice that the Roman poet Martial wrote a short quip about it way back in the first century A.D.:

> Tongilianus, you paid two hundred for your house;
> An accident too common in this city destroyed it.
> You collected ten times more. Doesn't it seem, I pray,
> That you set fire to your own house, Tongilianus?[12]

For a wealthy man whose money was mostly tied up in investments and real estate, the extravagant toys that enhanced his life of leisure could be of value even when their utility came to an end. The track had come to an end, driving as a fun and exciting hobby had come to an end, and the utility of his racers had come to an end. Why not let them burn? While this may seem like a leap to assume he held such a cynical view of the track and his car collection, there is a glimpse into this mind-set in a report from 1915.

In 1914, after Asa Sr. reacquired the land that the speedway had occupied, he considered a number of uses for it, none of which would permit auto racing. When Asa Jr. was reached for comment a year later, his response demonstrated a bitterness that leaked into the reporter's brief blurb.

> There is no chance of reopening the Atlanta speedway built some years ago but never profitably operated, as the splendid record breaking race course has been dismantled, according to a letter received from Asa Candler, Jr. This half million dollar track was constructed and proved a financial failure owing to an entire lack of national publicity and its consequent dependence upon local and surrounding territory for patronage.[13]

That was pretty much it for racing. In 1914, Buddie had emerged from a three-year hiatus to set the last driving record he would ever attempt on the route between Atlanta and Knoxville.[14] And then, aside from one paid promotion for Locomobile in 1917, Buddie pushed cars out of his public persona entirely.[15] He was in full retreat mode, done with his decade-long obsession with automobiles.

But that wasn't the end of Buddie the phoenix. He had big plans, and it was only a matter of time before he would emerge from the ashes, and the cycle would start again.

PART 3

WELCOME TO BRIARCLIFF

Undoubtedly Briarcliff dairy farm is as modern and scientifically conducted as the most exacting customer would desire.[1]

Build Your Own Empire

After the closure of the Atlanta Speedway and the fire that nearly killed him, Buddie took some time to live quietly and recover from the crash and burn of his grand endeavor. During this downtime, he and Helen welcomed twin daughters, Helen Jr. and Martha, into their family on August 14, 1911.

He then decided to try his hand at commercial farming. The land he'd relocated to in 1911 already had chicken coops that he could use, so his first agricultural venture was poultry. He bred Orpingtons and sold pullets from his newly named Briarcliff Farm. His flock competed for best of breed, bringing home second place honors initially, until he purchased enough winners to start taking blue ribbons.[2]

Poultry was a good distraction from the activity taking place at the site of the former speedway, where his father was busy demolishing the grandstands and trying to determine the best way to repurpose the land and recoup the debt. Asa Sr. considered parceling out the land to farmers, returning it to its original use. He also considered carving out space to relocate Emory College, a plan that built a small momentum before it was decided to migrate the college closer to the city. At no point, it appears, did he consult Buddie for ideas.

Throughout all of this, Buddie kept his head down, managed the Candler Investment Company properties, and farmed. Over the next couple of years, he shifted his focus from chickens to cattle. He bought 180 head of top-quality Holsteins, and when World War I operations ramped up he secured a deal with Fort McPherson to ship hundreds of gallons of milk to the doughboys in training who were stationed there. He also volunteered with the Red Cross to coordinate the flow of war support through Atlanta.[3]

The dairy farm transition shows the start of a new cycle. Steps 1 and 2 were already under way, and as he brought in more cows and built new barns, he transitioned into step 3: outlandish features and investments. A report in the *Electrical Review* trade magazine in 1918 provides a glimpse into the high overhead at Briarcliff Farm:

> Undoubtedly Briarcliff dairy farm is as modern and scientifically conducted as the most exacting customer would require. . . . The barn is provided with . . . electric lights and fans, steel frame stalls[,] . . . automatic drinking fountains, . . . milking machines, . . . and electric equipment for the silo and bottling the milk.
>
> The interior of the barn . . . reminds one of a hospital ward. Fresh air and light are supplied in abundance by the numerous windows on each side equipped for easy adjustment. The floors, walls and ceiling are of concrete and suggest cleanliness by their spotlessness. The barn is cooled in summer by means of Westinghouse ceiling fans, which also serve to furnish adequate ventilation in winter. Special attention was given to the lighting arrangements which would meet the requirements of the most modern office building.[4]

By 1918 Buddie's drive for superlatives had reasserted itself, and his small farm had become a massive, state-of-the-art operation, with electric fan ventilation, rail-mounted feed dispensers, and an automatic drinking fountain for each cow. Generating enough income to pay off his debts became secondary to his desire for recognition and success. He spent more than the farm could bring in, especially as World War I wound down and the demand at Fort McPherson dried up. He then tried to retarget the business to sell directly to consumers, but he couldn't generate enough sales to sustain the high-cost production model. From start to finish, Briarcliff Farm lasted just six years. But farming wasn't the only thing driving this cycle.

SPORTS MAKE GOOD INVESTMENTS

As he transitioned into an agrarian life in 1911, Buddie explored another venture: investing in athletics. Leveraging the connections he'd forged through auto racing, he was able to dabble in a new hobby—but purely as a financier this time, none of the pursuit of personal glory that he'd shown at the track.

He came to the world of athletics sideways. Using the speedway to get in good with famous drivers, he next connected with the growing popularity of baseball. The link was established in 1909, when Georgia native and popular player Ty Cobb drove in the New York to Atlanta Good Roads Tour, which ended in a lap around the newly opened Atlanta Speedway. Cobb was described by some at the event as an enthusiastic fan, and he and Buddie bonded over their mutual love of cars.[5] In September 1910, Buddie came up with an idea to drum up press for the track by staging a car race between Cobb and a fellow Georgia-grown baseball star, Nap Rucker. They were scheduled to compete in three heats, but at the last moment Cobb received a telegraph from the president of the Detroit Baseball Club, ordering him to bow out.[6] The race was off, but Buddie and baseball were now an item.

In October 1910, Buddie gave a spin around the track to the Southern Association's temperamental former baseball player Charlie Frank. Then manager of the New Orleans Pelicans, Frank toured the speedway during a visit to Atlanta. Buddie's associates lured Frank onto the track, and Buddie gave him a top-speed ride for laughs. Frank declared him "the worst" and said he would never get into a car with him again, but he rode back to town with Buddie, indicating they'd forged a friendship.[7]

Certainly, they talked baseball. In 1909, the same year the Atlanta Speedway opened, the Atlanta Crackers had won the Southern Association pennant. It was their second win in three years, but in 1910 they failed to rank high enough to get another shot at it. It was a time of high tension in the Atlanta baseball scene, and at the close of the season discontented rumbles circulated about the team's owner, the Georgia Railway and Electric Company.

In September 1911, after the track's foreclosure, Charlie Frank and Buddie put their heads together to discuss the Crackers' prospects. They put forth a proposal to buy the team and put it back on a winning path. The Georgia Railway and Electric Company set its selling price at $40,000, not including the players' contracts or the field. Frank and Buddie estimated that it would cost another $25,000 to recruit the players they needed to fix the team's prospects, and that made the total investment price too high. Buddie took his money and walked.[8] Given his financial landscape at the time, he could not accept a higher price tag than he'd already offered. But he wasn't out of the running yet.

In February 1915, Buddie became involved with the Atlanta Athletic Club. The organization had opened a new clubhouse and golf course and was struggling to make ends meet. Buddie attended a members meeting and offered to use his personal funds to set the finances straight, but only if the club adopted his terms. He proposed an overhaul of its bylaws that would grant him the power to appoint club leadership, and he offered to renegotiate its mortgage, which was held by his father, Asa Candler Sr.[9]

The club voted enthusiastically to approve his proposal. He was appointed president, and he named Preston Arkwright, president of the Georgia Railway and Electric Company, as one of the directors. In November, Buddie and Charlie Frank made another offer for the team. This time, they secured both the franchise and the players' contracts for $38,500.[10] Only the team's home field at Ponce de Leon Park was excluded from the deal. Charlie Frank took the reins, brought the team to fifth place in 1916, and then won pennants in 1917 and 1919.[11]

Over the years, many executives from Atlanta's biggest money-making companies, including Coca-Cola, Atlanta Steel Hoop Company (now Atlantic Steel), Georgia Electric Light Company (now Georgia Power), and the Industrial Aid Association (now Life Insurance Company of Georgia), were members of the Atlanta Athletic Club. The club was one of the places where men of power met and made alliances. The change in club directors at Asa Jr.'s discretion had been the key sticking point in his offer to head the club, and it may have been part of a backdoor deal by which Arkwright was willing to sell the Crackers for less than his original asking price.

Buddie stayed on as president of the Atlanta Athletic Club until 1917, at which point he stepped down without challenge or fanfare.

THE ATLANTA SPEEDWAY BECOMES CANDLER AIRFIELD

The Briarcliff Farm years were quieter than what was to come, but they were not without Candler family drama. In July 1911, Buddie's youngest brother, William, struck a man on Peachtree Street at "dead man's curve" while driving one of Buddie's cars. William was going twenty-five miles per hour and cracked the man's leg and ribs. No charges were filed.[12] Their uncle John Slaughter Candler was a city judge and alderman, and he was acting temporarily as Atlanta's mayor while the sitting mayor was on vacation.[13] Perhaps it's no mystery how the case slipped away.

In May 1912, Walter was arrested and charged with driving at least twenty miles per hour, five over the speed limit. Plainclothes police in a dragnet on Ponce de Leon Avenue took him and his passenger in, and while Walter claimed he stuck to fifteen miles per hour, his passenger told the judge that they averaged seventeen. Walter was charged five dollars and reminded to stick to the speed limit.[14] In September 1914, Walter found himself in court again after he pointed a gun at a streetcar driver who had shouted at him when he didn't yield the right of way. Again, the charges went away as quickly as they were brought.[15]

Throughout, the speedway property remained a contentious piece of the Candler Investment Company's portfolio. As previously mentioned, in 1914 Asa Candler Sr. formally reclaimed the foreclosed property. He had no intention of reinvigorating the track, and in fact told a reporter that he was considering selling it off as farmland. But then an interesting proposal crossed his desk, brought to him by his younger brother Bishop Warren Candler, the former president of Emory College.

THE VANDERBILT SPLIT

➔ Back in 1873, Cornelius Vanderbilt of the famously wealthy Vanderbilt family had pledged a million dollars to establish Vanderbilt University. A Methodist bishop based in Nashville, Tennessee, had convinced him to help fund a top-notch Southern Methodist college that would serve as a training ground for regional ministers. For the first several decades, the school operated with the oversight of the Methodist Episcopal Church, South, but in the early 1900s the board members faced a pressing question of the modern era: should they open up the teaching staff criteria to include non-Methodists? As part of the modernization movement, they also changed the structure of the board of trust to include just five bishops, reducing the influence of the church on the board's decisions.

In 1910, the board refused to seat three bishops, so the Methodist Episcopal Church, South, sued and won the right to influence the balance of power. But the school took the fight all the way to the Tennessee Supreme Court. In 1914, the court ruled that "The Commodore," Cornelius Vanderbilt, had established the college, not the Methodists. Thus, the board of trust called the shots. Angered by its ouster, the church voted to cut its ties with Vanderbilt and establish a new Southern Methodist college.

A key player in all of this was Bishop Warren Akin Candler, the former president of Emory College and younger brother of Asa Candler Sr. Warren was one of the loudest voices in the decision to sever the church's ties with the school. Feeling betrayed by the court system and angered by the power upset, he returned to Georgia and made a plea to his wealthy big brother to take charge and establish Atlanta as the site for Vandy's rival.

Asa Sr. was a devout man, deeply involved in the church and motivated by a strong moral sense of civic duty. He looked to Warren as a spiritual advisor and greatly appreciated his perspective on life and faith. Add to that the Candler family's competitive side-eye to the Vanderbilt family, and in short, Asa Sr. was receptive to Warren's idea.

They needed the church's buy-in before they could take action, however. Mirroring Cornelius Vanderbilt's original donation, Asa Sr. pledged $1 million to expand and relocate his family's alma mater, Emory College, to the Atlanta area, and he helped Warren put together a proposal to take to the General Conference of the Methodist Episcopal Church, South.

The big question was where to put the college. Fortunately, the Candler Investment Company had a large parcel of land that was doing nothing to earn its keep. The track had been dead for three years, and no viable proposal had turned up that looked like a worthwhile reinvestment. But for a college campus, it looked just about right.

Asa Sr. moved quickly. In August 1914, he rallied the residents of Hapeville to back the idea of hosting a prestigious institute of higher learning. It would cost more than Asa Sr.'s pledge to implement, so he motivated them to fundraise and campaign for the selection of the site in order to make the General Conference's decision easy.[16]

But the proposal never quite gelled. The site was too far from the city and too expensive, even with the community's support. So in 1915, Asa Sr. and Warren came up with an alternative plan. Asa Sr. had purchased the Druid Hills land development some years prior and could allocate property as he saw fit, so the brothers proposed to move Emory College to a parcel in Druid Hills. The General Conference members agreed. They accepted Asa Sr.'s land and monetary gifts and started the process of moving Emory from Oxford, Georgia, to Atlanta.

When the proposal flipped in this way, the land in Hapeville went idle again. The question remained: what could it be used for instead?

As far back as 1910, Asa Jr. had seen the potential in aviation. It was a new technology at the time, and if anything was novel, expensive, and fast, Buddie wanted in. During auto races, he would bring in pilots and hold flight exhibitions between heats. These were sensational, headline-grabbing shows, perfect for filling time with jaw-dropping demonstrations of aerial ingenuity.

When the track shut down, some of the pilots asked if they could continue to use the property as a landing field, offering to pay a small amount of rent. Doug Davis and Beeler Blevins, who led the initiative, had their eye on two business endeavors: flying lessons and airmail. Buddie negotiated the arrangements and permitted them to use the land until other prospects came along.

When the proposal to move Emory to Hapeville fell through, Davis and Blevins felt confident that they could continue to use what was becoming known as Candler Field. After all, no one else wanted it. But there was one other important event that helped to clinch the land as an airfield: Asa Candler Jr. received his inheritance and took up the hobby of aviation.

SUDDEN WEALTH

In 1916, Asa Candler Sr. was elected mayor of Atlanta. Keen to off-load some of his business demands, he shifted more of the management of the Candler Investment Company to Buddie. This included oversight of the Candler Warehouse, which had relocated to Stewart Avenue—currently named Metropolitan Parkway—and expanded significantly in 1914. Asa Sr. also stepped down from Coca-Cola, granting Howard the presidency in his place. His youngest son, William, was at Coca-Cola too, and his son Walter was deeply involved in the Central Bank and Trust. Asa Sr. had a child in place everywhere he needed one, all based out of the Candler Building, where he would spend half of his time during his mayoral term. These arrangements made stepping down more symbolic than actual.

Sadly, his wife, Lucy Elizabeth, had fallen ill with breast cancer.[17] She and Asa Sr. moved from Inman Park to a new mansion in Druid Hills with Lucy Jr. and her young family, as well as Asa Sr.'s widowed older sister, Florence, his beloved Sissie. Asa Sr. and Lucy Elizabeth decided to give their children their inheritances early, so in 1916 they put the ownership of Coca-Cola into their collective hands and issued payouts, minus any debts owed.

The reduced inheritance put a cramp in Buddie's aspirations. Howard, on the other hand, had his full inheritance to play with, as well as a highly compensated position as the president of Coca-Cola. Howard broke ground on his dream mansion, Callanwolde, just up the road from his younger brother's property.[18]

In 1917, fires sparked around the metro area, one of which was at the Candler Warehouse. A high, dry wind carried embers and flames north into the city, cutting a furious swath across Fourth Ward, including North Jackson Street, where Buddie and his family had once lived. The fire left a

Candler Warehouses sign, corner of Metropolitan Parkway and Ralph David Abernathy Boulevard, circa 2019. Photo by the author.

path of destruction in its wake. But Atlanta's symbol is the phoenix, which is seen on manhole covers and government buildings throughout the city. Its motto, "Resurgens," honors the citizens of Atlanta, who rose from the ashes of the Civil War and regrew their city in the aftermath of fire. In 1917, the city burned and rose from the ashes again. Mayor Asa Candler Sr. is credited by some historians with pulling the community together to rise and recover from the disaster. He personally financed some of the recovery efforts, offering fair home loans to people who had lost everything in the blaze.[19]

While Atlanta figured out how to move forward after the fire, Coca-Cola figured out how to move forward after the reorganization of its leadership. Howard was technically in charge, but all five siblings shared ownership, which meant they had to agree on business matters. It didn't go smoothly. Now enjoying their inheritances, the Candler heirs had little patience for the demands of managing the company as a team.

In 1919, they decided to sell Coca-Cola for $25 million and remove the hassle from their lives. They arranged to sell to a consortium headed by Ernest Woodruff, their father's lifelong rival. This was a contentious moment in Coca-Cola's history. Some historians believe the sale was against Asa Sr.'s wishes. Some believe he was insulted that he wasn't consulted in the sale. Others believe he wasn't bothered, since he'd tried to sell Coca-Cola for nearly the same price a few years prior.[20] But the deed was done, Asa Sr. wasn't consulted, and the strain on his relationship with his children is broadly accepted lore.

When the sale went through, each of the siblings was instantly $5 million richer. That's more than $73 million in 2020 dollars. Buddie's Briarcliff Farm had struggled since the end of World War I, so this windfall couldn't have come at a better time.

His first order of business was to invest in something huge, befitting the fortune he now controlled. Just before the Coca-Cola deal was finalized, he had announced a $2 million expansion of the existing Hotel Ansley, of which he was the lessor. The upgraded property would be valued at more than $4 million. Always one to speak in superlatives, Asa Jr. claimed it would be the largest hotel in the Southeast, with eight hundred rooms and a massive, opulent lobby.[21] The project never happened. It was outrageous in scope, and two years later Buddie had moved on. An announcement in the local newspaper noted that Louis J. Dinkler had taken over the lease and would manage the hotel effective immediately.[22]

The year 1919 wasn't as joyous as it should have been. Lucy Elizabeth Candler, love of Asa Sr.'s life and devoted mother to their children, passed away on February 22. The loss hit the family hard. In spite of Buddie's childhood exile and his occasional expressions of hurt, he loved his mother dearly. Family descendants claimed he would sometimes recite a poem titled *If I Only Was the Fellow* well into his later years.[23] Although the poem's provenance is somewhat murky, it appears to have been written by Will S. Adkin and was first published sometime between 1905 and 1910. It peaked in popularity between 1912 and 1914, a prime time in Buddie's life for a poem about mothers to make an impression. This particular message struck a lifelong chord with him.

IF I ONLY WAS THE FELLOW

While walking down a crowded
City street the other day,
I heard a little urchin
To a comrade turn and say,
"Say, Chimmey, lemme tell youse,
I'd be happy as a clam
If I only was de feller dat
Me mudder t'inks I am.

"She t'inks I am a wonder,
An' she knows her little lad
Could never mix wit' nuttin'
Dat was ugly, mean or bad.
Oh, lot o' times I sit and t'ink
How nice, 'twould be, gee whiz!
If a feller was de feller
Dat his mudder t'inks he is."

My friends, be yours a life of toil
Or undiluted joy,
You can learn a wholesome lesson
From that small, untutored boy.
Don't aim to be an earthly saint,
With eyes fixed on a star:
Just try to be the fellow that
Your mother thinks you are.

—WILL S. ADKIN

In the aftermath of the loss of his mother and the sale of Coca-Cola, Buddie whirled into a spending frenzy. Finally, he could afford to break ground on the palace he'd always wanted and felt he deserved, a mansion that would put Howard's to shame and even outclass his father's home. In January 1920, he sold off his herd of Holsteins, including a prized bull named Superba Lord Ragapple.[24]

He hired a demolition crew, temporarily relocated to a home on Oakdale Road in Druid Hills, and two years later he moved Helen and their children—Lucy III, John, Laura, Martha, Helen Jr., and Samuel—into Briarcliff Mansion.[25] The Roaring Twenties had arrived, and Buddie the phoenix was on the rise.

There are many poor boys who attend schools and buckle down
to their work in earnest because they have no other interests.
But there are many sons of rich men who have their cars and
their clubs and find too much to do other than to study.[1]

CHAPTER 12

A New Cycle Begins

We now enter the most visible and infamous period of Buddie's life, which started in the early 1920s. After the sale of Coca-Cola in 1919, Buddie's big plans were launched with gusto, and they included scraping away all remnants of the farm and laying the foundation of his family's new mansion in 1920. To escape the bother of construction, Buddie and Helen blossomed into socialites and seafarers. They purchased and sailed around the Gulf of Mexico in a new, luxurious, ninety-one-foot, twin-screw yacht and made a splash in the local society pages.[2]

> Asa Candler, Jr., owns the yacht "Helasa" which is 100 feet long, and is built with four staterooms, thereby accommodating quite a large party aboard. Likewise, every modern comfort and convenience has been placed on this yacht. The name was selected from the given names of Mr. and Mrs. Candler, being a combination of the names Helen and Asa.
>
> Mrs. Candler's stateroom is done in blue chintz, with draperies upholstered in this effective color. The other staterooms are in rose, yellow and lavender.
>
> Mr. and Mrs. Candler and family made trips from Atlantic City and up the Hudson river during the past summer. In winter many trips are made to Miami, Palm Beach and other noted resorts along the Florida coast.[3]

In August 1921, Asa Jr. invited journalists to tour the grounds of his upgraded property, showing off the lighted formal garden, the family pool, the greenhouses, and more. One newspaper dubbed it "Forty Acres of Fairyland."[4] Similar to the press tour that he hosted at the incomplete Atlanta Speedway in 1909, he ensured that the town was buzzing about his home in advance of its debut. In 1922, he celebrated the opening of Briarcliff Mansion, carrying over the name of the farm—and the car that originally bore it. He made Briarcliff a site for public and private gatherings, a venue worthy of mention in the society pages. Helen hosted high teas and the Rotary Club, and Buddie hosted pool parties and fine dinners. Over the years he revamped the property again and again, adding a golf course, tennis courts, a mini-farm, a public pool, a private zoo, and a laundry facility. References also exist to fish farming on the property.[5] On the top floor of the mansion was a gold-leaf-detailed ballroom, where he and Helen hosted galas for Atlanta's social elite.

Meanwhile, Buddie made dozens of real estate deals, large and small. Mostly large. He aimed for superlatives again, always trying to build the largest, most innovative structures. He continued to bring in income via his Coca-Cola stockholdings, his property management, and his real estate business. He was truly flush with cash, and he was ready to turn wealth into power and influence.

Buddie invested in grand ideas and cast a wide net across an array of industries. He did his best to balance the hedonism that only wealth could buy with the drive to build his financial empire. But whenever he had a moment to spare, he went out on his yacht, pulled between Atlanta and the open waters. He was on the hunt for new opportunities while the lure of the sea called him and filled his head with ideas.

Around this time, the Candler family was having a tough run with extortionists and bad press. In the late summer and fall of 1922, Asa Sr. and Walter each made headlines with not-so-private indiscretions. In August, Walter sexually assaulted a friend's wife on a passenger ship bound for France. A month later, the couple sued him for reneging on a promise to pay them hush money.[6] Then, Asa Sr. was accused of reneging on a marriage proposal to a younger socialite, who sued him for breach of contract over the canceled engagement.[7] Both Candler men landed in court with the eyes of the public scrutinizing them.

Fiercely loyal to his family and highly aware of the benefits of sailing in international waters, Buddie hatched a plan—a wild, ambitious plan that only he could believe in. He would launch a prep school for rich boys on a boat that would sail around the world with his family on board, carrying them far away from their troubles.

THE CANDLER FLOATING SCHOOL

First, he needed investors. In November 1922, he convinced a group of wealthy Atlantans—although, notably, none of his relatives—to see the potential in his proposal. He persuaded Harry P. Hermance of the Central Bank and Trust board of directors to come aboard. He won over Lindsey Hopkins, a Coca-Cola executive and later the second biggest Coca-Cola stockholder behind Ernest Woodruff. He got buy-in from Harold Hirsch, the general counsel of the Coca-Cola Company. He even sold the idea to Equifax founder and fellow Central Bank and Trust director Cator Woolford.[8] These were big men with deep pockets, and all were intrigued by Buddie's grand plan.

Next, he needed a boat. The investors' pledges reportedly totaled $2.5 million, of which $180,000 came directly out of Buddie's own pocket for the initial purchase.[9] He acquired a decommissioned U.S. Army transport ship named the USS *Logan*. Soon to be renamed the SS *Candler*, the steamliner would be fully overhauled to accommodate a roster of staff and students from fifty private prep schools, as well as a couple of troubled Candler men who couldn't be prosecuted if they were in international waters. Rumor had it that Buddie's real plan was to take the ship around the world on a personal tour before returning to take on his first class-load of kids. Asa Sr. was resistant to the idea at first, but Buddie intended to keep him on board until the drama back home died down.[10]

The *Logan* had a long history of service. Formerly the *Manitoba*, it was built in 1893 by the Atlantic Transport Company in Belfast, Ireland. The U.S. government bought it in 1898, renamed it the *Logan*, and used it as a transport vessel during the Spanish-American War.[11] The steel-hull ship could carry more than two thousand passengers and measured 465.5 feet long and 49 feet wide. A sizable craft for one man to own.

Before it crossed Buddie's desk, the proposal had been assembled by Atlanta Public Schools superintendent Willis Sutton, for whom Willis A. Sutton Middle School is named, and Lieutenant Colonel E. T. Winston, U.S. Army, retired, who had previously proposed a similar idea to the U.S. War Department without success.[12] Buddie offered Sutton a five-year contract to be the school's executive head and ship's commander. He hired Professor Zebulon Judd, head of the College of Education at what is now Auburn University, to act as dean.[13] The ship would sail from San Francisco to Baltimore, where it would be transformed into what would be known henceforth as the Candler Floating School.

Meanwhile, Buddie's PR machine hyped up prospective customers. He put out press statements and advertisements, making the kinds of grandiose, dubious claims typical in step 3 of his cycle. He and his staff claimed the school would charter a train and take students on a six-week tour of the United States before putting out to sea. Once aboard, between September and June the students would visit ports around the world, including London, Edinburgh, Antwerp, Gibraltar, Barcelona, Marseilles, Nice, Monaco, Naples, Athens, Constantinople, Jaffa, Port Said, Bombay, Colombo, Calcutta, Rangoon, Singapore, Batavia, Manila, Hong Kong, Shanghai, Nagasaki, Yokohama, Honolulu, Hilo, San Francisco, Panama, Colón, Havana, and Bermuda.[14] If that wasn't enough, they planned to add a land-based institution with two campuses, one in the United States and one in Europe.[15] They would also eventually purchase a second ship for an all-girls roster.[16]

All of these claims were made before the *Logan* left San Francisco.

The list of planned amenities was also impressive. In addition to living quarters for students and staff, the ship would have twenty-two classrooms, a 450-seat assembly hall, a library, science laboratories, athletic courts, a swimming pool, an infirmary, dental services, a full operating room, two dining rooms, and a lounge larger than that of the steamship RMS *Aquitania*, a luxurious contemporary of the *Titanic*. Quite a lofty comparison. The ship would offer the use of its powerful wireless transmitter to homesick boys, and a daily paper would keep the students apprised of happenings in the rest of the world.[17]

It was an impressive vision. To support the promoters' claim that the program would be no more expensive than a standard preparatory school, tuition was set at $1,000–$1,200 annually and would cover all expenses. This is where the business plan started to show the cracks. Only the ship had been paid for thus far, and that expense didn't include the cost of the major renovations, staff salaries, fuel, food, port fees, and all of the other necessities for ten months at sea. It would take years to recoup the money required to make the project viable. Anyone could see that the initial outlay was monumental, and the timeline for returns on the investment extended far into the future. But Buddie, Sutton, Winston, and Judd were confident that the future was worth waiting for:

> It is our belief that this school will exert a profound influence over future international thought and understanding. It is certain to promote international peace. Let the boys in America see the people of other nations and learn to understand them, and future international relations, so far as America is concerned, will be easy.[18]—WILLIS A. SUTTON

The *Logan* arrived in Baltimore in January 1923. Contractors from the Bethlehem Shipbuilding Corporation began the process of estimating the remodeling costs to convert the vessel into an institute of learning. As the tally climbed, Buddie published ads to start bringing in tuition to fund the renovations. Note the superlatives:

UNEXCELLED EDUCATIONAL ADVANTAGES:
270 DAYS' UNSURPASSED WORLD CRUISE

Only boys' school of its kind in the world. Last two years of High School and first two years of Liberal Arts College. Accredited by leading educational institutions. Strong faculty. Ideal conditions and facilities for study. Calls made at most interesting ports of both hemispheres. Interior excursions to Paris, war zones, "The Eternal City," Holy Land, Pyramids, etc. Noted institutions, libraries, museums, art galleries, palaces, cathedrals, capitals visited under the direction of faculty members and competent guides.

Ship noted for good behavior in all weather. Remodeled for floating school by naval and school architects. Free services of school surgeons, dentists, and nurses. Everything for students' welfare and happiness and for physical, educational, cultural, and moral development. Enrollment lists closed after acceptance of only 400 students. Write for complete information, tuition rates, etc.[19]

Buddie wanted it to be known that the Candler Floating School was not a philanthropic endeavor. It was a premium educational opportunity for families of means, intended to better their children's standings. In a telling statement that seems to echo his personal experience and perhaps gives a glimpse into the regrets of his youth, he said:

The view I take is this. There are many poor boys who attend schools and buckle down to their work in earnest because they have no other interests. But there are many sons of rich men who have their cars and their clubs and find too much to do other than to study. If rich men's sons are sent to my school, they will enjoy themselves, but at the same time they will see that they must concentrate on their studies.[20]

Then, the scheme hit a major snag. Before the executive team could do a walk-through of the ship they'd purchased, Winston fell ill and passed away.[21] This put a serious crimp in their plan, as Winston's idea was the impetus, and he alone had the practical experience to make the endeavor seaworthy. They had to regroup.

Buddie issued a revised schedule for the school's maiden voyage. Rather than September 1923, they would put to sea with their first class in June

1924.[22] To shore up confidence, he claimed his son John and his nephew Howard Jr. would join the student roster, although evidence suggests that Charles Howard would not have gone along with a plan of this nature.

In February 1923, Buddie arrived in Baltimore to inspect the *Logan* and finalize the remodeling estimates. Two months later, he rescheduled the maiden voyage again, this time pushing out to September 1924, and increased the tuition to $2,000 per year.[23] To quell any doubts, he claimed that he'd already received six hundred applications from interested parties. He also made grand claims about the salaries of the ship's educational staff, said that his critics were now praising his idea, and was sure that the venture would be so successful that within a year he would launch not one, but two more ships.

And then, much like the Hotel Ansley project, the deal went silent. In early 1924, the Candler Floating School investors cut their losses and sold the *Logan* for scrap.[24]

By this time, Asa Sr. had successfully proved to the court that he couldn't have been engaged to his accuser, so the case against him was dismissed.[25] Walter was slowly making headway in his extortion case and was in too deep to sail off into international waters. Buddie could walk away from his eponymous school without harming his family, and so he did.

Besides, he'd already replaced the school with other big ideas. Investing locally seemed like a better prospect, and there were opportunities galore. Just before he sent the *Logan* to the scrapyard, he came up with an even bigger idea than the floating school, one that rivaled the scale of the Atlanta Speedway. He decided to build an agricultural empire right in the heart of Atlanta.

While these big ideas were taking shape, he also had worked on climbing the social ladder, hosting events at his home and making public shows of his new, extravagant lifestyle. In January 1923, Buddie and Helen threw an elaborate reception with more than four hundred guests at Briarcliff Mansion in honor of their twenty-one-year-old debutante daughter, Lucy III. Later that evening, they celebrated her coming out with a lavish ball at the Piedmont Driving Club, one of the most elite venues in Atlanta. They spared no expense, outfitting the ballroom in a Japanese theme with pergolas and lanterns, and they even had two small replicas of Japanese houses built near the entrance, where costumed Japanese servers provided punch for guests. The ostentatious show of wealth and seemingly bottomless budget for the event caused ripples in the debutante community that season.[26]

The idea was for Lucy III to mingle with eligible bachelors, and of course Buddie had vocal opinions about what made a bachelor eligible. Money, for one. Membership in social clubs, for another.[27] Unfortunately for him, but fortunately for Lucy III, she'd already met the love of her life: a young man named Homer Thompson who was well liked among their peers but had no financial or networking prospects. Buddie didn't want them courting, and gossip circulated that he was vehemently opposed to the couple's growing affection.[28]

Right around the time that the Candler Floating School went belly up in early 1924, Buddie and Helen took Lucy III away on an extended trip around Asia. This was rumored to be an effort to distract her so she would forget about her beau. She didn't forget him. Upon their return, Thompson proposed, and Lucy III accepted.

Her parents acquiesced, the wedding was set for June, and the family went all out on the event, celebrating al fresco in the formal garden on the front lawn. They built a second solarium on the side of the porte cochere for the event, and a line of pergolas descended the hill from the solarium to the gardens, where a row of arches served as the altar. Bishop Warren Candler officiated, and Lucy wore a veil of delicate lace that she'd bought during her Far East voyage for this purpose. Despite her father's efforts, she hadn't forgotten Thompson at all.

AN EMPIRE IN THE SOUTH

An extensive investing spree followed the sale of Buddie's ill-fated school ship and the marriage of his first-born child. Each of his next moves followed a similar arc from entry to exit over the subsequent four years.

- Launched the Graphic Films Corporation, an industrial film production company
- Laid the groundwork to build the first Macy's store in the Southeast
- Bought the land to build what would eventually become the Briarcliff Hotel
- Leased the old Atlanta Speedway to the city of Atlanta as a municipal airfield
- Purchased a stockyard and built an expansive agricultural complex

➜ Graphic Films Corporation

In February 1924, Buddie announced the formation of a film production company in partnership with industry professional Robert B. Strickland, Graphic Films Corporation, to be headquartered at 24 Nassau Street in Atlanta.[29] Their new company would produce corporate, documentary, and educational films, rather than Hollywood blockbusters.[30] They brought in Joseph W. Coffman, who was the visual education supervisor for Atlanta schools from 1916 to 1923, to help manage the business.[31] They started production in earnest in April 1925, claiming to be the South's only full-service film production house with an "as fully complete plant as anywhere."[32]

The next year, they produced a film on diversified farming. After that, they completed a film on social progress starring Thomas Edison, a film about salmon canning, and another about the *Atlanta Constitution*. In 1927, they produced a documentary that followed the University of Alabama's Crimson Tide football team to Pasadena to play against Stanford in the annual Rose Bowl game.[33]

By the end of 1927, Buddie started ramping down many of his less profitable ventures, including Graphic Films. In 1928 the company produced a film about swimming featuring the Atlanta Athletic Club's swim team, and that appears to be the end of its run. Buddie had shuffled around the management structure, appointing his son John to the role of general manager after the resignation of cofounder Robert Strickland. Strickland then returned to buy out Buddie's half of the business and renamed it Strickland Industrial Film Corporation.[34]

➜ Macy's

In October 1924, the vice president of R. H. Macy & Company, Percy S. Straus, visited Atlanta, kicking off a spate of wild speculation. Macy's was a nationally known department store, but it hadn't expanded into the Southeast yet. Upon his arrival, Straus was greeted by press conjecture, but he chose to neither confirm nor deny rumors. While he claimed to be in town for a political dinner and a sporting event, he spent the day riding around Atlanta with Buddie, who happened to own the property rumored to be the store's future site. In an aside to reporters, Straus expressed surprise and delight at the large, beautiful homes that Buddie showed him, in what was likely an

The original facade
and windows of the
first Davison-Paxon
store in Atlanta at 200
Peachtree Street, 2019.
Photo by the author.

effort to convince the Macy's executive that Atlantans could indeed afford
the company's wares and keep a future store lucrative.[35]

By March 1925, the rumors were confirmed: Macy's would construct a $6
million store in Atlanta on Candler land under its Davison-Paxon brand.
The grand store would consist of six floors and a theater right on Peachtree
Street, a block north of the Candler Building and across from the Loew's
Grand Theater. At an event hosted at the fashionable Biltmore Hotel—built
and owned by Buddie's youngest brother, William—speeches were given by
Macy's head Jesse I. Straus, Governor Clifford Walker, Mayor Walter Sims,
and Asa Candler Jr., all of whom praised the deal as marking a pivotal moment in Atlanta's growth. The *Atlanta Constitution* promoted Buddie's "pa-
triotic spirit" and said no one in Atlanta deserved more credit for developing
the city than him and his brothers. Said the *Constitution*, "These men are

standing on the threshold of Atlanta's most brilliant era of prosperity and you will share the benefits with them."[36]

In 1927, as the Macy's building neared completion, Nathan Straus returned for an inspection and gave the following statement:

> It is a material and unquestioned tribute to Asa G. Candler, Jr., that the work has gone along so spiritedly. While I am not at liberty to announce any definite date for the opening, I must say that I can hardly wait until that time to see how Atlanta takes to the new store. . . . We have a peculiar faith in Atlanta. In building the structure Mr. Candler has done his part.[37]

On March 21, 1927, the Davison-Paxon store opened. It was the largest department store south of Philadelphia, with the longest expanse of store windows in the country.[38] Of course it was, with Buddie running the project. Superlatives, as always.

➔ Briarcliff Hotel and Apartments

Also in 1924, Buddie broke ground on a new project up the road from his impressive Druid Hills mansion. Originally named "The 750," the development was intended to be an upscale living option in the suburbs, perched on the corner of Ponce de Leon and North Highland avenues.

Featuring the kind of grandiose architectural details that Buddie loved, it was designed in an H shape by G. Lloyd Preacher, the architect also known for designing Atlanta's city hall. Nine stories tall, featuring twenty-four apartments per floor, it spent a scant few years living up to Buddie's expectations. When the Great Depression hit, however, luxury hotels and apartments fell hard. Just look at his brother William's Biltmore Hotel and Apartments for another example of Depression-strangled real estate.

By 1935, The 750 offered commercial services, including a barbershop and a pharmacy, but it was going to be a long journey back to its original luxury status.[39] In 1938 the building was rebranded as Briarcliff Hotel and Apartments, and Buddie's Briarcliff Investment Company located its headquarters there. Following a renumbering of Atlanta street addresses, the site became known locally as The 1050.

Years later, after Buddie sold Briarcliff Mansion in 1948, he moved to a nine-room penthouse on the top floor. Major remodeling subdivided the units, and by the 1950s it was advertising four hundred rooms and suites, double its original capacity within the same footprint. After Buddie's death, the remaining prominent residents moved on, and his heirs sold the property.

A well-loved local legend claims that Al Capone kept an apartment at the Briarcliff Hotel and Apartments, but little evidence exists. It is possible that Capone's wife rented a room there while her husband was incarcerated in Atlanta's prison, but Capone himself is unlikely to have called the hotel home.

➔ Fox Theater

In 1925, Buddie assumed full control of the Asa G. Candler Investment Company, which meant owning all decisions for the valuable portfolio of real estate assets.[40] That year, the local business community noted that he and his brother Walter owned five thousand square feet of property worth more than $30 million along Peachtree Street.[41]

As the failure of the Candler Floating School drifted into memory, Buddie's new business ventures held nothing but bright promise. So when the Shriners of the Yaarab Temple, of which Buddie was a member, decided they'd outgrown their meeting space, real estate became a critical topic for the brotherhood. Enter Asa Candler Jr., who took the lead on the financial team, known as the Special Loan Committee. At a group meeting on September 9, 1925, Buddie took the podium and gave a rousing speech along with his brother-in-law and past potentate Henry Heinz. They presented what Heinz claimed was "the most practical, the most feasible, and in all ways the finest financing plan."[42]

They intended to build a meeting space for their organization along with a great auditorium, which could be rented out and serve as a revenue generator for the club. At a meeting in October, the Yaarab Shriners announced that the hall would be named the Asa G. Candler Sr. Memorial Auditorium, despite the fact that Asa Sr. was still alive.[43] Given that Buddie, William, and Heinz were on the committee, it's plausible that they proposed the auditorium name, including the suffix to distinguish the honoree from Asa Jr.

The meeting was also a celebration of the end of their drive to raise $1 million to break ground. Their fundraising efforts had brought the group within reach of their goal, coming in around $900,000. Asa Sr. donated $1,000 personally to help close the remaining gap. The organization then asked individual members to pledge donations, and Buddie pledged $10,000 of his own money on top of the $10,000 he'd already promised.[44]

Fox Theater cornerstone on the northeast corner, which shows the Yaarab Temple dedication, 2018. Photo by the author.

Although only "noble" in Shriner rank, he was named the temple's chief of staff and spent 1926 riding around with high-ranking, influential Shriners in his private luxury railcar.[45] The project managers hired an architectural firm in 1927 and quickly discovered that the scope of their plans far exceeded their budget. They negotiated a deal with Fox Films Corporation to share the cost burden and gave Fox a twenty-one-year lease on the auditorium. That agreement enabled the Shriners to break ground and lay the cornerstone in 1928, but they hit the financial skids again. They revised their plans once more and continued plowing forward toward completion.

In 1929, the Great Depression put pressure on the project again, but by now they were in too deep to walk away. They eliminated some of the planned details and devised work-arounds when construction materials became scarce. The theater opened on Christmas 1929, and the mosque portion, which was retained by the Shriners, was dedicated on New Year's Day 1930.

But where was Buddie in all of this? In 1932 a small blurb appeared in the *Atlanta Constitution*: "Judgment given the Shrine[rs] Building Company against Asa G. Candler, Jr., for $10,000 on an allegation that Candler refused to pay a stock subscription for the Shrine[rs] Mosque was upheld by the court of appeals in a decision handed down on Friday."[46] It raises the question, what happened between the pledge of $10,000 in 1925 and the calling of that debt?

Although the Fox Theater retained no records indicating which specific members were involved during the construction phase, the project had Buddie's fingerprints all over it. Grandiose ideas with good-on-paper proposals that unraveled financially once set in motion were Buddie's specialty. The Atlanta Speedway, the Hotel Ansley expansion, the Candler Floating School, the Atlanta Union Stockyards, and other future projects all followed the same pattern as the Fox.

➔ Candler Field

Given that Buddie saw himself as a guiding force in Atlanta's growth in the early 1920s, it's no surprise that in 1924 he offered a lease to the city for the grassy expanse of land where the Atlanta Speedway formerly stood.

By that time, Doug Davis and Beeler Blevins had built up enough business to attract other aviation enthusiasts, and the promise of airmail had caught the eye of municipalities and business owners as public interest gained ground. Anticipating growth in the flight industry, Buddie approached Mayor Sims with his proposal, but it was Alderman William B. Hartsfield who appreciated the growing value of air service and campaigned hard to close the deal.

On April 16, 1925, Sims signed an agreement for a five-year lease, which specified that the city only had to pay taxes and upkeep. The contract also included a provision permitting the city to buy the land outright at any time during the lease term for $100,000.[47] In 1926, Davis and Blevins each built hangars, and on September 15, the first plane carrying mail from Jacksonville, Florida, landed at Candler Field.

On October 11, 1927, Hartsfield pulled some strings and convinced Charles Lindbergh to fly to Candler Field in the *Spirit of St. Louis* for a public appearance. Lindbergh was carried by a grand parade into the city, where he spoke to the citizens of Atlanta about the potential of commercial flight. The excitement over Lucky Lindy's visit clinched air travel as a part of Atlanta's identity. Just in the nick of time too. Asa Jr. was bailing out of business ventures and liquidating assets, which meant he wanted Candler Field sold and settled.

The five-year lease with the city should have carried through to 1930. But in 1928, Asa Jr. demanded $100,000 or he would cancel the lease. Alderman Hartsfield, now chair of the city council's Aviation Committee, drove a hard campaign to convince the city to come up with the funds, even though its financial outlook for the coming year wasn't good.

In March 1929, the deal became official with a purchase price of $94,500. Money changed hands on April 13, 1929, making the land officially Atlanta city property.

> It was one of the most important transactions by the city in years. With one airplane factory and an airport, Atlanta is in a dominant position in the aviation of the Southeast.—MAYOR ISAAC RAGSDALE, SPEECH TO THE ATLANTA CITY COUNCIL, 1930[48]

That airfield became what is now Hartsfield-Jackson International Airport, busiest in the world.

✹ Cotton, Cattle, and the Great Mule Mart Drama

The biggest and most ambitious project from the 1924–1928 cycle was the Atlanta Union Stockyards. This story started in 1924, but it might as well have been 1909. The venture played out in a way that closely mirrored the downfall of the Atlanta Speedway.

Back in 1919, right around when the sale of Coca-Cola made Buddie an attractive target for anyone with an investment opportunity, a man named William H. White Jr. approached him and asked if he would like to buy stock in his meat-packing business, White Provisions Company. This wasn't their first meeting. A few years earlier, White had made an investment in Candler Field, expressing an interest in learning how airmail might benefit the livestock business. Buddie passed on the offer in 1919, but when White approached him again in 1922, he found that Buddie was primed for the opportunity and looking for a way to turn his wealth into something big.[49]

In 1923, Buddie crafted a grand plan to make Atlanta the agricultural capital of the southeastern United States. He intended to combine the Candler Warehouse megaplex with a new cotton compress system and an expansive stockyard, which would create a consolidated trade hub and bring in business from the surrounding region. In November of that year, he and White announced that they were partnering to bring Buddie into White Provisions Company.[50] Together, they purchased the existing Miller Union Stockyards property and in early 1924 incorporated the Atlanta Union Stockyards, of which White Provisions was a subsidiary. Buddie then pumped money into building a huge, state-of-the-art livestock complex, complete with auction blocks and office spaces for sellers to lease to set up headquarters on-site. This was step 1 of his signature cycle starting up again.

Once the creation and announcement of the Atlanta Union Stockyards were complete, Buddie moved on to step 2, but things quickly went wrong. In July, Buddie leaked information to the press about a merger between two major regional livestock dealers, the Smyths and the Maxwells, and claimed that they would relocate their consolidated headquarters and establish a mule mart at the Atlanta Union Stockyards. This unprecedented news had the potential to upend the markets in which both companies were headquartered at the time. To hold off any possible panic, the brothers James Clarence Smyth and Thomas Albert Smyth made a statement claiming they were only considering a temporary move, nothing permanent.[51]

Behind the scenes, the deal must have been in turmoil, because William White Jr. did the unthinkable. He turned on Asa Candler Jr.—in public, no less. He went to the papers and said that he had no part in the decision to release the news of the merger and relocation: "Premature publication in an afternoon newspaper of this matter has proved greatly embarrassing to me. I had taken steps to secure cooperation of all Atlanta newspapers in handling details of the important transactions only after final consummation and approval of the plans, and ill-advised publication has caused me great distress."[52]

White should have known that you don't cross Asa Candler Jr. and get away with it. That was the harsh lesson that Edward Durant learned in 1910. Following a similar arc, Buddie called a meeting of the board of directors of White Provisions Company in December 1925, while White was out of town, and voted him out of its leadership.[53] It was the Atlanta Automobile Association's ejection of Durant all over again. This time, it was arguably worse, because White was out of town at a livestock event in Chicago that Buddie had insisted he attend. By the time White arrived back in Atlanta, it was all over. Buddie was now the president of White Provisions and Atlanta Union Stockyards.

In early 1926, the situation escalated further when William White Jr. was charged with embezzling funds from White Provisions Company. The charges alleged that he had cooked the books every year until 1925 and had taken more than $200,000 from the company's holdings for his own personal use. He was accused of using the ill-gotten money to speculate on cotton, cattle, and other agricultural exchanges.[54]

If one pays close attention to the patterns, another emerges here. Back in the early 1900s, Asa Sr. had sent Asa Jr. up north to Hartwell, Georgia, to manage the cotton mill owned by family friend William "Billy" Witham. The business struggled and never found its financial footing. When Asa Sr. asked Buddie why the mill was losing money, Buddie accused Witham of cooking the books, borrowing money, and speculating on stocks.

The nineteen-aughts were a period of big spending and reputation building for Asa Jr. It was when he discovered cars, started a family, and bought his first house. In the 1920s, he was in another big spending and reputation-building phase. The financials went badly in both eras. Perhaps a coincidence, perhaps a pattern. Either way, in both the aughts and the twenties, Buddie attributed his business struggles to a partner falsifying records and using company money to speculate. Since he was a former bucket shop speculator, perhaps it took one to know one.

Back to William White Jr. In July 1926, witnesses gave testimony and the prosecution claimed he'd juggled the company's debt by rolling various loans into each other and misrecording the financials in the business's records. He held three different accounts with his broker, one of which was under his secretary's name. Prosecutors recounted dates and dollar amounts that simply didn't add up.

In August, Asa Candler Jr. took the stand and testified against his former business partner. In simple terms he explained that White had approached him to buy stocks, that White had asked him to go into business with him, that White had asked him to lend the money to get their operations' improvements started, and that White was solely responsible for mismanaging the mule mart money, unbeknown to him.[55] There were no asides to soften his testimony with praise for White's character, as would have befitted a friend. He left no room for interpretation. He wanted the jury to come back with a guilty verdict.

The prosecution rested, and William White took the stand in his own defense. He gave long, rambling, sometimes confusing explanations for the financial questions the prosecution had raised. He pointed out multiple occasions in which he had personally paid expenses because the business wasn't able to cover its costs. He pointed out that he was never insolvent, never in enough debt to need misappropriated money. He spoke candidly about the way he and the board of directors had crisscrossed business and personal funds to help grow the company, not always recording transactions with complete transparency. He had invested twenty years of his life into White Provisions Company, starting out as a jobber and rising to the presidency of a major meat-processing concern. His question was plain: why would he rob the business he had poured his life into?

The jury entered deliberations on August 7. The verdict was returned quickly: not guilty. In spite of the questions that the prosecution had raised about White's activities, the consensus was that he was simply a lousy bookkeeper.[56]

Acquitted of the charges against him, William H. White Jr. left court a free man. He had won the lawsuit, and that was what mattered, right? Well, just ask Ed Durant, who took Asa Jr. to court when he evicted Durant from the Candler Building. Durant won the lawsuit and regained access to his office, but in the end it didn't matter. Soon after, Durant disappeared from the social scene. His name disappeared from event rosters and society pages, and history recorded virtually nothing of him past 1910. It seems Asa Jr. successfully squashed him.

White also won his court case. He was vindicated, although exposed as a poor financial manager. He should have been able to resume his life and business, but he didn't. Although he lived out his years in the Atlanta area, he ended his local business interests and joined a stockyard in Montgomery, Alabama. After that, the story of his life and trial faded into history.[57] It seems Asa Jr. successfully squashed him too.

What about the company itself? It continued on, and in early 1928, Atlanta Union Stockyards reported record business, more than it had the capacity to accept. The company was booming.[58]

Then in May, out of the blue, Asa Jr. announced that he was shutting the whole thing down. No reason was given, only a statement that he would be repurposing the land for other uses.[59] He then evicted the Smyth brothers, which ended their right to auction livestock on-site. This was a major blow to their regional business. The Smyths protested the decision and refused to leave. Asa Jr. insisted, so the Smyth brothers took him to court. By then, Buddie was spiraling, and nothing would stop him from shedding expensive investments from his portfolio. The court case dragged into 1929 and made its way to the Georgia Supreme Court. In the end, the court upheld his right to evict his tenants, and that was that.[60]

In June 1929, Atlanta Union Stockyards made a call for the redemption of all issued bonds. The mule mart upheaval went quiet as Buddie searched for opportunities to off-load the property, although it continued operating. In May 1930, he sold the stockyard property for $250,000, less than his original investment.[61]

CHAPTER 13

Buddie the Phoenix

The Great Sell-Off (Love, Loss, and Real Estate)

In 1924, Buddie started step 1 of his cycle by launching several grand projects. By 1925, he was deep into steps 3 and 4, spending extravagantly on lavish purchases, such as his personal railcar and a set of pearls worth $30,000 in 2020 dollars, which were discovered to have been illegally smuggled and were seized by U.S. authorities.[2] By the end of 1927, he was floundering in step 5 and moving rapidly into step 6, liquidation. By 1928, he was out of nearly every venture and was already lying low in step 7. What happened in 1927 and 1928 to inspire the great sell-off? The answer requires a more holistic look at what was going on in his life at the time.

In September 1925, Asa Candler Sr. fell ill with a kidney ailment, which landed him in the hospital under critical care. He spent a year languishing there until a debilitating stroke struck in September 1926, which left him bedridden for the next three years. It was an unexpected and ignoble turn for the man who had meant so much to the Atlanta community at large and who was the load-bearing pillar of the Candler family.

But Asa Sr. wasn't the only person close to Buddie's heart who suffered during this period. Helen, his wife of twenty-five years, was in declining health, and nothing seemed to improve her condition. In January 1927, Helen passed away, leaving her husband and six children devastated. Buddie had her buried in Westview Cemetery next to Asa III, their first-born son. This is when Buddie began to spiral. The timing of his exit from most of his business ventures coincided with this personal tragedy.

He was drinking heavily by this time. His son John recounted to family later that the Briarcliff Candlers lived like a real-life version of *The Great Gatsby*, always socializing and indulging in alcohol-fueled merriment, in spite of Prohibition.[3] Buddie wasn't new to booze, of course. He'd always indulged when it suited him. But during this period it became a major fixture in his life and began to affect his judgment and relationships.

In October 1927, nine months after Helen died, Buddie married his stenographer, Florence Adeline Stephenson, under intense public scrutiny. The newlyweds tried to shun press attention, boarded an ocean liner named the *President Adams*, and departed for passage through the Panama Canal.[4]

The ship stopped in Los Angeles before continuing to Hawaii, where Buddie and Florence intended to spend several weeks honeymooning on the beach. While in Hawaii they fended off newspaper reporters, who scrambled for details about their surprise union. The short interval between the death of his first wife and his second marriage along with Florence's status as a working-class woman on the Candler payroll made gossipy headlines during a time when Asa Jr. was struggling with loss and major life changes.[5]

In early 1928, around the time that he was bailing out of the stockyard and sinking deeper into alcoholism, Buddie sold the *Helasa* and purchased a new yacht named the *Amphitrite*. This larger boat spent much of its life in Gulf of Mexico waters, sailing through the Caribbean and visiting Cuba.[6] The Candler family had ties to Cuba due to Bishop Warren Candler's ministry work there, which resulted in the establishment of Candler College. Cuba was also a relatively close location where one could procure alcohol and imbibe freely during Prohibition.

On the second of two March voyages, the couple sailed to Haiti, where they were approached by a military boat that carried a U.S. naval commander and a U.S. marine lieutenant, who intended to board their craft. Halfway to the yacht, the military boat caught fire and required assistance. The *Amphitrite* crew tossed it a line, towed it to another ship, and then set sail for Miami, never having allowed the military staff to board.[7]

But when the *Amphitrite* arrived in Miami, the Coast Guard was waiting for them. The guards performed a search, during which they discovered eighty-eight illegal bottles of "assorted liquors." The passenger roster included friends of Buddie's twin sixteen-year-old daughters, Martha and Helen Jr., and the girls' fathers. The dads blamed their daughters for the booze and claimed the stash consisted only of "small souvenir bottles," which the girls had attempted to bring back.[8]

However, this claim did not hold up when the customs agents logged the inventory. Among the contraband was a gallon of standard rum, four quarts and two pints of scotch, two quarts and ten pints of rye, twelve quarts of champagne, seven quarts of gin, two quarts of vermouth, three quarts of high-grade rum, three quarts of low-grade rum, three quarts and three pints of wine, one quart of crème de menthe, sixteen bottles of beer, and nineteen bottles of fine liqueurs. This reported volume alone totaled more than ten gallons of booze. The remaining inventory was not made public. This was a serious issue, given that it was peak Prohibition, and bootlegging from Cuba was illegal.[9]

The timing of the liquidation step of Buddie's cycle raises the question of whether he was fined for rum-running. Soon after this event, in early June, he began to negotiate with the city of Atlanta for it to purchase Candler Field once and for all. In late June 1928, he sold his controlling interest in most of his industrial ventures for a cash consideration of $4 million. This deal included the massive, forty-acre Candler Warehouse and other facilities. He also announced that he would close and repurpose the reportedly successful Atlanta Union Stockyards property, and he sold his interest in Graphic Films Corporation. During this period he also reneged on his pledge of $10,000 for the Shriners' Fox Theater project.

Selling his interest in Candler Warehouse in 1928 was particularly significant. Besides contributing strategic value to the grand agricultural plan, the 1.25-million-square-foot facility on Stewart Avenue had been a major piece of the Candler portfolio for many years. Buddie claimed the sale was purely an investment decision, but it was an investment decision to sell off a legacy family business as his father languished in a hospital, progressing slowly but surely toward his end.

In January 1929, Buddie left on another trip, this time to Egypt and the Mediterranean.[10] On March 12, Asa Sr. passed away. Buddie was overseas during his final hours.

Throughout the remainder of 1929, Buddie wrapped up loose ends in the great sell-off, including winning the eviction court case against the Smyth brothers, finalizing the sale of Candler Field, and recalling bonds for the Atlanta Union Stockyards. In May 1930, Buddie acquired a fifty-year leasehold on the Robert Fulton Hotel for $800,000 and sold the Atlanta Union Stockyards for $250,000 of the hotel's purchase price. That transaction was the final nail in his agricultural empire's coffin. The great sell-off was over.

It might be tempting to chalk this all up to the pressures of the Great Depression, but Asa Jr.'s spiral and the majority of his liquidation efforts

Westside Provisions (formerly White Provisions) was part of Asa Candler Jr.'s short-lived agricultural empire, circa 2021. Photo by the author.

preceded Black Tuesday by more than a year. In fact, following his usual pattern, he emerged from 1929 flush with cash. Also as part of his pattern, after a brief quiet period he ramped up his spending again. The market crash didn't slow him down.

The years between 1923 and 1929 are when his reputation for being an eccentric, mercurial alcoholic took root. But his smart business skills are evidenced in the closing of big deals with influential players in key industries. His ability to network and win over business partners with the power of his personality is evident in each of these moves. But starting with the Candler Floating School idea in 1922–1923, some fuzzy logic started to manifest, along with a reemergence of his trouble in balancing the cost of his vision with the income potential of the final product, similar to the issues with the Atlanta Speedway and Briarcliff Farm. And problems in his personal life once again created financial pressures as he tried to maneuver in business.

Thanks to the influx of cash from the sale of Coca-Cola and the control he had over the Candler Investment Company, Buddie could afford to wager on big ideas and more than occasionally lose the bet. A burn-and-rebirth cycle necessitates some financial privilege, so failure ends in a soft landing, not a crash. Thus, in spite of the nation's economic troubles as the United States entered the 1930s, Buddie had already regained a firm financial footing and was ready to start a new cycle.

PART 4

MIDLIFE AND MORE

*This is my last trick and I hope you will
enjoy the performance.*[1]

CHAPTER 14

Airplanes and the Dark Arts

Airplanes were a part of Asa Candler Jr.'s life from the earliest days of flight.
And like bicycles and automobiles, airplanes (at the time, commonly spelled
aeroplanes) were destined to become an obsession. Buddie's earliest en-
counter with flying was in 1910, when he invited daredevils to do exhibition
flights from midfield between races at the Atlanta Speedway. Following the
closure of the speedway, he permitted Atlanta's first pilots to use the property
and thus maintained a connection with the local flying community.

When the Coca-Cola sale was finalized in 1919, Buddie joined the executive committee of the Southern Aero Club with the goal of promoting
flying at Candler Field. The club proposed repurposing the former Atlanta
Automobile Association clubhouse as a gathering place for flying enthusiasts. The plans were typically grandiose, as described by Southern Aero Club
president R. E. L. Cone:

> The club, which we expect to make one of the [liveliest] organizations in the
> South, will establish a training school for flyers, and will operate a regular fly-
> ing course with rides for the public at graduated prices, according to the length
> of time a passenger stays in the air. We have been given the use of the Candler
> field, and here we propose to put up a clubhouse for the use of the aviators
> and a gun club. It has been suggested that we have a ladies' auxiliary, and plans
> for this will probably be worked out a little later. There are undoubtedly many
> women in Atlanta who are enthusiasts over the possibilities of air transporta-
> tion. We now have under consideration contracts furnished by plane manufac-
> turers, but their acceptance will be determined by the executive committee.[2]

Over the decade that followed, Buddie maintained his flying business relationships, and even after he sold his interest in the future site of the world's busiest airport, he maintained a lifelong enthusiasm for aeronautics.

In October 1929, Asa Candler Jr. emerged from the great sell-off and began his cycle anew with a big purchase: his very own private airplane. It was a 165-horsepower, open-cockpit, maroon Waco BSO-A biplane with a Wright R-540A engine and "Briarcliff" stenciled on the side.[3] As in his auto-racing and pathfinder days, he needed a pilot to operate his vehicle. In Atlanta, if you wanted the best, you hired aeronautics pioneer Beeler Blevins. Blevins became Buddie's private pilot for the next five years.

Throughout 1930, Blevins raced Asa Jr.'s airplane and attempted to set speed and distance records.[4] He was paid handsomely to be at Buddie's beck and call, and he continued to grow his private business as well. That year, he and Asa Jr.'s twenty-five-year-old son, John, formed the Blevins Aircraft Company and offered airplane storage for wealthy Atlantans who were stricken with flying fever.

Unfortunately, flying fever was no match for the spiraling economy. Rich men who had lived large in the 1920s suddenly found themselves in dire financial straits, including those who had bought into the private airplane fad. And, of course, arson rates tend to rise during financial downturns, so when a fire broke out at Blevins's brand-new hangar on March 4, 1930, the papers claimed it was a mystery, but it was no mystery at all.

The blaze consumed twenty-one airplanes and the hangar.[5] Buddie's airplane was lost, along with three belonging to Blevins. The total cost of the damage was around $140,000. The worst part was that John and Blevins claimed they carried no insurance on the structure or the aircraft.[6] Still, Blevins somehow found the means to rebuild bigger and better than before. No details are available about how he managed to reestablish his business, build an improved hangar, and acquire new planes, but his close association with Buddie and John suggests that they may have helped him out.

One additional note is necessary here. Although evidence suggests that Buddie likely started his garage fire in 1911, no evidence suggests that he was behind this act of arson. He had purchased a new $20,000 closed-cockpit Lockheed Vega just three days prior. It was a Vega 5B NC49M, the same model that Amelia Earhart flew,[7] and after the fire destroyed it, he replaced it with a similar model, not an upgrade. That was hardly the act of someone who had received a windfall from insurance.

In June, Buddie added to his collection when he bought a plane for his daughter Martha as a college graduation present. At that time, only six women in the state of Georgia had a pilot's license. Martha's twin sister, Helen Jr., kept her feet on the ground and received a shiny new car.[8] John got his own plane too.

It's important to remember that this was well before the advent of passenger planes and casual air travel. Buddie's first plane, the Waco, had an open cockpit, which meant helmets and goggles were required, and wind and cold were limiting factors. It wasn't a commuter plane; it was for joyriding at high altitudes. But the purchase of the Vega greatly increased his range, which enabled him to embrace his other growing obsession: magic.

MAGIC MANIA

Flying wasn't the only rich man's hobby that flourished as Buddie's new cycle began. In May 1930, he was reported as one of the many wealthy men who had taken fondly to the practice of magic, and he frequently hopped into his airplane to fly up to New York City to shop for the latest and greatest magic tricks.[9]

Following the end of World War I, a fascination with the dark arts of magic, conjuring, and spiritualism swept through the United States, particularly among the affluent, fashionable set. There were a number of cultural elements at play during this time, all threaded together with the themes of mysticism, spirituality, and life after death. Seances, mediums, and phantom writing became parlor games, and the discovery of King Tut's tomb in 1922 spread Egyptomania and notions of the afterlife through every cultural corner, from architecture to fashion to home decor. This time period is associated with two so-called golden ages: that of magic and that of fraternal orders. Quasi mystical social clubs like the Shriners, Odd Fellows, and Freemasons saw peak memberships before a Depression-era decline.

All of these fads—Egyptomania, fraternal orders, and magic—appealed to Asa Candler Jr. and sparked a keen interest that he put on display in his usual grandiose way. Combine those interests with celebrity worship, like in his automobile and sports days, and you've got a recipe for obsession. It all started with Harry Houdini.

For all of his endearing qualities, Buddie was also a fibber, a blowhard, and a bit of a narcissist. He told stories to friends and family well into his final years about his close friendship with Houdini, claiming that he learned a magic trick from him that he swore to take to his grave.[10] But his stories can't simply be believed at face value. After all, if given an opportunity to puff up his importance or claim a seat at the right hand of the most influential people in an industry, he'd take it and inflate it beyond belief. In 1951, for example, author David Wesley Soper in *These Found the Way: Thirteen Converts to Protestant Christianity* recorded Buddie's story about showing his Houdini trick to native Africans while on safari. Asa Jr. said: "Houdini was one of my closest friends. He gave me before his death four of his choicest tricks, with the understanding that the secret behind each of them must remain with me, and die with me."[11] However, to date, no evidence has emerged to indicate that Asa Candler Jr. played any significant role in Harry Houdini's well-documented life. In fact, there is no evidence of a personal relationship at all. So did Buddie really know Harry Houdini?

Surprisingly, the answer is yes. As with so much of his puffery, there was a kernel of truth to this one. He likely knew Houdini, and it's possible that Houdini taught him a trick or two. But although many famous magicians visited Atlanta's Briarcliff Mansion, Houdini doesn't seem to have ever made an appearance there. It was travel in the opposite direction, from Atlanta to New York, that brought them together.

Houdini's career had taken an interesting turn when he gained fame as an escape artist. He appeared early in film history in a 1901 short titled *The Wonderful Adventures of the Famous Houdini in Paris*. In 1916 he made another film appearance, and in 1919 he starred in the box-office hit *The Master Mystery*. He appeared in two more films before he decided to create his own production company in 1921, the Houdini Picture Corporation.

Houdini needed a headquarters for his business and returned to New York to set up shop. He had connections with the Cinema Camera Club, which kept its headquarters on the sixteenth floor of the New York City Candler Building, which had been erected by Asa Sr. in 1912. This may have been the route by which he chose to lease space there.[12] As the manager of the Candler Investment Company's holdings, Buddie oversaw the leasing and maintenance of the New York City office building, including signing agreements with tenants like Harry Houdini. This was their connection.

The film company folded two years later, and then in 1926, Harry Houdini passed away. As a lover of celebrity, Buddie had probably been immediately taken by him. If history is any indicator of behavior, he latched onto the idea of friendship with the famous escape artist and started learning magic to forge a connection.

The enchanting hobby took hold of Asa Jr. as he decided to make his first major renovation to Briarcliff Mansion in 1925. His vision included a grand music hall and a dining room fit for galas of dignitaries, which also necessitated greater kitchen capacity for large-scale events. The music hall would be a performance venue and house the largest Aeolian pipe organ in Georgia—the eighth largest Aeolian built at the time. Buddie's father owned an Aeolian organ that was integrated into the ductwork surrounding a glass canopy above the living room at his Ponce de Leon Avenue home. His older brother and lifelong rival, Howard, owned an Aeolian organ that was integrated into the entryway arch at Callanwolde, with separate chambers set behind an elaborate rosette above the staircase and in the ceiling of his own great hall.[13] Callanwolde's great hall, incidentally, has an undeniable resemblance to Buddie's grander vision. Briarcliff's larger music hall and organ were intended to establish his dominance over his brother.

To escape the hubbub of construction, Buddie and his family left for another tour through Asia. During their stay in the Philippines, he encountered a young local magician named José Cruz. Something about Cruz must have made an impression, because Buddie arranged for him to migrate to the United States to be his personal butler and magic instructor. On April 7, 1925, twenty-four-year-old José arrived in San Francisco aboard the SS *President Taft*. With him were Philemon Cruz, presumably his younger brother, and Vincenzio DeVera, relationship unknown.[14] José's official capacity was butler, but his duties included teaching Buddie and his ten-year-old son, Sam, how to do magic tricks and assisting them in their acts. By Buddie's own account, his interest blossomed during his 1923–1925 trips to Asia: "Mr. Candler's hobby is the study of magic, sleight of hand tricks and many others which he learned in China and India."[15]

To review: in 1925 Buddie had just crashed out of the Candler Floating School and was now fully in control of the Candler Investment Company's portfolio. He was producing movies with the Graphic Films Corporation and had signed a deal to build the Southeast's first and biggest Macy's department store. Nine days after José's arrival, Atlanta signed a five-year lease for Candler Field, giving the land purpose for the first time in fourteen years. And he had recently orchestrated a full take-over of the Atlanta Union Stockyards and White Provisions Company. Soon after, the Shriners kicked off financial planning for their new temple, the future Fox Theater. Buddie was busy. Magic faced stiff competition for his time and attention.

Then the great sell-off began. Buddie pulled back from his many endeavors, and he lost his wife of twenty-five years, remarried, and sailed overseas to escape the spotlight. His father suffered a stroke, and Asa Jr. was caught smuggling a load of booze to the United States from Cuba. He sold the Candler Warehouse, the stockyards, Graphic Films, and Candler Field. And then everything quieted down. Finally, he had time to focus on other interests.

Magic took center stage, and José Cruz became a key player in Buddie's life. In June 1928, Buddie took his new private railcar to Lima, Ohio, so Sam could compete in an amateur event at a convention for professional magicians. The International Brotherhood of Magicians brought celebrity performer the Great Blackstone to judge the talent show. Sam and Buddie were listed as attendees, and in an interview with the local paper, Sam gave credit to Cruz as his teacher and assistant.[16]

As the stress of building an agricultural empire faded away in 1929, Buddie cofounded the Atlanta Society of Magicians.[17] The club was aligned with the Society of American Magicians, which Harry Houdini had led as president for many years before his death. Buddie also forged connections with the International Brotherhood of Magicians, establishing friendships with famous headlining performers.

In 1930, an article about the popularity of magic spoke of Buddie's obsession and its intersection with his love of airplanes: "One of the most incurable fans, and one of the master tricksters, is Asa Candler, son of the millionaire soft drink magnate. It is recorded that Candler jumps into his airplane and rides to Manhattan at regular intervals to pick up the best examples of mystification lying about the market."[18]

The number one magic shop in New York City for high-quality illusions was Martinka & Company, which was owned at one point by Harry Houdini and served as headquarters for the Society of American Magicians. It is likely that this was Buddie's vendor for all things magic when he visited New York.

But he didn't always travel to the apparatuses; sometimes, the apparatuses traveled to him. According to a story still circulating in Atlanta's magician community, Buddie contacted Floyd G. Thayer of the Thayer Magic Company, then regarded to be the best of the best, and ordered a magic trick. He liked it so much that he sent Thayer a check for $10,000 ($150,000 in 2020 dollars) and asked for one of everything in his catalog.[19] The illusions

The Thayer Phantom Cargo Cage, formerly part of Asa Candler Jr.'s magic collection.
Courtesy of William Schulert (aka Baffling Bill).

purchased in this set, many of which bore Egyptian motifs, included a
Thayer Phantom Cargo Cage, a Thayer Tea Chest, and a Thayer Egyptian
Princess Head illusion, all of which have survived and are still in working
order. Another item from Asa Candler Jr.'s impressive collection that is still
in use is his Noma Sword Cabinet, a rare illusion with few remaining models
in existence today.[20]

By 1930, Buddie's third-floor ballroom was stuffed to the rafters with
magic apparatuses, because, as with all of his hobbies, he eschewed moderation. Visiting magicians and fellow members of Atlanta's magic club were
permitted to select from his vast collection and perform at any gathering. He
started holding magic soirées, which were attended by society's elite. Dante
the Great, the Great Blackstone, Howard Thurston, and the Great Raymond
all attended Briarcliff soirées, flown in by Beeler Blevins in Buddie's private
plane.[21] And Buddie and Sam weren't the only Candlers who got in on the act
at these events. Sources claim he used his twin daughters, Martha and Helen
Jr., in his performances. Martha, in particular, was noted as his assistant.[22]

Then, it all came to a sudden halt. By the spring of 1931, magic was over. Buddie was no longer interested. Over the next few years, he occasionally appeared in magic-related media, but only in retrospectives or as the owner of apparatuses on loan to other acts.

In the early 1950s, a beat reporter for *Billboard* magazine, Bill Sachs, wrote about a trip to Atlanta, where he met up with magic duo Torrini and Phyllis, who owned a magic shop in the Peachtree Arcade. They had acquired the right to act as the selling agent for Asa Candler Jr.'s valuable magic collection, which was appraised at around a half million dollars (in 2020 dollars).[23] The collection was sold off piece by piece, dispersed through the magic community, and lost to history. Sachs bought some items as did Blackstone and Lieutenant Lee Allen Estes of the Kentucky State Police. The collection was said to contain "all Conradi and Thayer made equipment . . . the best."[24] It was by all accounts an astounding collection. This raises the question, what went wrong?

MURDER AT THE MANSION

Local lore says Briarcliff Mansion is haunted. Perhaps it's due to Asa Candler Jr.'s enduring reputation as an eccentric, depressed alcoholic. Undoubtedly, the building's time as a mental health facility after his death contributes to the legend. Some locals believe that Buddie's soul collected bad karma from conducting shady real estate deals during his life. The myth endures because it's an abandoned, decaying mansion that fits the haunted house trope perfectly.

But abandonment alone doesn't a haunted house make. Something tragic has to happen on the premises in order to fit the stereotype. At the heart of every good haunted house story is a macabre tale of suffering and death, something to validate the notion that a restless spirit lingers on. The news for those who would like to believe that Briarcliff is haunted is promising: there was, in fact, a murder that took place there.[25]

When the story broke in 1931, it made national headlines from coast to coast. But through the collective efforts of law enforcement and Buddie himself, the story faded away, and the world moved on. People who were alive at the time knew all about it, but it was impolite to gossip about such a grim event.[26] The story was quashed, one of the victims quite literally buried in an unmarked grave. The whole thing started with the hiring of José Cruz.

In April 1925, José, Philemon, and Vincenzio arrived at Briarcliff Mansion, ready to take their places as employees on the estate. Buddie gave them an apartment above the garage to share. This wasn't unusual; he had other servants living on-site, including his groundskeeper, James Stark, who lived in a cottage near the greenhouses. Buddie's lifelong servant, Landrum Anderson, and his wife, Jessie, rented a house on the back property as well.

Officially, José was Buddie's butler, Philemon was his footman, and Vincenzio was his valet. If it sounds like Buddie was the ruler of his own kingdom, it's worthwhile to note that by 1930 there were twenty people who resided at 1260 Briarcliff Road. Five were Candler family members, and fifteen were servants and staff.[27]

Between 1925 and 1930, Cruz did his duty, teaching and assisting Buddie in magic. They traveled together to and from magic events and shops where Asa Candler Jr. acquired new apparatuses, and they performed together at parties. Very little documentation of Asa Jr.'s staff from this period exists. Cruz, however, was both photographed and named in print media. He was also reported as one of Buddie's favorites.[28] It seems he played a particularly important role in Buddie's life. Certainly, he was a key employee who supported Buddie's ostentatious, attention-seeking, gregarious social nature, right up until Cruz's sudden, gruesome death.

➔ How It Was Widely Reported

On the morning of January 18, 1931, Asa Candler Jr. was awoken at dawn by his groundskeeper with the news that José Cruz was dead. While doing his morning rounds, James Stark had spotted a car parked by the putting green on the southern side of the forty-two-acre property. At first, he assumed it belonged to an Emory College employee, since Briarcliff's grounds were open to the school's faculty. After he walked the course and realized no one was out there, he approached the car to see who it belonged to.

Inside the car, he found Cruz with a gunshot wound in his temple and a young woman with a gunshot wound in her abdomen. They were both dead. In shock, Stark ran to the house to wake his boss and call the police.

During the investigation, a note found in the car indicated that their deaths were a double suicide.

To whom it may concern:
We, Gladys Frix and José Cruz, are taking our lives because we love each other, but due to objections of Louise Frix and Mrs. J. T. Clay we can't find a way to be

together in peace. We love each other and we rather die and be together always than to be parted from each other, and good bye to all, and may God forgive us.

Investigators also found a pair of school slates in the back seat. One ominously read: "This is my last trick and I hope you will enjoy the performance." The other read: "Good-night, Happy New Year and Merry Christmas."

A coroner's jury was assembled, and after hearing testimony by investigators and friends of Gladys Frix, the jury determined that the event was not a double suicide. Gladys's note had blamed her sister and grandmother (Mrs. Clay), the signature on the note was not in her handwriting, and given the location of her gunshot wound, the jury declared it a murder-suicide. José had killed himself and taken her with him against her will.

The final detail reported in newspapers across the United States was about the murder weapon: José had used a nickel-plated pistol with an ivory grip. That pistol belonged to his employer, Asa Candler Jr.[29]

➔ What Happened?

The story varied widely in different publications. Newspapers cribbed from each other's reports without verification, twisting the story, confusing the timeline, and inventing sensationalistic details. In some cases, the wrong Asa Candler was cited as Cruz's employer. Journalists disagreed on how many notes were found, and what exactly they said. Some implied that the messages on the child's slates were meant as a warning, possibly targeting Cruz's magic-enthusiast employer.

What follows is a compilation of all the reported details and witness testimonies, with the obvious untruths and errors weeded out. This is the most accurate timeline of events possible. For the cast, see the table.

➔ Compiled Narrative

The Candler estate's groundskeeper, James Stark, first saw the car at about six o'clock on Sunday morning, January 18, 1931. It was standing in the west driveway about forty feet from the street. No lights were on, and he paid little attention to it for more than an hour.

As dawn broke, he happened to glance toward the car and thought he saw someone in it. He walked up to the vehicle, looked through the closed window, and found a young woman and José Cruz. She was sitting in his lap.

INVOLVED PARTIES

Victim	Gladys Frix
Murderer	José Cruz
Employer	Asa Candler Jr.
Groundskeeper	James Stark
Sheriff	Jake Hall
Undertaker and Special Officer	Addison Turner
Solicitor's Investigator	Johnny Jones
County Physician and Coroner	C. E. Pattillo
Sister	Louise Frix
Friend	Mae Adair
Friend	W. L. Bennett
Friend	Tom Reed
Friend	Stewart Clup
Acquaintance	Kate Christiansen
Family Friend	Walter Ansley
Neighbor	W. S. Heil

Her head was on his shoulder, and his arm was around her. Cruz held Asa Candler Jr.'s pistol tightly gripped in one hand. Stark touched the bodies and found them cold and dead. He ran as fast as he could to tell Asa Jr. and call the sheriff. However, in contradictory testimony, Stark also said that he saw the bodies but didn't open the car door.

Sheriff Jake Hall and undertaker Addison Turner answered the call to the Candler estate. The door of the car was closed when they reached the scene. The young woman, later identified as Gladys Frix, was lying across Cruz's lap. Her arm was cast around his neck, and her head was resting on his left shoulder. Her body leaned against the steering wheel and the driver's side door. José Cruz's left arm was around Gladys, and his right was down on the seat.

A few inches from his right hand was an automatic .32-caliber pearl-handled and nickel-plated pistol. He carried thirteen dollars in cash, and she had twenty cents in her purse.

Hall and Turner agreed that death had occurred six or eight hours before the two were found, around eleven or twelve o'clock Saturday night. The sheriff ordered the bodies removed, and they were examined by Turner. He found that Frix had been shot through her left side, the bullet piercing her abdomen and emerging from her right side. Cruz was shot through the brain. The bullet entered through his right temple above his ear and came out through the left side of his head near the top of the skull, about two inches above and an inch or more behind his left temple. Turner believed it was evident that death in each case had been instantaneous. He and Hall were asked by coroner and county physician C. E. Pattillo if they thought the young woman would have lived several minutes after she was wounded. Both believed she could have, but neither found any evidence of a struggle.

Investigators found one empty cartridge on the floor of the car, another empty in the pistol, and two loaded cartridges on the floor under the driver's seat. Hall learned on inquiry that the pistol used in the incident belonged to Asa Candler Jr., but Buddie said he didn't know it was in Cruz's possession or how long he'd had it. The investigators also found other significant items in the car: one suicide note, one love note, two slates, and one pearl-handled dagger. Upon searching Cruz's apartment above the garage, they found two additional notes. None of the notes bore Frix's handwriting or signature.

NOTE 1 (FOUND ON A BODY)

An unsigned note on Cruz's body told of thwarted love and appeared to be written by the young woman, but the penmanship matched his handwriting. The note read verbatim as mentioned above.

NOTE 2 (FOUND IN THE CAR)

A piece of soap was found by Sheriff Hall in the back of the car. A love message, in Cruz's handwriting, was scrawled on the outside of the soap wrapper. The contents of the message were not published.

NOTES 3 AND 4 (FOUND IN CRUZ'S APARTMENT)

Two other notes in Cruz's room were understood to be addressed to his employer, Asa Candler Jr. One of the notes declared the deaths a suicide pact, but the jury could find no corroborative evidence. The contents of the notes were not published.

SLATES 1 AND 2 (FOUND IN THE CAR)

On the back seat of the small sedan, Sheriff Hall found two slates, the kind used in schoolrooms. They were evidently part of the equipment that Cruz used in performing magic, likely for a phantom writing trick. The contents of both were as described above. Hall said he did not believe there was any significance to the messages on the slates. The inscriptions had been written for a performance given by Cruz around the holidays, and he had merely neglected to remove them from his car.

The coroner's jury was pulled together the same day that the murder was discovered. This was done in an effort to expedite the conclusions and finalize the causes of death for both parties. Hall and undertaker Turner both testified and displayed evidence to the jury. In his own testimony, solicitor's investigator Johnny Jones said he had evidence that compelled him to believe that the message found in the car had been concocted by Cruz as a small detail of a long-planned plot to murder the girl and kill himself. A juror asked if he was basing this statement on any evidence that the jury hadn't heard yet. Jones reportedly hesitated, then said he had nothing "except some notes." He explained about the notes found in Cruz's apartment that were addressed to Asa Jr. The jury asked to see them, but he refused.

It was rumored, however, that the private notes were shared with the jury when they retired to deliberate, after the press had left the room. No record of what was contained in those notes was preserved. The jury came back without much delay: José Cruz had murdered Gladys Frix and killed himself.

➔ Testimonials

The police investigation turned up all the evidence that was needed to declare Gladys Frix the victim of murder. Her lack of consent was never in doubt. But that wasn't enough for her family and friends. They pulled together a roster of witnesses who all wanted to speak to the press and testify to the jury, ostensibly to clear Gladys's good name and characterize Cruz as a dangerous psychopath bent on doing harm. Their testimonials were somewhat dramatic and inconsistent, perhaps exaggerated or partially fabricated.

LOUISE FRIX

Louise Frix claimed that her sister Gladys had told her more than once that she did not love Cruz, but she was afraid to stop going out with him because he had threatened her life. Louise described the long-bladed, ivory-handled dagger that she heard was found in the car. The coroner produced it for the jury to see and noted that he understood Cruz used it in sleight-of-hand tricks. Louise responded:

> What do you mean, sleight-of-hand? He used that murderous thing for protection. He has often showed it to me and told me that the tip of it was poisoned with deadly serum. He said that if he stuck the blade into someone that death would be a matter of but a few moments. He always carried it in his pocket.

W. S. HEIL

W. S. Heil, who lived next door to the Frixes, also weighed in. He told the *Atlanta Journal* that José Cruz had given him a scrapbook earlier in the week, told him of his love for the young woman, and added that he was "tired of this worldly strife to win her love."

W. L. BENNETT

W. L. Bennett, a friend of Gladys who attended but did not formally testify at the inquest, suggested that Cruz had killed Frix out of jealousy. After the hearing, Bennett stated to the press that he was engaged to marry Frix, although he had told investigators that he was not her fiancé. He explained that he changed his story when the Frix family agreed that it would be all right for him to make the announcement. Bennett claimed their impending wedding was several months away. However, when approached by the press before the inquest, Bennett's father had said that as far as he knew, his son was not engaged to Gladys Frix.

GLADYS'S OTHER FRIENDS

Several of Gladys's friends provided testimony during the inquiry and to the press, agreeing unanimously that Cruz's behavior had set off red flags the evening of the murder. In addition to W. L. Bennett's statements, Mae Adair, Tom Reed, Stewart Clup, Walter Ansley, and Kate Christiansen all gave their own versions, which are compiled and consolidated in the following timeline.

Saturday, January 10, 1931

One week before the murder, Gladys Frix asked her friend Mae Adair to set up a group date, with José Cruz included. The plan was to meet up at Mae's house, so Gladys's family wouldn't discover that they were going out together.

Saturday, January 17, 1931, 8:00 p.m.

José arrived at Mae's house, and together they went down to the corner to wait for their friends.

8:30 p.m.

The rest of Gladys's friends met at her house, and together they ran down the road to join with the others at the corner near Mae's house. Gladys jumped into José's car, and the group drove to the Green Dragon Roadhouse in Hapeville. José and Gladys stopped at a fueling station on the way.

10:00 p.m.

José and Gladys arrived at the Green Dragon. They were late, but they appeared to be having fun. Gladys seemed to be enjoying herself.

11:00 p.m.

Gladys said she had to go home, so everyone headed back to Atlanta, intending to meet at a diner. Her friends waited a long time for José and Gladys to arrive. When José's car finally appeared, it flew by at high speed, and during testimony two of the young women described his speed as reckless and dangerous. They agreed that they saw Gladys screaming and pounding her hands on the passenger side window as it went by. Another acquaintance described the drive-by in milder terms, and said she didn't see Gladys inside the car as it passed.

11:00 p.m.–12:00 a.m.

José and Gladys arrived at the Briarcliff estate and parked near the golf course. He soon shot her in the abdomen and himself in the head.

⇥ What *Really* Happened?

After sifting through the innuendo and conjecture of sloppy journalism, the evidence supports only one conclusion: José Cruz murdered Gladys Frix and killed himself. She did not consent to a double suicide, and given the description of her position and the location of her wound, she likely suffered at the hands of a man she trusted.

And she did appear to have trusted him. Her sister's claim that she was scared of Cruz and her friend's claim that she was secretly engaged to someone else were unsubstantiated. The testimonials of several friends indicated that she liked him but knew her family wouldn't approve. Saturday night's outing was set up at her request, and her friends observed that she appeared to be having fun. Cruz betrayed her trust. He held her in his lap, put his arms around her, and shot her. She was the victim, and she never saw it coming.

The evidence also suggests that Asa Candler Jr. knew something more about this incident. José Cruz was his right-hand man, frequently traveling and performing with him and living at his home. Cruz might have been struggling with mental illness, and likely believed what he said in his note. He thought the world wouldn't permit him and Gladys to be together, so he decided that death was the only way out. Buddie may not have known that a murder-suicide was coming, but he surely knew that something was off, which was why Cruz left not one but two notes addressed to him in his personal quarters. Based on testimony, Buddie did not seem to be surprised by the notes, and he may not have been as ignorant of Cruz's possession of his pistol as he claimed.

The reasons provided in the suicide note were likely based on truth. Her family didn't want them to be together, thanks to good old-fashioned racism. This was the American South in the 1930s, and Filipinos were outsiders, like other minorities. The following lightly edited passage appears in *A Different Shade of Justice* by Stephanie Hinnershitz:

> Filipinos, however, did not always identify as "colored," citing their American "national" status or even Spanish heritage (as evident in their surnames) as evidence that the laws did not necessarily apply to them. . . . The fact that Asian Americans were not black but, rather, "brown" or "yellow" provided them with some maneuverability within the binary black-and-white structure as reflected in Southern laws.
>
> Filipino Americans' potential for maneuverability within Georgia's antimiscegenation law did not mean that free intermingling between "Malays" and whites was acceptable. Asian Americans were still racial minorities perceived according to their own set of accompanying sexual stereotypes. . . . Asian Americans [were perceived as] a particularly dangerous threat to the economic, social, and political power structure in America as well as the South.[30]

➜ The Aftermath

Gladys Frix, just nineteen years old, was prepared for burial at H. M. Patterson Funeral Home on Spring Street. She was buried on January 20, 1931, in Rose Hill Cemetery in Austell, Georgia.[31] As for José Cruz, he had no family in the United States other than his brother Philemon, who returned to the Philippines with Vincenzio after this incident. José's boss claimed his body. Buddie provided a plain pine casket and buried him at West View Cemetery, of which he had recently taken controlling interest. As fitting for a murderer, Buddie had Cruz interred in an unmarked grave in a section that was set aside for similarly unmarked plots.[32] Buried in anonymity, not to be remembered.

➜ How Was This Story Forgotten?

The Candlers had a way of making trouble disappear. In this case, the family had a personal connection to law enforcement and the coroner through Asa Candler Sr. While they may not have covered up anything specifically, embarrassment was a big deal to Buddie, and there was no way he wanted this story associated with his name or with Coca-Cola. The investigators expedited their work and kept any evidence tied to him out of the press. They quickly put the story to bed, quieting any rumbles about what Asa Jr. could have known prior to the incident.

Buddie put it to bed too. In reviewing his social activities, it is clear that his interest in magic came to a stop following this tragedy. He didn't get rid of his apparatuses yet, and he lent them to local magicians for shows over the years. But his soirée days were behind him. Magic was tainted now.

Fortunately, Asa Jr. had another hobby, an attention-grabbing hobby that he could use to garner new headlines. And thanks to a carefully orchestrated airplane stunt, the world forgot all about the murder at Briarcliff Mansion.

FLYING LIKE CHARLES LINDBERGH

In July 1931, Buddie sold his Vega and bought a $25,000 Lockheed Orion, a superspeed monoplane. Charles Lindbergh also flew an Orion, but Buddie's was reported as the only one privately purchased for the purpose of ferrying around business associates.[33]

This wasn't his only link to Charles Lindbergh. The first was in 1927, when Lindbergh flew to Atlanta to build public approval for the city's proposal to buy Candler Field. As an active member of this burgeoning, elite hobby, Buddie naturally would cross paths with him again. In fact, Lindbergh flew in Buddie's former Vega after he sold it.[34]

For his 1931 publicity stunt and much-needed distraction, Buddie traveled with his wife to United Airport (later, Bob Hope Airport and currently Hollywood Burbank Airport) in California to pick up his new airplane and take it on its maiden voyage. While standing on the tarmac with Lockheed executives and a few members of the press, he announced that he intended to break Lindbergh's transcontinental flight record when flying from Los Angeles to Atlanta. He called it an alternative transcontinental route, declaring that Los Angeles to Atlanta was far more important than San Francisco to New York.[35] This was a bold but not unexpected claim from a man whose family worked tirelessly to promote Georgia's reputation as the Empire State of the South.

It was a daring flight plan. Buddie and Florence brought no food and packed no bags. They would fly directly from Los Angeles to Dallas, Texas, stop for lunch, and then continue on to Atlanta. The first leg was reportedly uneventful, and they made good time until they entered Dallas air space. Then a great storm rose up around them, and the wind and rain forced them to make an emergency landing at Love Airfield. It was a close call, nearly a crash landing, as a wind shear cut across the landing strip and tilted the craft, digging its left wing into the ground as they touched down. The wing needed repairs, ruining any chance at breaking the speed record.[36] Buddie never attempted the transcontinental record again.

But the stunt did exactly what it was intended to do. It replaced the headlines about his murderous butler and the lingering questions about what he knew and how his personal pistol had been involved. No one cared about that unfortunate event anymore. Magic was over. Flying was where it was at.

After the failed record attempt, Buddie sent out Blevins to fly on his behalf in races all over the country as often as he could arrange it. It was the auto-racing days all over again. And when the governor of Georgia needed an appointee to represent the state's interests at a three-day aviation law conference in St. Louis in December 1931, he asked Buddie and Blevins to promote the need for uniform aviation regulations.[37]

Unfortunately, those days came to an end when Beeler Blevins died in an automobile accident in 1934. Rather than hiring a new daredevil pilot, Buddie withdrew from racing and used his planes for transporting important associates and taking hunting trips up to Jackson Hole, Wyoming, and other wildernesses. Edward W. Hightower, a former Blevins Aircraft employee, took over as his personal pilot until Hightower enlisted with the Royal Air Force and departed to serve in World War II over North Africa.[38]

Even without a daredevil in the cockpit, early air travel wasn't without risk. In 1951, Buddie recounted a story about a close call:

> At one time a group of friends were flying with me in my plane to Alaska on a hunting expedition. We were flying at 16,000 feet in a heavy fog to clear the mountaintops. But the ice formed rapidly on the wings, and we had only a limited supply of de-icing fluid. We were cruising at about 220 miles an hour.
>
> After a time my pilot, who had been with me for fifteen years, came back into the cabin and said, "Mr. Candler, we are out of de-icing fluid. At this altitude, ice will form rapidly, and slow us down. We cannot maintain a safe altitude when the plane slows to 160 miles an hour. When that happens, we have exhausted the possibilities. I want to ask you to be prepared for the end."[39]

Fortunately, the pilot was able to coast to an open field and make an emergency landing, but the scary experience stuck with Buddie and quickly became one of his gripping tales of adventure.

The failed transcontinental flight wasn't the last time the name Lindbergh would cross paths with the name Candler. The next time it came up, however, was in connection to Buddie's next obsession: the Briarcliff Zoological Park.

Buddy [sic], I believe this is the biggest fool thing you've done yet.[1]

CHAPTER 15

Lions and Tigers and . . . Elephants?

It all started at the end of 1931, when Buddie bought a bear.

The story says that a young student at Mercer University took ownership of the school's mascot but quickly found himself overwhelmed by the responsibility. Neighbors didn't appreciate a backyard bear in their midst, and as the student made plans to leave town for a work opportunity, it became clear that the bear needed a new home. He took the bear to Petland, a store that peddled all species of animals. And just in time for Christmas, the bear found a new home at Briarcliff Mansion.[2]

Of course, that was just the beginning. A few months later, Buddie bought an elephant, perhaps to keep the bear company. The large pachyderm was permitted to roam the back portion of the property, eating the underbrush and clearing land. It could have stopped there, but Buddie never believed in moderation. Once you buy an elephant and a bear, naturally you buy the rest of the menagerie.

By March 1932, Asa Jr. had acquired several monkeys, a second bear, two elk, a buffalo, and flocks of exotic birds were en route to Atlanta. He opened Briarcliff's gates to the public and invited locals to bring their children to meet his small collection up close. Meanwhile, he was busy making arrangements to buy many, many more animals, including Rosie, an African elephant that was purchased from a Miami Beach real estate developer who could no longer afford to feed her.[3] Rosie was reputedly mean—although evidence suggests she was mistreated rather than mean by nature—so the only handler she would tolerate came with her to Briarcliff and went on the payroll.[4]

An anecdote claims that Buddie—while drunk—next purchased animals from a defunct circus in Germany. As the story goes, he telegraphed his architects, Charles Frazier and Dan Bodin, to tell them that he'd bought a zoo and instructed them to build cages. Another anecdote claims the builders were not given advance notice, and construction only began after the animals arrived. Both versions have been repeated so many times with no attribution that they're impossible to verify. The first version reeks of Buddie's own flare for autobiographical exaggeration, and the second came straight from his former zookeeper's mouth decades later. What can be verified is that he completed a $30,000 transaction through Benson Animal Farms in Nashua, New Hampshire, and brought in the animals by train on April 20, 1932.[5]

The train story is probably the most well-known Asa Candler Jr. anecdote in the Atlanta area. He brought in his entire menagerie all at once, unloaded the animals at the Emory University train depot on Eagle Row, and marched them in a line through the residential streets of Druid Hills to Briarcliff Mansion. The unloading process was well documented by the press. The *Atlanta Constitution* journalist Ernest Rogers was there, and he described it as follows: "I was assigned to cover the unloading of the zoo the morning it arrived by rail at the Emory University station, and as tigers, elephants, monkeys, and whatnot were making their appearance Asa's brother, Walter, remarked, 'Buddy [*sic*], I believe this is the biggest fool thing you've done yet.'"[6]

Buddie relandscaped his front lawn, and the northeast corner of the property was leveled and cleared for cages and picnic areas. A large concrete structure contained a series of enclosures for some of the carnivores, and a separate enclosure housed the elephants. The list of creatures now occupying the front lawn of his suburban home included a Bengal tiger named Jimmy Walker, four more elephants, a troop of baboons, two black leopards, two llamas, three Shetland ponies, a camel, eight bears of assorted species, two Barbary lions, a zebra, Himalayan goats, four chimpanzees, and Japanese macaques. A suite of cages contained flamingos, parakeets, eagles, and more.[7] He later added to his collection by digging a water feature and adding a sea lion exhibit. He officially named the enterprise Briarcliff Zoological Park, and after throwing a few fundraisers for local causes, he officially invited everyone to visit his exotic collection starting in September for just twenty-five cents admission.[8]

During this acquisition phase, his life intersected with Charles Lindbergh's one more time. All of Buddie's zoo activity had taken place while the nation was transfixed by the sensational search for Lindbergh's kidnapped baby. One night, police in Newark, N.J., received a tip that a Lockheed monoplane

Candler Jr. (*right*) showing a guest an ostrich at Briarcliff Zoological Park, 1932 (digitally restored). Courtesy of the *Atlanta Journal-Constitution*.

had landed with two passengers and a bundle containing "something alive." Suspecting that the bundle might contain the missing baby, officers rushed to the scene to investigate. Rather than a baby, they found two small monkeys, which the travelers were handing off to friends in New Hampshire on Asa Jr.'s behalf.[9] In retrospect, the reporter likely misunderstood, and the monkeys probably were a delivery from the New Hampshire–based Benson Animal Farms to Buddie's delegates.

In Atlanta, Asa Jr. needed to keep the animals fed and cared for. He hired a man named Fletcher Reynolds, a violinist turned animal collector who had done a stint in Honduras as a fruit distributor and sold exotic creatures to Benson Animal Farms. Buddie had informed John T. Benson that he required an experienced caretaker along with his shipment of live animals, and Benson recommended Reynolds, who oversaw the construction of the zoo enclosures. Asa Jr. hired trainers to teach his more agreeable elephants, named Coca, Cola, Pause, Refreshes, and Delicious, to perform for paying guests. The zoo also offered a trained bear act and a Shetland pony show. By Reynolds's estimate, Buddie poured more than $1 million into this passion project.[10] In 2020 dollars, that's more than $18 million.

Briarcliff had one major natural asset that made owning a zoo possible: an artesian well. The high-pressure spring issued an endless bounty of water at a flow rate of five thousand gallons per minute.[11] His first use of the well had been for Briarcliff Farm's cattle barns, where automated drinking fountains were continually refreshed with pure, clean water. After the farm was leveled, the spring water filled his substantial family pool on the side lawn and fed his botanical collection in the greenhouses. He would tap the well again and again throughout his life for various projects, and in the 1930s, it gave him a bountiful supply for his animals with enough left over for swans and sea lions to cavort in. However, the water ended up being a source of complaint from his neighbors, whose concerns over odors and disease due to runoff and standing wastewater grew by the day.[12]

That wasn't his neighbors' only complaint. They claimed the animals' noises kept them up at night and that they heard gunshots over the wall, which concerned them. While Buddie claimed that wasn't true and suggested that the shots might have come from scoundrels out on Briarcliff Road, there may have been some veracity to the reports.[13] It should be noted that he was a lifelong game hunter whose growing passion for flying off to various hunting grounds to collect trophies coincided in timing with the acquisition of his menagerie. In August 1932, prior to the zoo's official opening, Buddie even had referred to his property as Briarcliff Lodge rather than Briarcliff Zoological Park.[14] Perhaps he looked to emulate other wealthy men, like William Randolph Hearst, who occasionally used his private zoo for hunting fodder, and wished to demonstrate a similar show of money and joie de vivre.[15]

The gunshot accusations didn't stick, but other charges had merit. Neighbors claimed that sometimes the large carnivores escaped from their enclosures and roamed Druid Hills unrestrained. An urban legend claims that zoo staff would walk the residential streets pulling wagons loaded with drug-laced meat, hoping to lure the big cats out of hiding. One neighbor said that sometimes the monkeys would break free and gather in the treetops above his home.[16] Another neighbor claimed that a baboon broke into her car, snatched her purse, and ate sixty dollars.[17] (This is perhaps the most enduring incident associated with Asa Candler Jr.'s local history.)

Buddie took umbrage at these claims. He swore his enclosures were above reproach and insisted that he had summoned the head of security at the DeKalb County Jail to inspect his cages: "As for the animals escaping and going on the rampage, the jailer down at Decatur told me he wished his cells would hold his inmates half as well as mine did these animals."[18] He spoke of the utmost care with which his staff handled sanitation, and he refuted claims that standing water bred odors and mosquitoes that lowered his neighbors' property values.[19] True to step 5 of his typical cycle, he was floundering and fighting criticism with preposterous claims.

But the venture was starting to spiral out of control. By 1933 the zoo was financially insolvent, which was leaked to the public by unhappy staff.[20] In an effort to drum up more business, Buddie tapped his well again and opened a public pool. The pool was popular with the locals, but the money it brought in wasn't enough to offset the expense of the zoo. In March, a man named John Lee Butler tried his hand at extortion and threatened to kill Briarcliff's animals if Buddie didn't pay him $1,000.[21] The man was arrested without incident, but the stress added to the growing list of problems that the zoo had brought into Buddie's life.

Like so many of his big ideas, it was doomed. Admission fees weren't covering the cost of maintenance, and outside forces threatened to add to the expenses. DeKalb County drafted a plan to issue a tax on residential zoos, and given that there was only one residential zoo in the county, this move was clearly intended to target him. Asa Jr. was embroiled in many lawsuits by then too, and he had lost the case brought by the Yaarab Shriners to collect the $10,000 he owed for the Fox Theater construction.[22] Legal objections to the zoo filed by his neighbors gained traction, with one class action suit seeking $25,000 in damages.[23] Even his lawyer sued him: for back payment for ten court cases he'd worked on.[24] In August 1933, his father's widow sued him and his siblings for $250,000, claiming they had misinterpreted Asa Sr.'s will and shortchanged her on what she was owed.[25]

He was teetering on the brink of financial pandemonium, and so Buddie's cycle entered step 6: liquidation and abandoning the venture. The zoo's end was imminent.

BUDDIE THE PHOENIX: GOODBYE, ZOO

By this time, Asa Jr. was drinking a lot, his temper was short, and his behavior was becoming erratic. His adult children were, by all accounts, struggling as well. Lucy, Laura, and John were admitted alcoholics. If, in fact, Buddie was participating in a rum-running side hustle during Prohibition, he could have easily fueled his and his family's addictions with enough left over to bring in extra funds. A false floor panel discovered in a basement storage room adjacent to his walk-in safe concealed a sizable compartment, suggesting its function was for stashing valuables or contraband. His growing erratic behavior surrounding the zoo aligned with the Briarcliff Candlers' peak alcoholism, despite Prohibition.

One employee provided a glimpse of Buddie's irrational behavior. Fletcher Reynolds recalled that one day the bear trainer didn't show up for work, so Buddie declared himself fit to conduct the afternoon's performance. It didn't go well, and he emerged from the enclosure with a bitten finger. Taking no comfort in how much worse it could have been, Buddie became enraged and took his anger out on his zookeeper. He announced: "Reynolds, I've got news for you. You haven't got a job anymore. I'm getting rid of these animals. I'll give them away if I have to."[26]

And then he threatened to blow up the enclosures with dynamite.

Like in his run-ins with Edward Durant and William White Jr., Buddie and Reynolds duked it out in the papers. Buddie went to the press on September 21 and informed reporters that he would close the zoo and sell the animals and that Reynolds had been dismissed.[27] In response, Reynolds stated that he had been fired and that it all came down to money problems.[28] The very next day, Buddie retracted his statement: there were no money problems, the zoo would remain open, and Reynolds was simply off acquiring new animals.[29] Then, he named junior staff member Al Langdon to take Reynolds's place until a new hire named Johnny Dilbeck could take over.[30]

In October 1933, he quietly sold his Lockheed Orion and gave his first elephant, Coca, to Grant Park Zoo (Zoo Atlanta's predecessor).[31] Meanwhile, DeKalb County was in the process of pushing through its private zoo tax, and one of the biggest neighborhood lawsuits was going to trial.[32]

The year 1934 was rough. He couldn't find a buyer for his menagerie at a price that he felt was fair. He was in discussions with Grant Park Zoo and with a potential buyer in New York, but he could neither off-load the financial burden nor stop paying for the animals' upkeep. In July, a court handed down a judgment against him, sticking him with the bill for zoological park equipment, such as picnic tables and other furnishings. The judge denied his claim that because the zoo was incorporated, he was personally protected from having to pay the debt.[33] This is a key court finding in his history because it exhibits some of the legal wrangling that enabled him to take huge financial risks without going bankrupt, and it would come back to haunt him later.

Then, his daughter Helen Jr. hit a little boy with her car, which landed Buddie in court again when the boy's family sued for damages.[34] No matter

Asa Candler Jr. (*right*) with one of his elephants and an employee at Briarcliff Zoological Park (digitally restored), 1932. Courtesy of the *Atlanta Journal-Constitution*.

which way Buddie turned, angry accusers sought monetary recompense. This was in the midst of the Great Depression, so his real estate investments weren't making the kind of profit he was used to. Prohibition also had ended in 1933, which may have impacted him financially, if he was really rum-running. All signs pointed to Asa Jr.'s personal problems peaking again, just like in 1911, just like in 1928.

By 1935, Buddie had finalized the arrangements to sell his menagerie to the Grant Park Zoo for $20,000. Like with Candler Field and the Atlanta Union Stockyards, he settled for less than his original asking price and significantly less than what the endeavor had cost him, especially taking zoo operations and staff salaries into account. To get to his final asking price, he rallied the city to launch a campaign to raise 150,000 dimes for Grant Park Zoo's purchase. Children all over the city collected $15,000, one coin at a time.[35] The animals that the Grant Park Zoo didn't take went to farms and circuses. Rosie the elephant joined a circus, where she passed away a few years later.[36]

But the sale didn't stop his legal woes. By then, the case of the money-eating baboon had made its way up to the Georgia Superior Court, and the judgment against him was upheld, forcing him to pay $10,000 ($180,000 in 2020 dollars) in damages for the effects of his zoo on his neighbors, even though the Briarcliff Zoological Park was no more. As promised, dynamite blasts leveled the enclosures, leaving nothing but concrete footings, which remain on the property to this day.[37]

SMOKE ON THE WATER

On August 22, 1935, while driving back from his seaside summer home, Buddie lost control of the steering in his car, which spun off the road and overturned. His passengers—his wife, Florence, and two nephews—were all injured and taken to the hospital. Florence sprained her back, and one of the boys broke three ribs. The other boy escaped with some scrapes and bruises, and Buddie was nearly unscathed.[38] Perhaps not coincidentally, he started questioning his alcoholism around this time.[39]

The route was a familiar one that he had driven many times. His property on Bunkers Cove Road in Panama City, Florida, was his home base when he had the urge to go sailing.[40] In June 1936, he sponsored the first annual Candler Regatta at the St. Andrews Bay Yacht Club, with the stipulation that the race route pass directly in front of his house so he could watch from the comfort of his patio.[41] He provided a silver punch bowl as a trophy for the winner, and at the award ceremony he described the event in typical superlative fashion as "the most colorful regatta" he had ever seen.[42]

A month later, a fire broke out on board the *Amphitrite*, causing at least $10,000 of damage. His insurance policy paid for his losses.

My self was my trouble—my love of myself, my fear of anything that might frustrate my wishes. My will had always been the central interest in my life.[1]

CHAPTER 16

Laundry and the Eternal

Two life choices coincided to upend Asa Candler Jr.'s last grasp at superlative greatness. The first concerned a graveyard and the second concerned a laundry. To get there, we have to go back to 1930.

That year, while deep in his magic phase and regrouping from the great sell-off, Buddie made a unique business decision. He decided to buy a controlling interest in Westview Cemetery (then called West View Cemetery), a massive burial ground west of downtown Atlanta. Once the site of the bloody Battle of Ezra Church during the Civil War, the cemetery served as the final resting place for many of the city's most prominent white citizens. So, of course, it was the Candler family burial ground. Asa Jr.'s first-born son was buried there, along with his first wife, Helen, his mother and father, his brother Walter's first wife, his sister Lucy's first husband, his cousin Asa W. Candler, and several other relatives. The sections flanking the obelisk that marks Asa Candler Sr.'s grave contain a who's who of early 1900s white Atlanta business figures. And West View had another quality that surely appealed to Buddie's extravagant nature. It encompassed more than 580 acres of land, mostly undeveloped, making it the largest cemetery in the Southeast.

Buddie's investment in the cemetery represented a shift from his previous endeavors, but it may not have been entirely spontaneous. Back in 1909, when he and Edward Durant were in Hapeville scouting land for the future site of the Atlanta Speedway, Asa Jr. informed nosy journalists that they were simply considering establishing a vast cemetery.[2] This claim came back around during the Durant kerfuffle when one of the Atlanta Automobile

Association directors suggested that the speedway might become a large cemetery if finances didn't improve. Twenty years later, Buddie took control of a large cemetery. Perhaps a lifelong ambition came to fruition.

He wasn't heavily involved in the cemetery at first. He had magic parties to throw, airplanes to fly, and wild animals to collect. But in 1933, when Briarcliff Zoological Park started to flounder, he fired his zookeeper, announced he would close the attraction, and turned his attention to West View to distance himself from his woes.

Up until that point, he had delegated decision-making to Forrest and George Adair Jr., two prominent real estate investors whose late father had a close working relationship with Asa Sr. Buddie gave the brothers free rein to run things, and for the first few years not much changed in the daily management of the property. However, sales were sluggish, and the Adairs' improvements weren't adding value to the business. In fact, quite the opposite. They lowered plot prices again and again, and Depression-era economic woes put luxuries like high-status monuments out of reach for customers who had lost their financial standing. When Buddie decided to get more involved in 1933, he took the Adairs' place as head of management and focused his energy on creating a profitable business and a clean public image for himself in the noble field of mortuary services.[3]

Buddie had big plans for West View. He wanted to make it the most beautiful memorial park in Atlanta, possibly in all of America, and he was confident that he could make money on the venture. His vision included revamping the landscaping, removing monuments and decorative shrubberies, and installing stone walls, fountains, and statuary around the grounds. He also intended to grow and arrange flowers on-site, sell caskets, and provide embalming services. In 1935, he eliminated some overhead by adding offices to the historic gatehouse, and soon after that he started reporting profits.[4]

West View's turnaround was a lifeline after Buddie had suffered the financial slings and arrows of his ill-fated zoo and the resulting legal challenges. It heralded an upswing in his fortunes as new real estate opportunities came his way, including the outright purchase of the Robert Fulton Hotel by his Briarcliff Investment Company in 1935.[5] He made his son John second-in-command and put him in charge of the investment company's portfolio with a mandate to keep it growing.

West View was a family affair too. Buddie's wife, Florence, ran the office, drawing on her skills as an experienced executive stenographer. His daughter

Laura and her husband, Edgar Chambers Jr., helped to run daily operations. Things seemed to be looking up.

Then, tragedy struck. William Candler, owner of the Biltmore Hotel and Buddie's youngest brother, died in a car accident on his way home from Florida. It wasn't William's first accident. He liked to speed and always had since the early days of the Atlanta Speedway, where he had raced his SPO in 1910. He'd struck a man while speeding in one of Buddie's cars in 1911, and he'd crashed once before on a similar trip back from Florida, landing in a rural hospital with injuries. This time, his car rolled, trapping him inside as it caught fire. He died at forty-six, leaving a wife and two young children behind.[6]

Buddie and William had shared a special bond. They were ten years apart in age, William looked up to Buddie, and they shared none of the acrimony that existed between Buddie and Howard. William was reportedly kind, thoughtful, and disinclined to create splashy headlines with poor behavior or business follies, like Buddie and Walter. He didn't spread himself thin and overextend his investments, and unlike his three older brothers he refrained from pouring his wealth into a mega-mansion or other ostentatious demonstrations. Of all of the Candler siblings, he left the quietest legacy, so quiet that he's occasionally forgotten in historical accounts.

William and Buddie also shared a love of cars. Their Druid Hills houses are closer to each other than to any other Candler family homes. Briarcliff and Rest Haven, William's home on Springdale Road, are remarkably similar in brick, roof, and design. Briarcliff is like Rest Haven's big brother. When William died, Buddie honored him by providing a space at West View, not down with their father and extended family, but up the hill closer to his own more prominent future plot. William's grave is unique in the family, set apart in a white marble private mausoleum just steps away from his big brother.

Then, another tragedy. Five months after William's death, Buddie's son-in-law Edgar passed away from complications during surgery. Buddie went quiet after this, and over the next few years he discovered a religious faith that had never come easily before. Later in life, he would reflect on this period as the end of his struggle with alcoholism and the start of his religious devotion.

Based on clues in Asa Jr.'s personal testimonials, his troubles with alcohol began well before Helen died, around the mid-1920s, and he likely gave it up between 1936 and 1938, after the zoo was demolished and before his uncle Warren passed away. According to Buddie, Warren tried his hardest to free him from the grips of alcohol addiction with patience and love, but he continued to fall deeper and deeper under its influence. One day on his way home, drunk in the back seat of his limousine, Buddie heard a voice from within, telling him to give himself up to God.

> The voice said to me, "You must get rid of your self; you must renounce your self; you must reject your self." These were surprising words. I should not have been surprised if the voice had commanded me to stop drinking. But this was not the message at all. It was my self that I was commanded to give up. My self was my trouble—my love of myself, my fear of anything that might frustrate my wishes. My will had always been the central interest in my life.[7]

He claimed that this epiphany drove him into the house, where he summoned Florence and asked her to tie a ribbon around a bottle of liquor to symbolize his rejection of alcohol: "Then we put the bottle in the closet, and there it sits until this day. From that hour I was delivered from the desire for drink—but more, I was delivered from the selfishness and the love of money."[8] After nearly forty years of vice, Buddie was finally going clean.

THE LAUNDRY

In the mid-1930s, Briarcliff Investment Company started righting the financial ship by making new moves in the real estate market. Buddie and John purchased several apartment complexes and listed units for rent in what appears to have been a strategic plan to return to Buddie's roots in rental property management.[9] They also formed the Briarcliff Laundry Company and erected a massive commercial facility on Briarcliff Mansion's property, utilizing the artesian well's generous output to supply fresh water for its services. It was the largest cleaning and cold storage facility in the Southeast. Step 1 of his signature cycle.

Buddie installed his sons John and Samuel to oversee operations. John managed the finances, and Samuel oversaw the day-to-day tasks. The facility was truly huge, rivaling Briarcliff Mansion in footprint. On one side, employees processed clothes in large drum-style washing machines, and others pressed each item on a fleet of 140 Pantex laundry presses.[10] Broad high-set windows dotted the walls, letting in natural light for the dozens of workers tasked with processing each load. On the other side, a cold storage warehouse offered temperature-controlled housing for off-season clothing, especially furs that could only be worn a few months of the year.

Briarcliff Laundry delivery truck with Briarcliff Mansion visible in the background (digitally restored), circa 1938. Courtesy of Georgia State University Library.

Customers entered through Briarcliff's front gates and drove up the long, curved driveway to the house, where they dropped off their laundry at the solarium on the left of the porte cochere. They received a ticket that bore information about the service, including a one-cent surcharge per bundle for insurance to guarantee that their clothes would be handled with care and kept safe from incident.[11] When they arrived to pick up, customers received their fresh, clean, pressed, and folded garments in a cotton Briarcliff Laundry duffel bag.

The endless outflow of money that had dogged Buddie was slowly turning around. In 1930, a struggling commercial property on Ponce de Leon Avenue called the Bonaventure Arms Hotel and Apartments went up for sale, and Buddie had swept in with an offer. Once a luxury property near Ponce de Leon Park and the Atlanta Crackers' baseball field, Bonaventure Arms had fallen on hard times.

The Candlers were familiar with the Depression's effect on luxury housing. William's premier rental property, the Biltmore Hotel and Apartments, had hit rough financial waters before his death, but by the close of the 1930s was slowly righting itself under the managerial hand of William's widow, Bennie.

Briarcliff Laundry truck with driver outside the property gates, circa 1938.
Courtesy of Georgia State University Library.

And Buddie's hotel on the corner of Ponce de Leon and North Highland avenues, The 750, had struggles of its own. He'd already subdivided the units and turned the property into a commercial hotel by the time he acquired the Bonaventure Arms just up the road.

The Bonaventure property limped along for the next few years, advertising reduced prices in a desperate effort to bring in residents. But successful investment returns and an infusion of income from Briarcliff Laundry in the latter half of the decade enabled Buddie to remodel the property and reshape its future.

His successes funded the purchase in 1939 of a new boat, this time a Chris-Craft cruiser that he named the *Clermont*. Rather than following his old Gulf of Mexico routes, he mostly kept to the eastern seaboard with his new yacht, docking it in the Savannah area between voyages. Also in 1939, he decided to break ground on a new enterprise, a yacht basin in Thunderbolt, Georgia, where he could moor the *Clermont* and a smaller craft named the *Esperanza*, as well as lease space to yacht-owning customers.[12] He cut the ribbon in November aboard his ship to celebrate the project's completion. That same month, he reopened the Bonaventure Arms as the rebranded Clermont

Hotel and Apartments, which still stands today as a beloved Atlanta land-mark. Just like when he named Briarcliff Farm after his favorite automobile, he named the Clermont Hotel after his current favorite yacht.

The year 1939 was one of peak acquisition for the Briarcliff Investment Company. Buddie was back in the swing of things and buying properties all over the city with his son John. But Briarcliff Laundry, like Briarcliff Farm twenty years before, struggled to stay in the black. The scale of the facility and the overhead required to keep it profitable exceeded demand. Advertisements proclaimed the highest quality of services and offered fair prices, but an operation that size required large sales and a massive customer base, which the local market couldn't support long term.

This was a problem because Briarcliff Laundry was about to be tasked with a new purpose. At the dawn of the 1940s, Buddie became fixed on a grand vision for West View Cemetery. He'd discovered God, given up alcohol, and had a desire to build something enduring and transcendent. The laundry was to be his cash cow, the income generator that would enable him to launch and sustain his final project, his gift to Atlanta and the eternal: the West View Mausoleum.

WEST VIEW MAUSOLEUM AND ABBEY

As Buddie moved into the 1940s, his attention narrowed in on what would become his magnum opus. His whole world and public image became de-fined by one purpose: turning West View Cemetery into the most beautiful memorial park in the nation, and at the core of this vision was the West View Mausoleum and Abbey.

West View's mausoleum was to be the largest structure of its kind under one roof in the entire United States—superlative, as always. It would be the focal point of West View's rolling lawns and terraced memorial sections, an ornate, awe-inspiring burial option for those with the means to choose eter-nity in its marble-clad halls. Visually, it would evoke opulent old Europe, and as a born-again Christian, Buddie hoped it would be a grand statement of faith and devotion in tribute to God's grandeur. Every detail would be selected by Buddie himself. In his own superlative words:

> It is my purpose to make West View a place where men's hearts and minds are lifted to God and immortality, to Life. . . . It is my plan to make of West View, and especially of its abbey, a whole series of sermons in stone and marble,

where men cannot walk without praying, without an increase of faith and joy in God. The abbey is, in fact, the New Testament in marble. . . . For hundreds of years, if the earth stands, the abbey will go right on preaching the gospel of Jesus Christ, long after my voice is still.

. . . Throughout the abbey, over six-hundred feet long, which I have designed and built, the choicest passages of Scripture are found. I believe no man can walk through the halls of the abbey—unless his heart is utterly closed against God, closed up in self—without receiving new spiritual power and vitality, without a new vision of Christ's claim upon him. That is why I built it, literally to the glory of God. I cannot always tell the story of God's love with my lips. As long as the abbey stands, it will tell my story, and the story of all Christians.[13]

But the project needed money, lots of money, and as the United States ramped up its involvement in World War II at the end of 1941, construction materials became expensive and scarce. While Asa Jr. had managed to turn around the struggling cemetery in the 1930s, it wasn't yet a money machine. He formulated a plan to bring in more income by broadening the services he could offer to grieving families, but expanded services alone wouldn't fund the massive construction project he had in mind.

His yacht, the *Clermont*, was seized by the U.S. Navy for troop transport, so he couldn't sell it for cash. His rental properties were too valuable to his portfolio to sell off. And while West View was intended to eventually be self-sustaining, with an on-site morgue, casket sales, and floral arrangements, it would take time to ramp up those departments and start generating sufficient revenue. But he wasn't willing to put the project on hold. The vision would become reality one way or another.

Buddie announced the mausoleum project in February 1942, describing it as "one of America's largest and finest community mausoleums—a great and beautiful structure of stone-concrete-marble and bronze" amid "surroundings of enduring beauty."[14] He encouraged forward-thinking Atlantans to make an advance purchase of a vault in the forthcoming structure as a means of raising the funds to break ground and start construction.

But like the Atlanta Speedway, the Candler Floating School, and Briarcliff Zoological Park, his idea dwarfed the proposed business model and could never be self-sustaining. Advance vault sales alone wouldn't fund his vision. He needed more money. That was where Briarcliff Laundry factored into the equation.

The laundry, fed by an unending supply of fresh water, seemed to be well positioned to fund West View Cemetery's development. Perhaps a smaller facility with an overhead more equal to the size of the customer base could have been the easy revenue generator he needed it to be. But overscaled as it was, and with construction costs higher than ever, it wasn't turning a sufficient profit quickly enough.

So Buddie rolled out his next idea, this time tapping into his experience in tontine life insurance. He hired a staff of salesmen headed by W. L. Halberstadt, who had experience in selling advance plot contracts. In this program, buyers would pay in installments for their plot over time, and as with tontine insurance, the policyholder gambled that they would financially benefit from a fortuitous timing of their own death. If they passed before their plan was paid in full, they got the plot for the amount already paid, which meant the purchase was incentivized by the discount one would earn by dying early. Of course, the business came out ahead because customers rarely died on a timetable that benefited them.

The advance plot contracts sold well. Perhaps too well. They drew the attention of Homer C. Parker, the state insurance commissioner, who inspected the contracts and concluded that they amounted to life insurance policies. In June 1942, Parker filed a class action lawsuit against West View, seeking a judgment of $700,000 to be returned to the policyholders.[15] A month later, Buddie conceded and promised the court that West View would cease issuing advance contracts and would seek a licensed insurance provider to cover the policies already sold. Just like that, a promising source of funding for the mausoleum project dried up.

BUDDIE THE PHOENIX: THE FINAL FIRE

Although the mausoleum wasn't as magnificently flamboyant as a zoo, an agricultural empire, or a racetrack, Asa Jr.'s trademark cycle was fully in effect. He breezed through steps 1–3 by releasing detailed architectural renderings of the finished mausoleum, which included coffered ceilings, arched stone bridges, a chapel with a pipe organ loft, and elaborate water features. He'd already started revising the landscaping and installing stone walls, decorative shrubberies, sculptures, and monuments. He hired security staff to protect the grounds at night, when sticky-fingered ne'er-do-wells attempted to purloin his upgraded features.[16]

Outside of work, he was proceeding into a modified step 4 by spending more time with top leadership in the Southern Baptist and Methodist churches, such as Dr. Louie Newton and Bishop Arthur J. Moore. He personally flew key religious figures around the country and hosted them at his home, drawing them into his inner circle. Rather than making showy purchases on his own behalf, he participated in well-publicized fundraising and helped to break ground on new church construction. This intense affiliation with his rediscovered faith served to reinforce his vision of the grand mausoleum, so he redoubled his dedication to his plans.

Although by this time he was no longer drinking alcohol, he made headlines once again with his antics. In October 1942, Buddie welcomed his former personal pilot, Edward W. Hightower, for a dinner at Briarcliff Mansion. Hightower had stopped over in Atlanta with fellow Royal Air Force pilots who flew B-24 Liberators across northern Africa. The men enjoyed Buddie's hospitality, including a delicious cured ham that had been raised, slaughtered, and prepared on Briarcliff's own mini-farm.[17]

The ham was something of a wartime luxury. Meat rationing for British citizens, including the R.A.F. pilots, had gone into effect the previous week, creating long lines at butcher shops all over the country. The practice of raising and butchering one's own meat might have been commonplace when Buddie was a child, but by the 1940s it had fallen out of practice in urban and suburban neighborhoods. The Candlers had always run mini-farms, owing their self-sufficiency to Asa Sr. So while the large, homegrown ham may have been a novelty to his guests, it was just another seasonal crop for Buddie, like his annual sausage production.[18]

Toward the end of the dinner, one of the Royal Air Force pilots, Captain Wally Siple, suggested that such a high-quality ham would surely be appreciated back home in England. His fellow crewmen agreed that even Prime Minister Winston Churchill would be delighted to taste Briarcliff's meats. One of the men placed a phone call, and sure enough, Churchill himself called back and spoke to Buddie directly, requesting one of his hams. Flattered by the prestigious request, Buddie had his staff crate his largest ham and prepare it for a flight to London, including cooking instructions. He expressed his pleasure at having received the request and hoped that Churchill would share the southern delicacy with King George.[19]

But before the men could depart with the meat, the call was revealed to be a prank. Winston Churchill hadn't phoned to request a ham; a friend of the crew had impersonated him in the hopes of bypassing the meat rationing. Buddie had a laugh, and he circulated the anecdote in the name of good fun. In many ways, this story resembled the one Buddie had invented in 1911 about his son driving his Lozier Briarcliff at the Atlanta Speedway. Because of how hyperbolic his tall tales typically were, it becomes impossible to know how much was truth and how much was punch line.

True or not, the published ham story contributes evidence for a set of assumptions:

1. Buddie was still his jovial, friendly, entertaining self who enjoyed a good laugh with friends.
2. He was out of touch with the problems facing everyday people, grandiose in his self-perception, and eager to publish stories about his life of luxury.
3. He may have been exhibiting what's known as "dry drunk" behavior, wherein alcoholics abstain from drinking but continue to demonstrate actions, emotions, and/or compromised judgment associated with their addiction.[20]

Following the typical Buddie Candler cycle, the public-facing merriment served as cover as he entered step 5. The mausoleum project was floundering. Although West View hadn't become profitable enough on its own to fund the expensive construction, he was too far under way on the structure to back out now. He'd already compromised on many of the most expensive architectural details, but completion was still beyond reach. So is it any wonder that step 6—liquidate assets—was right around the corner?

Just past noon on June 17, 1943, the Druid Hills Fire Department received a call for help at Briarcliff Laundry. A fire had broken out in the drying room and spread too rapidly to be extinguished by the employees. The staff evacuated, and firefighters from stations in Decatur and Atlanta joined the Druid Hills team to fight the blaze. But the flames engulfed the entire complex, destroying equipment and bringing down walls.

By the time the fire was brought under control, there was little left to save. Highly flammable dry-cleaning chemicals had fueled the blaze, which consumed customers' property along with the facility. With wartime demands making building materials scarce, Buddie declared the loss total and irreparable.[21]

This is where the cycle should have returned to the beginning. This is where insurance should have paid out and Buddie should have walked away with renewed purchasing power. But this time, something went wrong that nearly landed the sixty-two-year-old untouchable multimillionaire in jail.

Let it ride.[1]

CHAPTER 17

Buddie Candler on Trial

After Briarcliff Laundry burned to the ground in June 1943, trouble soon followed. Customers whose belongings were damaged or destroyed naturally wanted compensation for their losses. After all, their claim checks showed they had paid a one-cent charge per bundle to provide insurance for all garments. This coverage provided assurance that the staff would provide the utmost care, and given that they only had to properly process items as trained, it had been easy money in the business's pocket every time a load of laundry was dropped off.

The problems started when customers tried to file claims and receive compensation for their losses. One by one, they learned that there was no coverage and therefore no funds to pay out. To dodge culpability, the company mailed a letter to customers who had not yet filed claims, advising them that the laundry had held all garments at the customers' risk, and unless the remaining property was reclaimed immediately, it would be disposed of.[2] Four customers who had been denied recompense brought a lawsuit, and as the business entered receivership, the failings of its financial management came to light.

As it turned out, there was an insurance policy, but it was woefully underfunded. While the customers' losses were initially estimated to total around $100,000, the policy only provided $1,000 in fire damages to items serviced as laundry, and it provided zero coverage for the approximately four thousand items kept in the cold storage section of the facility. Attorneys representing the four customers claimed that two other policies existed, which totaled $265,000, covering equipment and the structure itself, benefiting the business's owners. These policies, the lawyers said, were subject to claims for the customers' damages.[3]

The lawsuit sought $35,000, which was based on a calculation of one cent per bundle over the seven years that the business was in operation, multiplied by an estimated number of customers during that time. The attorneys asserted that Briarcliff Laundry had paid just $50 per year for the $1,000 policy, far less than should have been secured for the fees taken.[4]

In August, the attorneys added more claims. They alleged that Buddie, John, and Samuel Candler had arranged their business in such a way as to "relieve Asa G. Candler, Jr., and Briarcliff, Inc., of legal responsibility for the goods of customers in their possession."[5] The case was assigned to Fulton County Superior Court judge Virlyn Moore, who issued a deadline of September 3 for the Candlers to demonstrate why they shouldn't be held liable. As they were unable to present any convincing argument, the case proceeded.

On December 14, 1943, testimony began, starting with the issue of whether Buddie and his sons should be named as codefendants in the lawsuit. The receiver, Bond Almand, noted that more than 2,500 customers had filed claims, which now totaled $150,000.[6] Evidence submitted included soot-blackened paper records that had been recovered from the fire-damaged property, confirming that the company had only secured a $1,000 customer property policy.[7]

These kinds of civil lawsuits were not unfamiliar to the Candlers. Buddie had dealt with more than his fair share over the decades. It is possible that he and his sons could have ridden the case to the very top of the appeals process, shuffled around assets, and settled for a lesser amount, paid out of their other holdings. That would have been an unfortunate and unforeseen loss for Buddie. The $265,000 of coverage on the structure and equipment should have been collected and put to good use for his mausoleum project. The oversight that had led to an underfunded policy on customer property would potentially halve the payout he expected, but it wouldn't ruin him.

Unfortunately, this "oversight" had much greater consequences. On February 1, 1944, the U.S. government stepped in and filed via federal grand jury an eight-count indictment for mail fraud. Buddie and his sons were charged with "devising a scheme and artifice to defraud and for obtaining

Aerial photo of the Briarcliff property showing the fire-damaged ruins of Briarcliff Laundry, circa 1948. Courtesy of Georgia State University Library.

money and property by means of false pretenses to customers, patrons and competitors of Briarcliff Laundry, Inc."[8]

According to the attorneys representing the government, Briarcliff Laundry had utilized the U.S. Postal Service to advertise its services, which included a guarantee of insurance for all items in exchange for a service charge—insurance that was never secured. The government estimated that the business had collected as much as $5,000 annually in service charges, one penny at a time. It also claimed that between the cleaning facility and the cold storage warehouse, the business sometimes held as much as $300,000 worth of customers' property on the premises. With only $1,000 in coverage, the gap between what was promised and what was provided was enormous.

Worse still, the assessment of damages continued to rise. Based on the estimate put forth by the government, the grand jury had determined that the customers' losses potentially amounted to as much as $300,000. Anything held on the premises should have been counted as a total loss, burnt or not.

Added to the accusations was a claim that Briarcliff Laundry, Inc., was intentionally established as an insolvent entity. Being insolvent, the business was positioned from the very start to be immune from any potential claims against it. The charges asserted that this was by design. The Candlers had knowingly structured the business to eliminate any liability that could have financial consequences if something went wrong, and they did so just before something went wrong.

These charges provide unique insight into Buddie's work behind the scenes before the incident. On March 1, 1942, one year before the fire broke out, he had acted as president of Briarcliff, Inc., to create Briarcliff Laundry, Inc., and then transferred Briarcliff Laundry to the newly established company. The so-called sale of the laundry to Briarcliff Laundry, Inc., provided $400,000 in bonds to Briarcliff, Inc., essentially paying with promised money that didn't exist yet. Ownership and management of Briarcliff Laundry, Inc., was passed to John Candler, who stood to earn 60 percent of the business's profits, and Samuel Candler, who would earn 40 percent.[9] Buddie, at least on paper, would no longer have any stake in the laundry. Put simply, Buddie arranged a "sale" of the laundry business to his sons in exchange for $400,000 in bonds.

Soon after the fire made headlines in 1943 and before the trial began, Buddie wrote a letter to the editor of the *Atlanta Constitution*, declaring himself innocent of all responsibility for the fire. He stated that he was in no way connected to Briarcliff Laundry, Inc., and had never been an officer or a stockholder or otherwise connected in any way to its operations.[10] When he made that claim, he was referring to the "sale" described above. It was an arrangement designed to protect him from any risk associated with the business and to make the company that held the laundry insolvent before a massive fire destroyed the well-insured structure and equipment.

The government wasn't buying it. The attorneys saw through the maneuvering and held firm that Buddie's exclusion from the laundry's management was in name only and that he had continued to provide guidance to his sons over the next year. This meant all three Candler men were potentially facing up to five years in prison for each of the eight counts they were charged with.[11]

Buddie was in the fight of his life now. While his father had faced the federal government in defense of Coca-Cola, Buddie had never taken heat from such a high authority. He put his team of lawyers on it and threw himself into his work at West View. Perhaps in an effort to improve his public image, he announced that he would soon build a soldiers chapel, which was intended to honor the servicemen who died fighting overseas. In a public statement, he said:

> Mrs. Candler and I have wanted to do something for the men of our home counties who are fighting this war. It seemed to us that providing this perpetual memorial was something we could do. It will be a place where families may place their soldier dead by a beautiful memorial to them and their fellow soldiers and sailors. We are deeding it to the Legion for them to manage. Details of this will be worked out by attorneys so that it may continue through the years. There will be no cost to the Legion insofar as upkeep goes, because a fund already in trust provides for the perpetual upkeep of the cemetery.[12]

Of course, there was no money for a soldiers chapel and no real plan beyond an artist's rendering. The project never broke ground.

Testimony continued throughout the spring of 1944. In April, James Dunlap of the insurance provider Dunlap & Company confirmed that Buddie, John, and Samuel had secured $265,000 in coverage on the facility and equipment, and that John personally had instructed Dunlap to forgo sufficient coverage for their customers' property. In March 1942, when ownership of the laundry had passed from Briarcliff, Inc., to Briarcliff Laundry, Inc., Dunlap had advised John to increase his policy to $85,000 in total coverage for customers' property, with an annual premium increase from $50 to $1,000. But John, Dunlap claimed, had instructed him to "let it ride" because he "didn't have the money at the time."[13]

This testimony served to support the federal attorneys' claim that Briarcliff Laundry, Inc., was designed to be insolvent from the start. As the charges stated, the one-cent insurance surcharge per bundle totaled $5,000 annually, and that was on top of the cleaning and storage fees. Yet John claimed the business couldn't afford a $1,000 annual premium. This was visible evidence of how the business's revenue was funneled away.

On April 19, the defense started calling character witnesses. Methodist Episcopal Church bishop Arthur J. Moore, Southern Baptist Convention president Dr. Louie Newton, and Georgia Power president Preston S. Arkwright all took the stand to praise Asa Candler Jr. They testified that he had a good reputation and was an upright member of the community. All that time spent flying Newton and Moore to various religious events had paid off. It was good to have friends in high places.

Next, the Candler sons took the stand. Samuel, the secretary and treasurer of Briarcliff Laundry, Inc., explained that he'd had little to do with running the business. At twenty-nine years old, his job was to learn how to run the laundry, starting in the washroom and working his way up through every facet of the operations. Therefore, he claimed, he could not have knowingly defrauded anyone.

John's testimony supported his younger brother's claims. He testified that as president of the laundry, he was in charge of office matters, and that included securing insurance policies. He admitted that while the business held a number of high-value policies on everything from the equipment to the employees, he'd never secured sufficient coverage for the customers' property.[14]

Two days later, the court determined that Samuel Candler should be acquitted, as he clearly had no knowledge or decision-making power that could constitute fraud, mail or otherwise. He was released from the trial and exonerated of all charges, leaving his brother and father to face the jury without him.[15] The jury then retired to deliberate for several hours, returning with a decision late in the afternoon.[16] Although Buddie's demeanor was noted as characteristically jovial throughout the trial, he and John were stoic as the federal judge called the deputy clerk to read the verdict. They were found not guilty on all counts.[17]

This decision released the Candler men from the threat of fines and jail time, which was worthy of celebration. But it did not release Briarcliff Laundry from the claims pending against it for lost property. In September 1944, three of the four claimants in the original suit requested a rehearing, but the request was denied.[18] Presumably, that enabled Buddie to keep his facility insurance payout.

In June, another fire had broken out at Briarcliff, this time in a barn and storage shed. No estimate for those damages has been located.[19]

If the Lord lets me live long enough and if the people of
Atlanta will cooperate, West View will be the most beautiful
place in the world.[1]

CHAPTER 18

The Long, Slow Slide

Buddie turned his back on the defunct laundry as soon as the court case was put to bed. In fact, the rubble of the destroyed facility remained on the property for years following the event. He simply ignored the destruction on his lawn and poured every ounce of his energy into his remaining obsession, West View Cemetery.

His plans were bigger than ever. He wanted to modernize the landscaping, following a different concept in cemetery design. Inspired by Forest Lawn Memorial Park in Glendale, California, which likewise had an impressive mausoleum as its focal point and offered on-site funerary services, he planned to replace large monuments with flat stones, which would open up the vistas and create a more park-like green space. The flat stones would also cut the groundskeeping overhead significantly since mowing and trimming around bulky monuments required more time and manpower. He intended to feature artwork throughout the cemetery and brought in bronze and marble sculptures to add to the serene landscape. He also planned a water feature adjacent to the mausoleum, so he dammed a stream to create an artificial lake and installed an illuminated fountain.

To move the plans along, West View purchased a funeral home on Peachtree Street that offered competitively priced services. Buddie hired a staff of forty salesmen and incentivized them to increase sales, which reached $1.2 million in 1945. Following the Buddie cycle, he celebrated this new, growing endeavor by splurging on a Cadillac ambulance and, of course, a private airplane with "West View" stenciled on the side. By 1946, his sales team was bringing in $250,000 per month.[2]

Meanwhile, Buddie was indulging in big game hunting, a hobby that he'd pursued on and off throughout his life, starting with a trip to Pikes Peak to hunt bighorn rams when he was twenty years old.[3] By the mid-1940s, he was taking frequent trips to Tifton, Georgia, and flying to Montana and other big game hotspots. In a typically hyperbolic moment, he even announced that he planned to invest in Tifton property development, including building a second home or a hunting lodge.[4] Evidence suggests, however, that he was not financially positioned to do anything of the sort by that time.

In fact, by 1946 he was embarking on his last mass liquidation of assets, starting with the sale of his yacht basin in Thunderbolt, Georgia. Since the government had failed to return the *Clermont* at the end of the war, he claimed he had no use for the business any longer.[5] But the truth was that he was freeing up funds to continue work on his mausoleum. Next, he sold his father's mansion on Ponce de Leon Avenue to the American Legion.[6]

Asa Jr. also initiated remodeling plans at his Briarcliff Hotel and Apartments, perhaps paving the way to relocate as he prepped Briarcliff Mansion for sale.[7] As in 1925 when he traveled by sea to escape the clamor of construction at home, he spent much of 1946 in the air, flying with high-ranking church officials, jaunting off on hunting trips, and ferrying fellow businessmen around.[8] He made grand claims, such as killing a moose and an elk with one shot each, although his family would later recount his practice of having hunting guides wear down his quarry, making his kill shots somewhat less impressive feats of marksmanship.[9]

In an odd story that demonstrates his continued capacity for sensational concepts that transcended reality, Buddie attended the Southern Baptist Convention annual meeting and gave a speech. He spoke of his divided devotion as a Methodist who had married a Baptist woman, and therefore attended both services every week. Then, according to those in attendance, he shared an idea worthy of science fiction: "Candler, with a mechanical invention of his own design, illustrated the Christian in his church. When the Christian went into his church with the spirit of God in his heart, the gadget worked. If the Christian entered alone, the machine would not operate."[10]

ASHES TO ASHES

If all of this sounds like he was winding through the steps of a new cycle, perhaps he was, but this time he rejected hedonism and focused on his goal, which was funding the completion of his great mausoleum and demonstrating his faith and devotion in the grandeur of its opulent design. Perhaps the scale of his ambition could have wound him up again, and perhaps he would have found the spark inside for one more cycle. But in February 1947, tragedy befell the Briarcliff Candlers one more time.

John Candler, Asa Jr.'s oldest surviving son and business partner, died of a heart attack after years of battling severe alcoholism. John, who had by his own admission followed his father into addiction but failed to follow him out the other side, had fallen deeper into the bottle after the laundry trial. His first wife, Elizabeth (née Brandon), had shielded their children from it before her death, and his second wife, Thesis (née Robinson), had encouraged him to seek help. It was no secret to anyone, including himself, that his addiction was out of control and that it was tied directly to his father. In Elizabeth Candler Graham and Ralph Roberts's book, *The Real Ones: Four Generations of the First Family of Coca-Cola*, one of his relatives reflected upon a conversation he had with John before his death: "'John, why do you drink like this after you lived with that at home the way you have?' He answered, 'If I analyze it myself I'm getting even with my father.'" In the same passage, his sister Laura—a self-admitted daddy's girl who insisted that she was always Buddie's favorite—had the following to say: "Papa knew about John, and it just killed him. ... I was almost tempted to say, 'Well you deserve it.'"[11]

After John's death, the fight went out of Buddie Candler. As he grieved the loss of his son, his health took a turn that signaled the beginning of the end. No longer inclined to channel his energy into supersized, whimsical ideas, he forged on in a manner that appeared to anticipate his own demise. He faced a decision point: either give up his work at West View and refocus on better investments, or sell off more of his portfolio to fund his cemetery work. He chose the latter, and the largest casualty was Briarcliff Mansion.

Preparing to part ways with his beloved home, he built a circular office around the base of the crenellated water tower at West View where he could relocate all of his hunting trophies, earning the title of the largest trophy room in the United States.[12] Superlative as always. He also forged ahead on the administration building that was attached to the mausoleum, which included a windowless room on the top floor where he planned to hold private movie showings. Now morbidly obese and relying heavily on a cane to get around, he continued to personally direct design decisions, material selection, and detail work at the mausoleum while Florence ran the front office.

In 1948 he found a buyer for Briarcliff Mansion and sold the whole property: public pool, laundry ruins, zoo foundations, and all. The U.S. General Services Administration purchased it with the intention of converting the house into a hospital for veterans with on-site quarters for nursing staff.[13]

In 1949 the deal was finalized, with a provision to permit Buddie and Florence to live on the premises until definitive decisions were made about the property's future. Buddie and Florence made plans to move to the penthouse suite at Briarcliff Hotel and Apartments and decided to leave most of their furnishings behind for the new hospital to utilize at its discretion. However, the Aeolian pipe organ was not included in the sale. Rather than abandoning it, Buddie boxed up the majority of the pipes and gifted them to Wesleyan College in Macon, Georgia, where they remain in use to this day. The solarium pipes were moved to the West View Mausoleum, taking up residence behind an ornate wooden reredos in what would be christened the Florence Candler Chapel.[14] Years later, the solarium pipes were relocated to Charleston Southern University, where the pipes were damaged by a storm and later restored to working order.[15]

The solarium's organ pipes weren't the only elements that linked the mausoleum to Briarcliff Mansion. The chapel also featured three tall arches framing high windows, reminiscent of the three bay windows in Briarcliff's music hall. The original chapel plan called for a barrel ceiling in the foyer, similar to the barrel ceiling in the entryway leading in from the porte cochere at Briarcliff Mansion. The chapel ceiling was to be clad in wood in a coffered design similar to the one in Briarcliff's formal dining room, but budget constraints forced Buddie to compromise and revise the plan to a fan design. In the grand atrium, which was originally intended to be the main entrance, he hung halo-style chandeliers that matched the ones in the music hall at Briarcliff. And outside the chapel, the location of the newly constructed Lake Palmyra and its adjacent fountain were curiously similar in orientation to his music hall and fountain-centric pool at home.

The similarities were no coincidence. Asa Jr. wasn't just building the mausoleum as a gift to the community and a tribute to God. It was also a gift to himself, his eternal Briarcliff, where he planned to be interred like a great

The partially furnished interior of the music hall at Briarcliff Mansion, circa 1953. The organ pipes, which were concealed behind the tapestry on the back wall, had already been removed. Courtesy of the *Atlanta Journal-Constitution*.

pharaoh of the Egypt he'd admired during the 1920s, his peak obsession years. Even as he made compromise after compromise in the building materials and nixed the elaborate Court of Transfiguration that he'd intended to dedicate to his father, he ensured the placement of one special vault, a large, polished granite sarcophagus set on a raised pedestal at the end of an ornate hall beneath a stained-glass window. The only one of its type in the mausoleum, it was to be his own place of eternal rest.[16]

That was why he had liquidated his holdings and poured his fortune into the immense structure. Like the pharaohs, he spent the end of his life directing the completion of his own tomb.

Unfortunately, the community didn't support all of Buddie's ideas. In July 1949, a group of frustrated West View patrons whose family members occupied plots at the cemetery held a rally with more than two hundred supporters in attendance. They were upset by Buddie's efforts to modernize the cemetery, since he had removed shrubberies and lowered monuments, substituting flat stones without consulting the plot holders. They were angry and demanded to be heard. They'd had enough of his lifetime of shenanigans, and their goal, some said, was to drive him out of town once and for all.[17]

So he obliged. Rather than hearing them out, Buddie boarded a flight with his grandson Asa V and flew to Africa for one last safari. They shot a colossal bull elephant and traveled across the continent, meeting with locals and bringing home outlandish stories. Buddie claimed to have been an inspiration to the African people, and said that he stunned them with magic tricks that he'd learned from Harry Houdini.[18] He seemed to have some awareness that this was likely his last opportunity for a trip of that magnitude, and he was determined to make the most of it.

When the two returned, Asa Jr. found the community's ire still waiting for him. The protestors filed an injunction to prevent him from making any additional changes to the cemetery grounds. In response, he ceased all landscaping maintenance at West View, refusing to permit his staff to mow or weed, and letting the plots become overgrown and unkempt. His point, it seemed, was to prove that caring for a cemetery with large monuments and shrubberies simply cost too much, and if forced to halt his improvements the standard of care would be reduced. His protesting customers didn't buy it and responded by filing a lawsuit. He pleaded for their understanding, hoping that they would feel empathy for his commitment to a higher calling.

> I am going to make West View Cemetery the most beautiful in the country. I have taken money from my own pocket for the beautification of the cemetery. I have sold tax-free bonds to pay for this beautification program. If the Lord lets me live long enough and if the people of Atlanta will co-operate, West View will be the most beautiful place in the world.[19]

Superlatives, as always.

The protestors' lawyers demanded to see West View's books to make sure the finances added up. Buddie refused but promised that he had personally funded the perpetual care shortfall.[20] In December 1949, the Georgia Funeral Directors Association expelled West View Cemetery from its organization for unfair business practices and ethics violations.[21] But work on the mausoleum continued unabated.

In 1950, Asa Jr.'s first elephant, Coca, died at Atlanta's zoo. The city's citizens were heartbroken over the loss of their beloved pachyderm, so he backed a campaign to find a replacement. His efforts demonstrated that the good-hearted Buddie who had charmed the community for years was still in there beneath all of the eccentric behavior, egotism, and greed. He was still capable of big ideas and still wanted to please his community. While he wasn't willing or able to fund the replacement, undoubtedly due to his finances being entirely dominated by the mausoleum project, he revived a fundraising program to have Atlanta's children raise dimes to purchase a new elephant. It was the same campaign he'd started to fund Grant Park's purchase of his menagerie in the 1930s. He hosted a fundraiser at the trophy room at West View, where he and his grandson shared stories, photos, and film footage of their African safari. Buddie said:

> I gave Coca to Atlanta's zoo several years ago, and it pleases me very much to see the interest people are showing in replacing her.... Coca's death has shown what an interest there is in Atlanta's zoo. And I sincerely hope that the people throughout the city will not only help the children to subscribe the money to replace Coca but I also hope they will give their unstinted support to our officials in a general zoo improvement program.[22]

When the community reached the fundraising goal, Asa Jr. flew two children to an exotic animal farm to handpick the new elephant. When Coca II arrived in Atlanta, she was greeted by a ticker tape parade.[23] Shortly thereafter, Buddie went into the hospital and stayed for more than a month.[24] His son Samuel gave statements, saying he was comfortable and improving, but Buddie's decisions following his release make it clear that he knew his remaining time was short.

He petitioned the court to be permitted to sell his remaining holdings and protect his assets from the pending West View court case. An injunction had previously stopped him from any further liquidation efforts, citing concerns that he would be unable to pay restitution if the case proved successful. The decision went all the way to the Georgia Supreme Court, which affirmed his right to sell while acknowledging his true intentions: "[Asa Candler Jr. is] 70 years old, in bad health and intends to give the proceeds to his children and render himself insolvent."[25]

Also in 1951, a new lawsuit was filed, this time alleging that Buddie had thrown parties at West View, personal events with merriment that grieving families found disrespectful to their lost loved ones.[26] It was well past time to step away from controversy. In February, Buddie sold West View Cemetery to new management and removed himself from day-to-day oversight.

In 1952, he and Florence completed their move to the Briarcliff Hotel and Apartments penthouse, and he sold his West View stock completely, finally severing all decision-making ties. The mausoleum was still incomplete, but he proclaimed his optimism that the new owners would see it through. The sale price was rumored to be around $2 million, a fraction of the money he'd fed into the property in the hopes of transforming it into something transcendent.[27] This would be his final major transaction.

FAREWELL, BUDDIE CANDLER

On January 11, 1953, Asa Griggs Candler Jr. passed away. The reported story was that he died of a "malignant condition" that was probably liver cancer.[28] Liver cancer is rare, but when it develops as a primary cancer it typically appears in people with cirrhosis or fatty liver disease. Since Buddie was widely known as a long-time alcoholic and was morbidly obese in his later years, liver cancer is a plausible diagnosis.

His estate was estimated to be around $2 million, although a court order barred the actual total from publication. He left most of the money to his wife, Florence, and his five living children, and he left $8,500 each to seven of his servants—more than $80,000 each in 2020 dollars.[29]

At one time, Asa Jr. had owned more than thirty major Atlanta rental properties and one of the largest and most beautiful estates in the city. At the time of his death, he had only a fraction of his fortune to leave behind. But his impact on the city of Atlanta was undeniable, and his legacy could not be overstated. As the *Atlanta Constitution*'s obituary stated: "Mr. Candler's death ended one of the most colorful and eventful lives of this century."[30]

At Buddie's funeral, his older brother, Howard, was one of his pallbearers, ending the lifelong bitter rivalry that had divided them. But his burial became a point of contention among his wife and children. Believing that West View Mausoleum and Abbey would be completed and that it would achieve the status he'd dreamed of, he had expected to be interred in his marble sarcophagus in a place of special honor in his mausoleum. But work on the structure had ground to a halt after the sale. Large sections, including most of the third floor, were still incomplete, and the new owners showed no intention of prioritizing additional funding.

Florence chose not to follow his plan. Some of his children fought her, believing that Buddie should have his final wish honored.[31] But she persevered and had him interred in his family's plot, next to his first wife, Helen, and

Unused sarcophagus at the Westview Cemetery mausoleum, which was originally intended to be Asa Candler Jr.'s final resting place, 2018. Photo by the author.

Asa Candler Jr.'s monument at Westview Cemetery, 2018. Headstones are behind the monument, flat to the ground. Photo by the author.

his first son, Asa III, and within view of his brother William's private mausoleum. Florence had a monument erected in his honor, something her husband's landscaping revisions had tried to eliminate. Later, Florence would be buried next to him, and some of his children would also eventually occupy spaces in the family plot.

Asa Jr.'s blue-gray Georgia granite monument is simple, based on a standard monument designed by the McNeel Marble-Granite Company, which appeared in its 1932 catalog.[32] Although much larger than the original stone, it is visually unobtrusive and easy to drive past without noticing. His headstone lies flat to the ground, consistent with his redesign if not his personality, and these days it is often covered in a layer of dried grass clippings. Seventy years after his passing, his grave is rarely visited, and no one leaves flowers for the forgotten Asa.

[Asa Candler Jr.] and his associates did much to build up the city, and to help it becme the great city that it is today.[1]

CHAPTER 19

Buddie's Best Buds

For all of the society headlines Asa Jr. made during his lifetime, not much is known about his inner circle of friends. However, it is possible to trace some names through various periods of his life. His friendship with Edward Durant was well documented in the first decade of the 1900s. But the friendship appeared to be short-lived and fraught with disagreements, and it ultimately ended in a firestorm of bad press. But Ed wasn't Buddie's only friend who can be traced through documentation. Some, like William Owens and Henry Heinz, married into the family, but Asa Jr.'s relationships with them can be documented prior to their nuptials. Another friend, J. Lee Barnes, was Buddie's pal during the Atlanta Speedway years and was still his friend when magic fever touched the wealthy men of Atlanta. But the more interesting friendship to trace is the one with Bill Stoddard.

DRY CLEANING IN A DRY TOWN

William J. Stoddard was probably the most frequent associate to show up in Buddie's social circle. Stoddard was a rare example of someone who was close with Buddie but didn't seem to go into business with him at any point. There was no financial power dynamic, which tended to be the trigger that caused many of Buddie's public fallings-out, but they appear to have eventually parted ways. As with so many stories in Buddie's life, it started with cars.

Stoddard was an early automobile adopter, and he and Buddie became fast friends—no pun intended—when they joined Ed Inman's automobile club in 1908. Later, Stoddard supported Asa Jr.'s personal automobile club, the AAA, as the leaders built and promoted their new racetrack. Stoddard competed in nearly every Atlanta amateur race on record and participated in most of the same road tours that Buddie reportedly drove in. He appeared throughout Atlanta Speedway media coverage until its closure in 1911, even after Asa Jr.'s nasty falling-out with Ed Durant. But their friendship didn't end with the speedway's closure, although Stoddard played a side role in most of the later stories.

On September 16, 1915, a painter from Cincinnati named S. B. Burnett arrived in Atlanta, looking for an end to his money woes. He hired a jitney cab and went to the Candler Building, where he asked for a meeting with Asa Candler Sr. He claimed to be a Coca-Cola shareholder and intended to demand money as an investor. Reportedly drunk and turned away with the excuse that Candler was in New York, Burnett returned to his hired car and started leafing through the Atlanta City Directory. Finding an entry for an Asa G. Candler—albeit the wrong Asa G. Candler—he placed a phone call to Briarcliff Farm and asked Helen if he could speak with her husband. She informed Burnett that he was dining at the home of Bill Stoddard and wouldn't be back until later. Concerned by the man's tone, she phoned the Stoddards to inform Buddie that someone was looking for him.[2]

Meanwhile, Burnett was back in his jitney, looking up Bill Stoddard's address, which was located in what is present-day midtown Atlanta. When he arrived at the Stoddard house, he asked for Buddie and pleaded his case. At first, he demanded $100. Buddie told him he wasn't carrying that kind of money, especially not for handing out to strangers. Burnett took that as an invitation to negotiate and asked for $50 instead. Buddie turned his pockets inside out, showed the man that he only had twenty-one cents, and sent him on his way again.

From there, Burnett directed his driver to Briarcliff Farm. Helen had left for an evening out with friends, so only the maid was home to answer the door. Burnett self-reported later that he was "crazy drunk" as he demanded to speak with the homeowners, and when the maid shut the door in his face, he tried to break it down and shouted profanities at her. Naturally, she was terribly frightened and called for help.[3]

Not willing to give up yet, Burnett got back into his hired car and drove to Lucy Candler's house. Buddie's sister was living on her own with her two children in a big house between Inman Park and Druid Hills. Her husband, Bill Owens, had passed away the previous December, and she had recently been ill herself. So when Burnett came knocking, she begged his forgiveness and tried to politely turn him away. He demanded to be let in, and out of fear she opened the door. He suggested to Lucy that anarchists had been giving rich people a lot of trouble recently, and they believed that people like the Candlers should be forced to contribute to the needs of those less fortunate. But she had nothing to give him, and eventually he left of his own accord.

He wasn't hard for police to track down since he'd paraded his protracted attempt at extortion in front of many witnesses. He was arrested, released on a technicality, and then arrested again. He never earned a dime from his master plan.[4]

Back to Bill Stoddard. He was an entrepreneur, one of the biggest laundry men in Atlanta, and an innovator in the dry-cleaning industry. In 1924, he developed a chemical solvent that became the industry standard for dry cleaning textiles until nonflammable alternatives arrived on the market years later.[5] The Stoddard solvent was a type of white spirit, or mineral turpentine, that was safer than the gasoline-based formulas that were more commonly in use. The Stoddard solvent is still used today as a paint thinner, in photocopier toner and printing inks, and as a degreaser.[6] Bill Stoddard also bred prize-winning cattle, learned to fly airplanes, was a member of the pipe aficionado community, and raced pigeons. He was a renaissance man.

It should be noted that while Stoddard's 1924 invention coincided with the leading edge of Buddie's biggest peak in investment in a variety of industries, no evidence suggests that Buddie bankrolled Stoddard's work or had any involvement in the solvent's promotion in the cleaning industry. It wasn't laundry that linked his name to the Candlers that year. And laundry wasn't what ended his friendship with Buddie either.

In June 1923, Asa Candler Sr. had married his stenographer, May Little Ragin, in an act of convenience that put an end to a lawsuit brought by a socialite named Onezima de Bouchel, who asserted that the Coca-Cola millionaire had reneged on a verbal contract to marry her. At the conclusion of the sensational lawsuit, the jury determined that Asa Sr. couldn't have made a promise of engagement to de Bouchel while she was still legally married to her first husband, and he couldn't have made a promise later because he was engaged to Ragin. Ragin's agreement to marry the aging industrialist put an end to the media circus and nationwide headlines.

That court case ended on February 5, 1924. Four days later, Atlanta's police chief, James L. Beavers, caught the new Mrs. Candler in an apartment drinking illegally with two men, one of whom was Buddie's dear friend William J. Stoddard. Beavers arrested all of them on the spot, but after Stoddard claimed sole ownership of the bottle of whiskey, May Candler and the other man were released. Stoddard was held on a $300 bond, and they were all ordered to appear in front of a judge.[7]

In the court testimony, Chief Beavers laid out in plain language what was going on. He claimed he had been contacted by Forrest Adair, one of the real estate Adairs who were lifelong business partners with the Candlers. Forrest Adair had worked as Asa Sr.'s proxy during a 1918 extortion lawsuit, and he later ran West View Cemetery on Buddie's behalf until Buddie took over in 1933. Adair notified Beavers that he'd hired men to follow around May Candler and Bill Stoddard for weeks, trying to catch them in a suspected extramarital affair. He gave the police chief the address of an apartment at the corner of Juniper Street and Ponce de Leon Avenue, just steps down the road from the iconic Georgian Terrace Apartments and the future site of the Yaarab Temple (later, the Fox Theater).[8]

When Beavers arrived at the apartment, he found a man named J. W. Keeling in the living room. In the bedroom, he found Stoddard and May Candler in a state of semi-undress. Stoddard was described as "in his shirt sleeves," which was enough to suggest what was going on. During his testimony, Beavers told the court that he asked Stoddard how long he and Mrs. Candler had been seeing each other in this way. Stoddard noted that she was a former employee of his and that they'd been seeing each other for at least six years. He also stated that his wife knew about the affair and didn't approve.[9]

As if this weren't messy enough, the trial of Keeling, Stoddard, and May Candler was delayed because Stoddard just so happened to hire an attorney who was busy representing an accuser in a lawsuit against Walter Candler.[10] His choice of counsel suggests a rift already had formed between Stoddard and the Candlers, and it was playing out publicly.

But it got messier still. Forrest Adair was, of course, working on behalf of Asa Candler Sr., and by all appearances, catching May and Bill together was an effort to acquire evidence that could be used against her in a divorce suit. Beavers had let it slip during the arrest of the trio that Asa Sr. wanted him to avoid showing them any special treatment and to march them down to the police station like anyone else.

That didn't sit well with one councilman in particular, who happened to be the chair of the city's police committee. Councilman Edward H. Inman, the man who had started Atlanta's first automobile club, who'd had a falling-out with Buddie over the formation of the AAA, whose uncle Samuel Inman had invested with Joel Hurt and Ernest Woodruff in the development of Inman Park, whose father had invested with Thomas K. Glenn and Ernest Woodruff in Atlantic Steel, and who seemed to run in competing circles with his own generation of Candlers, stepped forward to retaliate against the man who had arrested William Stoddard and splashed his indiscretions all over the society pages. Inman charged Beavers with misconduct, citing a regulation that forbade police officers from working privately to assist in the gathering of evidence for divorce proceedings.[11] This thrust Asa Candler Sr. into the spotlight again. The question was, did Atlanta's wealthiest citizen and former mayor abuse his power by leveraging his connection with the chief of police for private gain?

James Beavers was a controversial figure. Strongly anti-vice, he and Asa Sr. saw eye to eye on the prohibition of alcohol, and during Beavers's reign as police chief from 1911 to 1915, he formed a heavy-handed vice squad—literally, the morality police—which made plenty of citizens unhappy. He had been removed from his position in 1915 amid charges of incompetence, led by Ed Inman.

Upon assuming office in 1916, Mayor Asa Candler Sr. announced that James Beavers's trial would be postponed. In response, Inman sarcastically proposed to delay the trial until the day after Mayor Candler left office. Everyone knew that Beavers would be untouchable as long as his pal was leading the city. The courts put down the charges altogether, and Beavers was reinstated.[12] Beavers and Candler remained linked, and a copy of the original charges filed against Beavers in 1915 is preserved in the Asa Candler Papers at Emory University's library.

So when Chief Beavers arrested William Stoddard and May Candler at Asa Sr.'s request in 1924, Ed Inman pounced and pressed charges.[13] Inman and Beavers traded barbs in court, and Inman didn't deny that this time it was personal.[14] But in the end, Inman's case flopped. Beavers was reinstated as chief of police in May 1926.[15] By that point, Inman had resigned from the city council and the police committee and could no longer pursue him, and no one was talking about William Stoddard's affair anymore.

Unlike what happened to Ed Durant and William White, Stoddard's falling-out with the Candlers didn't drive him out of high society. He continued to enjoy success in business, participate in civics, fly his airplane, and race pigeons until his death in 1940. Perhaps the difference was social allegiance. Durant and White had no clear connections to the Woodruff camp. Stoddard may have had the unique honor of emerging from a Candler kerfuffle unscathed due to his place at the center of the Venn diagram of the intersection between the two wealthy old men.

THE SEARCH FOR LANDRUM ANDERSON

Asa Jr. and Helen employed many servants at Briarcliff Mansion. They came and went over the years, but the bulk of the workers were hired after 1922. There was, however, a man who served them from the time they were first married until his death: Landrum Anderson.

Anderson was known as "Brother Landrum," according to Candler family lore.[16] Landrum and Buddie met in Hartwell, Georgia, in 1901, right after Buddie was relocated to run his father's cotton mill. When Buddie returned to Atlanta in 1906, Brother Landrum came with him. When Asa Jr. and his family moved to Inman Park, Landrum moved with them. When they moved to Briarcliff Farm, Landrum went with them. When they tore down the farmhouse and built Briarcliff Mansion, Landrum was there. He lived in a small house on the back property, rented for one dollar per month from his employer. That's about fifteen dollars per month in 2020 dollars. Landrum was there until the very end, still working for Asa Jr. when the latter died in 1953. He lived only one more year and then passed in 1954.[17]

Landrum is unusually persistent throughout Buddie's history. Buddie had some friends and other servants who stayed with him for years, but no one other than blood relatives stuck by his side like Landrum. But who was he? That's not an easy question to answer.

Anderson was born in the rural South in the post–Civil War era. This was a murky time for records of Black Americans. During the slavery era, enslaved people were often listed as property, not as people with vital records. The 1870 Census was the first one that recorded African Americans by name, but it was hardly comprehensive. Further, even if names were noted accurately, they could have been changed, and birth names may have been lost to history. Residence locations often changed, and few records followed. Jim Crow laws suppressed Black voter registration, so those records were spotty for decades. We have very little to go on if we want to trace Anderson's history and find his family. His name appears in Census records, and accounts given by Asa Candler Jr.'s grandchildren and great-grandchildren capture some valuable anecdotes. But there are still many questions.

In 1910, Landrum Anderson first appeared on a U.S. Census at Asa Jr.'s house in Inman Park. He was listed as forty years old, and his occupation was given as butler. Elsewhere in the record, it was noted that he could not read or write and was born in Georgia. He was the only servant on staff at the time.[18] In 1920, Landrum was recorded again as a servant, this time living at Briarcliff Farm with the Candler family. Other servants appeared in this Census as well, including Landrum's wife, Jessy (maid); Fanny Upshaw (cook); and Eli Johnson (chauffeur, automobile). Once again, Landrum was noted as forty years old. It's evident throughout Census records that few people cared about capturing the correct vital statistics of servants. Sometimes, they didn't even bother spelling their names right. In the 1920 Briarcliff Farm record, all staff were noted as literate, although it's likely that this data point was also inaccurately reported.[19]

In the 1930 record, the Census taker noted in the margin, "West of Briarcliff Rd. (Candler Estate)" across several names, including José Cruz and James Stark, who would be involved in the murder-suicide incident in 1931. In this record, Landrum was listed as twenty-five years old. His wife's name was spelled Jessie instead of Jessy, and their daughter, Mary, was noted as six years old. This Census said Landrum couldn't read or write. By contrast, it said Jessie didn't attend school but was literate.[20]

When I began this research, the 1940 Census was the last one available, since the 1950 Census wouldn't be made public until 2022. In the 1940 document, Landrum's information was different. It was individualized, less generic. His birthplace was listed as South Carolina. His age was sixty-seven instead of a number ending in zero or five. And this time, his first name was spelled Landers. Jessie's name was spelled the same as in 1930, but Mary was now Alice, and she was listed as "Adopted Daughter, age 16." This 1940 information appears to have been self-reported rather than employer-reported, and therefore it is probably more accurate than the previous records. Landrum's legal name may have actually been Landers.[21]

In 1954, Landers Anderson, as he was officially recorded in the Georgia Death Index, passed away at the age of sixty-seven, having spent over fifty years of his life serving the Candler family. But here, too, we have problems. If he was sixty-seven at the time of his death, why was he listed as sixty-seven in the 1940 Census record? Which age was correct? Which of any of the ages were correct? If the 1910 record is correct, he would have been born in 1870 and would have been eighty-four at the time of his death. If the 1920 record is correct, he would have been born in 1880 and would have been seventy-four at the time of his death. It seems unlikely that the 1930 Census is correct, since he would have been born in 1905, four years after he met Asa Candler Jr. If the 1940 Census is correct, he would have been born in 1873 and died at the age of eighty-one. We may never know his actual year of birth nor how old he was when he died.

When researching where Landrum Anderson came from and whether he had any other family, what should an investigator do? Do you search for Landrum or Landers? Do you search for a birth date of 1870, 1873, 1880, or 1887? What if none of those are correct? Also, do you search for a birth location in Georgia or South Carolina?

One confirmed piece of information is that Anderson met the Candler family during their time in Hartwell, Georgia. In the 1992 Candler family biography, *The Real Ones: Four Generations of the First Family of Coca-Cola* by Elizabeth Candler Graham and Ralph Roberts, Landrum's story is captured in detail. According to that book, Landrum was in prison for murder, and he worked on a chain gang that was deployed to improve and repair the Witham Cotton Mill while Buddie was secretary and treasurer. The family claimed that he built trust with Buddie by tipping him off to prisoner rebellions, and Buddie rewarded him by successfully campaigning to the governor, a blood relative, to pardon him.[22]

But this history is also problematic. It's a sensational tale of heroism and loyalty; it shows off Buddie's importance and influence; and it's a classic Buddie tall tale, like so many others. It also plays on a number of racially charged stereotypes during a time when Black Americans were often depicted as criminals and the white savior perspective was commonly accepted.

There are no entries for Landrum Anderson or Landers Anderson in any published prison records from that time period. And it's highly unlikely that Buddie had the power or influence to get the state's governor to overturn a murder conviction, even if the governor at the time was related to him.

If you look at Hartwell's location on a map, you'll see that it's very close to the border of South Carolina. Just on the other side of the border is a town called Anderson. If you look for the surname Anderson in Anderson, South Carolina, during the immediate post–Civil War era, you'll find a large number of results for African American residents.

The town of Anderson's history is pertinent to Landrum's history. It was a cotton town, the first fully electrified town in the South with an electrically powered cotton gin at the mill. In 1901, a flood knocked out the hydroelectric dam that supplied power to the mill, putting it out of commission. The town remained dark until 1902. So in 1901, a lot of mill workers were put out of work. That year, Landrum Anderson met Asa Jr. at Witham Cotton Mill in Hartwell, Georgia, the next closest mill town. Rather than the lurid story of Landrum as a murderer-turned-snitch who was freed thanks to the generosity of his white employer, it's likely that Landrum arrived in Hartwell from Anderson, South Carolina, just across the border, looking for work when the cotton mill back home went out of business.

Regarding Landrum's family, two leads exist but have failed to turn up results. First, he might have had a brother who worked for Lucy Candler, Asa Jr.'s sister. Henry Anderson appeared on the 1930 Census under the household of Lucy's second husband, Henry Heinz. Henry Anderson's age was listed as a nice round number: fifty. He was also listed as Black, illiterate, and born in Georgia. This is probably no more accurate than any of Landrum's records. But because of the shared surname and the close relationship between their employers, it is possible that a link exists between Henry and Landrum. Unfortunately, Lucy's life was a tumultuous one, and her household changed frequently. Her Census data showed different locations, cohabitants, and staff on each record. Henry only showed up in 1930.

The other potential family member of Landrum was a woman named Lula Mae Ware, who worked for Laura Candler, Buddie's daughter, and died in 2012.[23] Laura's grandson recalls hearing from his family that Lula Mae was related to Landrum, although the nature of the relationship—by blood or by marriage—was not documented.[24] Records for Lula Mae Ware's parents and siblings are available, but no link to a Landrum Anderson has been established. At the start of the 2020s, verifiable confirmation of Landrum's identity remained elusive.

However, in the summer of 2022, a breakthrough finally shed light on Brother Landrum's story. The 1950 U.S. Census was released to the public, and I finally learned who he really was. It turns out that Landrum was not Landrum. He wasn't Landers either. His name was Lander Anderson.

After Briarcliff Mansion was sold in 1948, Lander moved off the property and became the head of his own household. In the 1950 Census, he self-reported his age as 74, making his birth date 1876, just four years before his lifelong employer's birth. He was born in Georgia, and he was employed in 1950 as a full-time cook at a cemetery restaurant. Although Buddie had long since sold off West View, it's likely that he arranged this employment after he let his personal staff go. Lander lived with his sister Ola Anderson (misspelled Ala) and a lodger named Annie Harper. He was listed as a widow, confirming Candler family stories that his wife, Jessie, had passed away sometime in the previous decade.[25]

With his real name, I could now find his obituary. Lander Anderson, Brother Landrum to the Candler family, died on September 11, 1954. He had lived in the Washington Park area of Atlanta—an easy commute to Westview Cemetery—attended Holsey Temple CME Church, and was a Freemason. It's worth noting that like Buddie, he was a Methodist and a member of a fraternal organization.

According to the obituary, Lander's siblings included Ola Anderson, Mary Bowers, and Mollie Reid. He was the father of Lillie Turner, Lews J. Barnes, and Alice King. Alice was listed in the 1940 Census as his sixteen-year-old adopted daughter, so this appears to clear up the inconsistency with her name. He was also married to Mary Anderson at the time of his death, indicating that he remarried after Jessie passed.[26] And one has to wonder, could his sister Ola, recorded in the 1950 Census as Ala, actually be Lula, whom Buddie's great-grandson recalls? Further investigation will hopefully reveal her identity too.

At the time of his passing, Lander Anderson appears to have been loved by many and actively involved in his community. And he likely lived comfortably after his former employer's death. In 1953, a newspaper report claimed that Buddie left $8,500 to each of his seven servants.[27] Certainly, Brother Landrum was one of the recipients. Candler family lore depicts a close relationship between the Candlers and Lander, although the stories are rife with the kind of overt racism that permeated the South during his lifetime, and therefore must be viewed through a skeptical lens.

Lander Anderson, along with all of the Candlers' servants, deserves to have his history recorded respectfully and accurately, and to have the skewed depictions of his life dismantled. With time and more publicly available information, we may be able to fill in more missing details and reconstruct a more equitable view of our community's past. Further research into Briarcliff's former residents may reveal lost connections and recover more forgotten history for other families in present-day Atlanta.

The grounds are not open to visitors now, but Mr. Candler
states that as soon as the residence is completed he will permit
visitors on the place during certain hours of the day.[1]

CHAPTER 20

What's Next for Briarcliff Mansion?

Briarcliff Mansion's journey became simultaneously more mundane and more sensational after Asa Candler Jr. left the premises. Initially intended to be used as a hospital, or perhaps as hospital staff housing, the property was met with some uncertainty by its new owners. Over time, it was modified and adapted to function as a medical facility rather than the glamorous home it once was. The house became an alcoholism treatment center, a fact that feeds many of the present-day rumors and myths about Buddie's own alcoholism.

In some rooms, drop ceilings were installed to cover up the aging plasterwork. In other rooms, walls were erected to provide office space for healthcare workers. The former ballroom was unceremoniously divided up into smaller functional spaces, and the original kitchen was converted into a medical wing.

The burnt-down rubble of the former laundry facility was bulldozed away, and in 1965 a new structure was built in its place. The Georgia Mental Health Institute operated on the Briarcliff property until 1997, at which point the facility was shut down, and the forty-two-acre property was sold to Emory University.

Emory already had experience maintaining a former Candler mansion. Lullwater House, built by Walter Candler at the edge of Emory's campus, now enjoys life as the residence of the university's reigning president. So when the university took on the Briarcliff property, it did so with a commitment to honor the intent of its original owner. That said, maintaining a mansion and forty-two acres of land is a costly endeavor, especially when that property is just far enough from the main college campus to make student commuting a challenge. While Emory University made a commitment to not tear down the mansion, the costs of maintenance, repairs, and upgrades were beyond the scope of its budget.

So from 1998 until today, Briarcliff Mansion has endured what could be called demolition by neglect. Broken windows and roof leaks have permitted water to enter the house and to damage walls, ceilings, and floors. The original construction materials included asbestos and lead paint, but the mansion developed a serious mold problem too. The house became a health hazard, and the cascading effect of compounding decay attracted urban explorers and photographers, creating an additional need for security and monitoring.

Campaigns to save the mansion have brought the property into the spotlight over the years, and community members with an interest in preserving history have done their best to remind Atlanta of Briarcliff's plight. But on Briarcliff Mansion's hundredth anniversary in the spring of 2022, the house still stood empty, overlooking an unkempt lawn and a filled-in pool, its lush gardens paved over with cracked, faded concrete.

Today, water damage has collapsed a section of ceiling above the magic performance area in the ballroom, and the paint peels in crisp, brittle flakes up and down the hallways. The northern wing cannot be entered without gloves and a respirator to protect one from mold and lead paint dust. Broken glass and ceramic tiles litter the floor, along with shreds of insulation and debris from halfhearted demolition attempts—both official and unofficial. Graffiti and discarded beer cans can be found here and there, a reminder that the greatest threat to the mansion's future may come in the form of careless urban explorers.

But it's not all bad news. As Briarcliff Mansion enters its second century, a thriving film industry in Atlanta has brought new attention and new interest to the property. Production crews visit frequently, and by sheer necessity they have repaired some of the leaky window casings. The roof was replaced, and although some preservationists cringe at the modern asphalt shingles that were selected in lieu of historically accurate green terra-cotta tiles, at least the rain isn't pouring in anymore. Call me a pragmatist, but I see repair happening where there once was only neglect.

Due to the extraordinary expense, a full restoration has been an ever-receding goal line. Over the years, Emory University has entertained

The Atlanta skyline from the repaired roof of Briarcliff Mansion, circa 2019.
Photo by the author.

proposals for adaptive reuse, such as a plan that would turn the mansion into a boutique hotel with additional lodging in newly constructed outbuildings. But even if the mansion itself were successfully restored, the property still contains the massive Georgia Mental Health Institute building, which is decaying just as rapidly. Finding—and funding—a proposal that will restore the mansion and grounds and also address the abandoned hospital is no small undertaking.

Briarcliff's status as a historical landmark protects the mansion from intentional demolition. Not that Emory has ever considered demolition an option. But for the university, it's difficult to justify the expense associated with renovating the satellite campus, which leaves the property in limbo even though intermittent efforts to stave off entropy have kept the structure standing.

According to Emory University's associate vice president of planning and engagement, David C. Payne, the search for a viable proposal is ongoing. He expressed optimism that the property has a bright future ahead of it and emphasized Emory's commitment to finding the right fit: "Emory has a real appreciation for the history of the property and [we] are interested in finding a way to activate or develop the property in a way that supports that history. We have maintained the mansion's structural integrity until we could determine a path forward to restore it to its grandeur."[2]

In June 2022, a promising proposal to revive Briarcliff as a senior living community was presented through a press release, a virtual webinar, and an in-person meeting. Architectural concept drawings and detailed renovation plans were shared, and the representatives for the developers and Emory answered questions from the public. The university is operating with such transparency because its leaders understand the importance of community buy-in and want the residents of Druid Hills to be comfortable with the adaptive reuse project.

This project, in my opinion, is one Buddie would be pleased with. The current proposal is to raze the hospital and replace it with accessible housing, complete with cottages and a main street of community-serving retail. The mansion would be repurposed into an events hall that the residents, their families, and the greater community can enjoy. Buddie's home would serve a public function similar to the Callanwolde Fine Arts Center, his older brother's former home just up the street. The proposal includes restoration of the greenhouses out back, preservation of James Stark's old groundskeeper cottage, and reuse of the Cruz brothers' apartment above the garages. The pool out front would be transformed into a garden, fitting for a property that once teemed with enough flowers to require a full-time gardener. The site of the former zoo, which once hosted community gatherings and family outings, would be restored to a park-like green space where outdoor events can take place. And up on the hill, that grand house at the end of a meandering driveway, that expanse of tan brick and white columns overlooking a vast lawn dotted with magnolia trees, will begin life again, better than the way Asa Candler Jr. left it.

Notes

CHAPTER 1. A Boy Named Buddie

1. Asa Candler Jr. to Lucy Candler, May 3, 1901. Letter. Emory University's Stuart A. Rose Manuscript, Archives and Rare Book Library. Asa Griggs Candler Papers, 1821–1951.

2. World Population Review. Cartersville, Georgia, Population 2020 (Demographics, Maps, Graphs). https://worldpopulationreview.com/us-cities /cartersville-ga-population/, accessed Oct. 18, 2020.

3. Head, J. "Asa G. Candler." Etowah Valley Historical Society. 2016. https:// evhsonline.org/archives/43069, accessed Oct. 18, 2020; U.S. Census, 1880. Cartersville, Bartow County, Georgia. https://familysearch.org/ark:/61903 /1:1:M8L4-P91, accessed Oct. 19, 2020.

4. Lucy Candler report card, West End Institute for Females, 1897. Emory University's Stuart A. Rose Manuscript, Archives and Rare Book Library. Asa Griggs Candler Papers, 1821–1951.

5. *Report of the Commissioner of Education Made to the Secretary of the Interior . . . with Accompanying Papers.* Washington, D.C.: U.S. Government Printing Office, 1891, 1031.

6. Roberts, Ralph, and Graham, Elizabeth Candler. *The Real Ones: Four Generations of the First Family of Coca-Cola.* Fort Lee, N.J.: Barricade Books, 1992, 170.

7. Asa Candler Jr. to Lucy Candler, May 3, 1901. Letter. Emory University's Stuart A. Rose Manuscript, Archives and Rare Book Library. Asa Griggs Candler Papers, 1821–1951.

8. Abrams, Ann Uhry. *Formula for Fortune: How Asa Candler Discovered Coca-Cola and Turned It into the Wealth His Children Enjoyed*. Bloomington, Ind.: iUniverse, 2012, 20.

9. Author's Note: There's a modern-day tendency to read between the lines and wonder whether Buddie had a learning disability or a neurodevelopmental disorder such as ADHD. He displayed behaviors throughout his life that can correlate anecdotally with dopamine-linked conditions such as ADHD, addiction, depression, and lack of impulse control. However, there is insufficient documentation for any diagnostic criteria, and while speculation can help us view his history with empathy, a diagnosis cannot be confirmed with any degree of accuracy.

CHAPTER 2. In the Heart of Dear Old Emory

1. Asa Candler to Charles Howard Candler, Jan. 20, 1897. Letter. Emory University's Stuart A. Rose Manuscript, Archives and Rare Book Library. Asa Griggs Candler Papers, 1821–1951.

2. Emory College, *Annual Catalog, 1895–98*. Franklin Printing and Publishing Co., Atlanta, Ga., 1896, 11. Digitized by University of Illinois, Urbana-Champaign.

3. "Georgia's Railroad History & Heritage: Streetcars in Covington." 1999. http://railga.com/oddend/streetrail/covingtonstr.html, accessed Dec. 10, 2018.

4. Reed, Mary Beth. *Historic Streetcar Systems in Georgia*. New South Associates Technical Report, Georgia Department of Transportation, 1987. http://www.dot.ga.gov/BuildSmart/research/Documents/GAStreetcar.pdf, accessed Oct. 18, 2020.

5. Oxford Historical Society. Self-Guided Tour. 2016. http://www.oxfordhistoricalsociety.org/self-guided-tour.html, accessed Oct. 19, 2020.

6. Emory College, *The Zodiac, 1895*. Atlanta, Ga.: Emory College, 1895, 160. Digitized by University of Illinois, Urbana-Champaign.

7. The term is from the yearbook and was a common spelling at the time. Feist is a breed of dog.

8. Emory College, *The Zodiac, 1898*. Atlanta, Ga.: Emory College, 1898, 214. Emory University Library.

9. Jarrell, Charles C. *Oxford Echoes*. Oxford, Ga., Historical Society of the North Georgia Conference and the Wesleyan Christian Advocate, 1967.

10. Bullock, Henry Morton. *A History of Emory University*. Nashville, Tenn.: Parthenon Press, 1936.

11. Asa Candler to Charles Howard Candler and Asa Griggs Candler Jr., Jan. 27, 1896. Letter. Emory University's Stuart A. Rose Manuscript, Archives and Rare Book Library. Asa Griggs Candler Papers, 1821–1951.

12. Candler, Charles Howard. *Asa Griggs Candler*. Atlanta, Ga.: Emory University, 1950, 229.

13. Asa Candler to Charles Howard Candler, Feb. 21, 1896. Letter. Emory University's Stuart A. Rose Manuscript, Archives and Rare Book Library. Asa Griggs Candler Papers, 1821–1951.

14. Roberts and Graham, *Real Ones*, 153.

15. Emory College, *The Zodiac, 1898*. Atlanta, Ga.: Emory College, 1898, 150. Emory University Library.

16. Kappa Alpha Order. "John Slaughter Candler." 2015. https://www. kappaalphaorder.org/knight-commanders/john-slaughter-candler/, accessed Oct. 18, 2020.

17. *Epsilon Enquirer*. Atlanta, Ga.: Epsilon Chapter, Kappa Alpha Order, 2005, 2. https://websites.omegafi.com/omegaws/kappaalphaorderemory/files/2014/06 /Epsilon-Enquirer-Dec.-2005.pdf, accessed Oct. 19, 2020.

18. Asa Candler to Charles Howard Candler and Asa Candler Jr., Nov. 27, 1895. Letter. Emory University's Stuart A. Rose Manuscript, Archives and Rare Book Library. Asa Griggs Candler Papers, 1821–1951.

19. Abrams, *Formula for Fortune*, 64; Emory College, *The Zodiac, 1895*. Atlanta, Ga.: Emory College, 1895, 230. Digitized by University of Illinois, Urbana-Champaign.

20. Emory College, *The Zodiac, 1897*. Atlanta, Ga.: Emory College, 1897, 39. Emory University Library.

21. Asa Candler to Charles Howard Candler, Jan. 20, 1897. Letter. Emory University's Stuart A. Rose Manuscript, Archives and Rare Book Library. Asa Griggs Candler Papers, 1821–1951.

22. Asa Candler to Charles Howard Candler and Asa Candler Jr., Oct. 16, 1897. Letter. Emory University's Stuart A. Rose Manuscript, Archives and Rare Book Library. Asa Griggs Candler Papers, 1821–1951.

23. Asa Candler to Charles Howard Candler, Oct. 16, 1897. Letter. Emory University's Stuart A. Rose Manuscript, Archives and Rare Book Library. Asa Griggs Candler Papers, 1821–1951.

24. Roberts and Graham, *Real Ones*, 173.

25. Candler, *Asa Griggs Candler*, 231.

26. Asa Candler to Charles Howard Candler, Oct. 8, 1897. Letter. Emory University's Stuart A. Rose Manuscript, Archives and Rare Book Library. Asa Griggs Candler Papers, 1821–1951.

27. Emory College, *The Zodiac, 1898*. Atlanta, Ga.: Emory College, 1898, 130. Emory University Library.

28. Ibid., 197.

29. Asa Candler to Charles Howard Candler, June 8, 1899. Letter. Emory University's Stuart A. Rose Manuscript, Archives and Rare Book Library. Asa Griggs Candler Papers, 1821–1951.

30. Ibid.

CHAPTER 3. Go West, Young Man

1. Asa Candler to Charles Howard Candler, June 8, 1899. Letter. Emory University's Stuart A. Rose Manuscript, Archives and Rare Book Library. Asa Griggs Candler Papers, 1821–1951.

2. Charles Howard Candler to Lucy Candler, July 13, 1899. Letter. Emory University's Stuart A. Rose Manuscript, Archives and Rare Book Library. Asa Griggs Candler Papers, 1821–1951.

3. Ibid.

4. Asa Candler to Charles Howard Candler, May 30, 1899. Letter. Emory University's Stuart A. Rose Manuscript, Archives and Rare Book Library. Asa Griggs Candler Papers, 1821–1951.

5. *Los Angeles City Directory, 1900–1901.* 1900. Los Angeles Public Library. https:// rescarta.lapl.org/, 907, accessed Oct. 19, 2020.

6. Asa Candler Jr. to Asa Griggs Candler Sr., July 10, 1899. Letter. Emory University's Stuart A. Rose Manuscript, Archives and Rare Book Library. Asa Griggs Candler Papers, 1821–1951.

7. Soper, David Wesley. *These Found the Way: Thirteen Converts to Protestant Christianity.* Louisville, Ky.: Westminster Press, 1951, 53.

8. Asa Candler Jr. to Lucy Candler, Mar. 1, 1901. Letter. Emory University's Stuart A. Rose Manuscript, Archives and Rare Book Library. Asa Griggs Candler Papers, 1821–1951.

9. Charles Howard Candler to Lucy Candler, July 13, 1899. Letter. Emory University's Stuart A. Rose Manuscript, Archives and Rare Book Library. Asa Griggs Candler Papers, 1821–1951.

10. Asa Candler to Charles Howard Candler, July 11, 1899. Letter. Emory University's Stuart A. Rose Manuscript, Archives and Rare Book Library. Asa Griggs Candler Papers, 1821–1951.

11. Asa Candler to Charles Howard Candler, Mar. 28, 1900. Letter. Emory University's Stuart A. Rose Manuscript, Archives and Rare Book Library. Asa Griggs Candler Papers, 1821–1951.

12. Asa Candler to Asa Candler Jr., Apr. 30, 1900. Letter. Emory University's Stuart A. Rose Manuscript, Archives and Rare Book Library. Asa Griggs Candler Papers, 1821–1951.

13. Asa Candler Jr. to Lucy Candler, Sept. 17, 1900. Letter. Emory University's Stuart A. Rose Manuscript, Archives and Rare Book Library. Asa Griggs Candler Papers, 1821–1951.

14. Asa Candler Jr. to Lucy Candler, Sept. 25, 1900. Letter. Emory University's Stuart A. Rose Manuscript, Archives and Rare Book Library. Asa Griggs Candler Papers, 1821–1951.

CHAPTER 4. Mill, Marriage, and Family

1. Asa Candler Jr. to Lucy Candler, September 25, 1900. Letter. Emory University's Stuart A. Rose Manuscript, Archives and Rare Book Library. Asa Griggs Candler Papers, 1821–1951.

2. Asa Candler Jr. to Lucy Candler, Sept. 17, 1900. Letter. Emory University's Stuart A. Rose Manuscript, Archives and Rare Book Library. Asa Griggs Candler Papers, 1821–1951.

3. Asa Candler Jr. to Lucy Candler, Apr. 27, 1901. Letter. Emory University's Stuart A. Rose Manuscript, Archives and Rare Book Library. Asa Griggs Candler Papers, 1821–1951.

4. Asa Candler Jr. to Lucy Candler, May 3, 1901. Letter. Emory University's Stuart A. Rose Manuscript, Archives and Rare Book Library. Asa Griggs Candler Papers, 1821–1951.

5. Ibid.

6. *Sanborn Fire Insurance Maps for Georgia Towns and Cities, 1884–1922.* Hartwell, Ga.: Sanborn Map & Publishing Co., 1901. Digital Library of Georgia. http://dlg.galileo.usg.edu/sanborn/CityCounty/Hartwell1901/Sheet1.html?Welcome, accessed Oct. 19, 2020.

7. Asa Candler Jr. to Lucy Candler, Mar. 1, 1901. Letter. Emory University's Stuart A. Rose Manuscript, Archives and Rare Book Library. Asa Griggs Candler Papers, 1821–1951.

8. *About Us: Hartwell Sun*, Hartwell, Ga., 2019. https://www.thehartwellsun.com/about, accessed Oct. 19, 2020.

9. Asa Candler Jr. to Lucy Candler, Jan. 22, 1901. Letter. Emory University's Stuart A. Rose Manuscript, Archives and Rare Book Library. Asa Griggs Candler Papers, 1821–1951.

10. Asa Candler Jr. to Lucy Candler, May 3, 1901. Letter. Emory University's Stuart A. Rose Manuscript, Archives and Rare Book Library. Asa Griggs Candler Papers, 1821–1951.

11. Asa Candler Jr. to Lucy Candler, May 9, 1901. Letter. Emory University's Stuart A. Rose Manuscript, Archives and Rare Book Library. Asa Griggs Candler Papers, 1821–1951.

12. Asa Candler Jr. to Lucy Candler, May 14, 1901. Letter. Emory University's Stuart A. Rose Manuscript, Archives and Rare Book Library. Asa Griggs Candler Papers, 1821–1951.

13. Asa Candler Jr. to Lucy Candler, May 18, 1901. Letter. Emory University's Stuart A. Rose Manuscript, Archives and Rare Book Library. Asa Griggs Candler Papers, 1821–1951.

14. Abrams, *Formula for Fortune*, 85.

15. Ibid., 91.

16. Asa Candler to Charles Howard Candler, Mar. 22, 1902. Letter. Emory University's Stuart A. Rose Manuscript, Archives and Rare Book Library. Asa Griggs Candler Papers, 1821–1951.

17. Hibbs, Henry Horace. "The Present Position of Infant Mortality: Its Recent Decline in the United States." *Publications of the American Statistical Association* 14, no. 112 (1915): 813–826. doi:10.2307/2965157, accessed Jan. 18, 2021.

18. Baker, Jeffrey P. "The Incubator Controversy: Pediatricians and the Origins of Premature Infant Technology in the United States, 1890 to 1910." *Pediatrics* 87, no. 5 (May 1991): 654–662. https://pediatrics.aappublications.org/content/87/5/654, accessed Jan. 18, 2020.

19. Candler, *Asa Griggs Candler*.

20. *Georgia Railway Map of Alabama and Georgia.* 1899. Georgiainfo: An Online Georgia Almanac. https://georgiainfo.galileo.usg.edu/histcountymaps/hart1899map.htm, accessed Oct. 20, 2020.

21. Asa Candler to Charles Howard Candler, Apr. 1, 1902. Letter. Emory University's Stuart A. Rose Manuscript, Archives and Rare Book Library. Asa Griggs Candler Papers, 1821–1951.

22. Asa Candler to Charles Howard Candler, May 7, 1902. Letter. Emory University's Stuart A. Rose Manuscript, Archives and Rare Book Library. Asa Griggs Candler Papers, 1821–1951.

23. Asa Candler to Charles Howard Candler, May 10, 1902. Letter. Emory University's Stuart A. Rose Manuscript, Archives and Rare Book Library. Asa Griggs Candler Papers, 1821–1951.

24. Asa Candler to Charles Howard Candler, 1902–1903. Letter. Emory University's Stuart A. Rose Manuscript, Archives and Rare Book Library. Asa Griggs Candler Papers, 1821–1951.

25. Candler, *Asa Griggs Candler*.

26. "Worst Weather of Many Winters Afflicting People of Atlanta." *Atlanta Constitution*, Feb. 5, 1905.

27. "His Iciness of the North Freezes Atlanta to His Car of Triumph." *Atlanta Constitution*, Feb. 6, 1905.

28. "Atlanta Is Still Cut Off from the World." *Atlanta Constitution*, Feb. 10, 1905.

29. "Wires Mended; News Comes in from Outside." *Atlanta Constitution*, Feb. 11, 1905.

30. "Georgia's Railroad History & Heritage: Hartwell Railroad." 1999. http://railga.com/hart.html, accessed Dec. 10, 2018.

31. "Special Notices: Funeral Notices." *Atlanta Constitution*, Feb. 11, 1905.

32. Roberts and Graham, *Real Ones*, 193.

33. *Cotton: Boston Journal of Commerce and Textile Industries and Southern Mills* 74, no. 3 (Jan. 1910): 136.

CHAPTER 5. The People's Buddie

1. "Asa G. Candler, Jr., President Atlanta Automobile Association, Owner of World's Greatest Speedway." *Greater Atlantan*, May 1910.

2. *Atlanta City Directory, 1906*. Foote and Davis Co. and Joseph W. Hill. Emory University Libraries. https://archive.org/details/atlantacitydirec1906foot, accessed Oct. 20, 2020.

3. *Atlanta City Directory, 1907*. Foote and Davis Co. and Joseph W. Hill, 498. Emory University Libraries. https://archive.org/details/atlantacitydirec1907foot, accessed Oct. 20, 2020.

4. *Atlanta City Directory, 1906*.

5. "Atlantans Form a Life Company." *Atlanta Constitution*, Mar. 4, 1906.

6. "Barbecue to Mr. Dawson." *Atlanta Constitution*, June 25, 1906.

7. Louisiana Attorney General's Office. *Opinions and Reports of the Attorney General*. Baton Rouge, La., 1908, 264.

8. "Asa Candler, Jr., in Politics." *Atlanta Constitution*, June 23, 1906.

9. "Many Citizens Sign Petition." *Atlanta Constitution*, June 24, 1906.

10. *United States of America v. the Coca-Cola Company*, Depositions of Ernest Woodruff and Asa Candler Sr., Jan. 27, 1925, 1–6.

11. Candler, *Asa Griggs Candler*, 258.

12. National Park Service. "Druid Hills Historic District." 2009. https://www.nps.gov/nr/travel/atlanta/dru.htm, accessed Oct. 19, 2020.

13. Fruchtman, T. "Glenridge Hall: A Little Known Sandy Springs Historic Gem." 2007. Reporter Newspapers. https://www.reporternewspapers.net/2007/06/01/glenridge-hall-a-little-known-sandy-springs-historic-gem/, accessed Oct. 20, 2020.

14. *United States of America v. the Coca-Cola Company*, No. 738, Deposition of Ernest Woodruff, Jan. 27, 1925, 3.

15. "City Politics Up to Date." *Atlanta Constitution*, June 30, 1906.

16. U.S. Census, 1910. Population Density, Ward 9, Fulton County, Georgia.

17. "Coal! Coal!" Asa G. Candler Jr. advertisement. *Atlanta Georgian and News*, June 20, 1907.

18. "104 Machines Parade Today." *Atlanta Constitution*, July 20, 1907.

19. "News Borne to Brown of Nomination." *Atlanta Georgian and News*, July 11, 1908.

20. *Southeastern Reporter* 55 (1907): 930.

21. Kroplick, H. *The Long Island Motor Parkway: Vanderbilt Cup Races.* 2012. https://www.vanderbiltcupraces.com/about/detail/the_long_island_motor_parkway, accessed Oct. 20, 2020.

22. "Ed H. Inman Heads Automobile Club." *Atlanta Georgian and News*, Nov. 6, 1908.

CHAPTER 6. Gentlemen, Start Your Engines

1. Untitled Auto Week article, *Atlanta Journal*, Nov. 14, 1909.

2. *1909 Balloon Race.* 2009. https://www.firstsuperspeedway.com/articles/category/126, accessed Oct. 23, 2020.

3. "Among the Automobilists." *Sun* (N.Y.), July 2, 1909.

4. "Georgia—South's Stepping Stone." *Motor Age* 16, no. 19 (Nov. 4, 1909): 21.

5. "One Big Ovation from Atlanta Down to Macon." *Atlanta Constitution,* May 25, 1909.

6. "Atlanta Builds Track, Prepares Motor Speedway." *Indianapolis Star*, July 9, 1909.

7. Chilton Company, Incorporated. *Automotive Industries* 21 (Nov. 4, 1909): 766.

8. "Atlanta Builds Track, Prepares Motor Speedway."

9. "Auto Show in Atlanta Begins on November 27." *Atlanta Constitution*, Apr. 30, 1909.

10. "How Atlanta's Great Speedway Was Built." *Automotive Industries* 21, no. 19 (Nov. 4, 1909).

11. "First Auto Races at the Indianapolis Motor Speedway—August 1909." 2009. http://www.firstsuperspeedway.com/articles/category/56, accessed Oct. 23, 2020.

12. "Atlanta Builds Track, Prepares Motor Speedway."

13. "Liberal Response Made to Call for Auto Funds." *Atlanta Constitution*, Sept. 12, 1909.

14. "Auto Barbeque Given at the New Autodrome." *Atlanta Constitution*, Sept. 12, 1909.

15. "Liberal Response Made to Call for Auto Funds."

16. Central of Georgia Railway Company, Fred Robinson to Brooks Morgan, Sept. 23, 1909. Letter. Emory University's Stuart A. Rose Manuscript, Archives and Rare Book Library. Asa Griggs Candler Papers, 1821–1951.

17. "Asks Charter for Warehouse." *Atlanta Constitution*, Apr. 20, 1908.

18. "Store Your Cars with Candler Garage." Walter T. Candler advertisement. *Atlanta Constitution*, Nov. 6, 1909.

19. "After Vanderbilt Come Auto Races at Atlanta." *Indianapolis News*, Oct. 19, 1909.

20. "Atlanta Builds Track, Vies with Local Speedway." *Indianapolis Star*, Sept. 12, 1909.

21. "Two Auto Clubs Will Not Merge." *Atlanta Constitution*, Sept. 25, 1909.

22. "On Georgia's Record Race Track." *Automotive Industries* 21, no. 18 (Oct. 28, 1909): 715.

23. "Insured, B'gosh! Speedway Promoters Raise Defiant and Triumphant Cry, 'Come on, You Rain!'" *Atlanta Constitution*, Nov. 6, 1909.

24. Untitled Auto Week article, *Atlanta Journal*, Nov. 14, 1909.

CHAPTER 7. The Legend of the Merry Widow

1. "This Car Goes Some." *Atlanta Georgian*, July 2, 1909.
2. "Two-Mile-a-Minute Car Owned by A. G. Candler, Jr." *Atlanta Constitution*, July 2, 1909.
3. Ibid.; "This Car Goes Some."
4. "Atlanta Auto Week Awakes South." *Automotive Industries* 21, no. 21 (Nov. 18, 1909): 861.
5. Ibid.
6. "Reaper Close to Kilpatrick." *Atlanta Constitution*, Nov. 13, 1909.
7. "Sixteen Racers Now at Speedway." *Atlanta Constitution*, Oct. 27, 1910.
8. "Reaper Close to Kilpatrick."

CHAPTER 8. Trouble at the Track

1. "Speedway Tangle Not Yet Unraveled." *Atlanta Georgian and News*, Feb. 2, 1910.
2. Ibid.
3. Ibid.
4. "Pickens and Oldfield Cause Stir in Gotham." *Los Angeles Herald*, Feb. 1, 1910.
5. "Speedway Tangle Not Yet Unraveled."
6. "Durant Gives Out Statement." *Atlanta Constitution*, Feb. 8, 1910.
7. "A Spoilt Child Causes Some Foolish Things." *Atlanta Georgian and News*, Feb. 7, 1910.
8. "Speedway Tangle Not Yet Unraveled."
9. "Races on the New Atlanta Speedway." *Horseless Age* 24, no. 20 (Nov. 17, 1909): 570.
10. "Speedway Tangle Not Yet Unraveled."
11. Ibid.
12. Ibid.
13. Ibid.
14. "Auto Track Men Agree to Disagree, Hot Talk Follows." *Atlanta Georgian and News*, Jan. 31, 1910.
15. "Speedway Tangle Not Yet Unraveled."
16. "Secret Service Man Conducts Auto Course." *Los Angeles Herald*, Jan. 24, 1910.
17. "Atlanta Automobile Speedway May Get That One Big Race." *Atlanta Georgian and News*, Jan. 31, 1910.
18. "Durant Refuses to Sign a Paper Denying Claims." *Atlanta Georgian and News*, Feb. 5, 1910.
19. Ibid.
20. "Durant Gives Out Statement."
21. "Spoilt Child Causes Some Foolish Things"; "Durant Is Invited to Vacate Office in Candler Bldg." *Atlanta Georgian and News*, Feb. 8, 1910; "Durant Got a Chill, Moved Out of Draught." *Atlanta Georgian and News*, Mar. 7, 1910.

22. "Durant Gives Out Statement."

23. Ibid.

24. "Durant Asked to Move from Candler Building." *Atlanta Constitution*, Feb. 9, 1910.

25. "Over $750,000 Will Be Spent for Homes in Druid Hills Park." *Atlanta Journal*, Dec. 12, 1909; "Railway Company May Take Charge of the Speedway." *Atlanta Georgian and News*, Feb. 9, 1910.

26. "Durant Got a Chill."

27. "Speedway Tangle Not Yet Unraveled."

CHAPTER 9. The Fall of the Atlanta Speedway

1. "Asa G. Candler, Jr., President Atlanta Automobile Association, Owner of World's Greatest Speedway." *Greater Atlantan*, May 1910.

2. Asa G. Candler and Atlanta Automobile Association, Contract. Emory University's Stuart A. Rose Manuscript, Archives and Rare Book Library. Asa Griggs Candler Papers, 1821–1951.

3. "Speedway Officials Off to New York." *Atlanta Georgian and News*, Mar. 8, 1910.

4. "Durant Refuses to Sign."

5. "Asa Candler, Jr., Tells Grand Jury of 'Wire Houses.'" *Atlanta Georgian and News*, Apr. 2, 1910.

6. "The History of Dry Cleaning." 2017. http://www.drycleaningchiller.com /historyo-dry-cleaning/, accessed Oct. 25, 2020.

7. "Asa G. Candler, Jr., President Atlanta Automobile Association, Owner of World's Greatest Speedway." *Greater Atlantan*, May 1910; "Greater Atlantan Is a Lively Number." *Atlanta Georgian and News*, May 2, 1910.

8. "Asa Candler, Jr., Sells Cotton Exchange Seat." *Atlanta Georgian and News*, May 13, 1910; "Candler Swaps Fiat for Big Limousine." *Atlanta Georgian and News*, Mar. 7, 1910.

9. "Candler Buys Another Car." *Daily Times Enterprise* (Thomasville, Ga.), May 17, 1910.

10. "Lozier Car Taken by Speedway Owner." *San Francisco Chronicle*, May 29, 1910.

11. "Automobilists of Good Roads Tour Given Hearty Welcome in Charlotte." *Charlotte Observer* (N.C.), June 8, 1910.

12. "Good Roads." *Motor Age* 22, no. 23 (June 9, 1910): 1034.

13. "Winners in Good Roads Tour." *Motor Age* 22, no. 25 (June 23, 1910): 1152.

14. "Lozier Breaks Atlanta–New York Record!" advertisement. *New York Times*, June 17, 1910.

15. "List of Registered Chauffeurs," in *Report of the Secretary of State of the State of Florida*. Tallahassee, Fla.: Secretary of State, 1906, 238.

16. "Faster Far than Real Race Drivers Are Local Men Sending Speedway Cars." *Atlanta Georgian and News*, July 20, 1910.

17. "Many Entries for Speedway." *Atlanta Georgian and News*, July 19, 1910.

18. "All 15 Races in Afternoon." *Atlanta Georgian and News*, July 14, 1910.

19. "Some New Entries for Auto Races." *Atlanta Constitution*, July 26, 1910.

20. "Is Fined for Striking Match on Candler's Auto." *Atlanta Georgian and News*, Aug. 27, 1910.

21. "Three Cars Which Will Tour the State This Week." *Atlanta Constitution*, Sept. 8, 1910.

22. Weldon, Frank. "Run Is Made around the State in under 6 Days." *Atlanta Constitution*, Sept. 25, 1910.

23. "Some of the Big Racers All of Them Beefy Men." *Wilmington Morning Star* (N.C.), Sept. 28, 1910.

24. "Races to Start Soon." *Atlanta Georgian and News*, Oct. 20, 1910.

25. "Asa G. Candler, Jr." *Atlanta Constitution*, Nov. 27, 1910.

26. "Atlanta Motordrome Enterprise in the Balance." *Horseless Age* 26, no. 25 (Dec. 21, 1910): 871.

27. "Automobile News and Gossip." *Washington Herald*, Jan. 15, 1911.

28. "Four-Year-Old Pilot of a Racing Lozier." *San Francisco Chronicle*, Jan. 22, 1911.

29. "Sleuth 'Bill' Nye Grabs Big Counterfeiting Gang." *Atlanta Georgian and News*, Aug. 31, 1911.

CHAPTER 10. Buddie the Phoenix: The Great Garage Fire of 1911

1. "Candler's Autos Prey to Flames." *Atlanta Constitution*, Feb. 8, 1911.

2. Ibid.

3. "Asa Candler, Jr., Injured." *Tennessean* (Nashville), Feb. 8, 1911.

4. "Over $750,000 Will Be Spent for Homes in Druid Hills Park." *Atlanta Journal*, Dec. 12, 1909.

5. "Ten Atlantans Go to Chattanooga to Indorse [*sic*] Coca-Cola." *Atlanta Georgian and News*, Mar. 31, 1911.

6. "May Race This Fall on Atlanta Speedway." *Atlanta Georgian and News*, May 11, 1911.

7. "Personal Mention." *Atlanta Georgian*, June 11, 1911.

8. Advertisement, *Atlanta Constitution*, Nov. 3, 1912.

9. Candler, Asa Griggs, Sr., 1910–1916. Letters. Emory University's Stuart A. Rose Manuscript, Archives and Rare Book Library. Asa Griggs Candler Papers, 1821–1951.

10. Abrams, *Formula for Fortune*.

11. Kearney, Paul W. "Burn Your Own Home." *New Outlook*, Aug. 1933, 22.

12. Shelton, Jo-Ann. *As the Romans Did: A Sourcebook in Roman Social History*. New York: Oxford University Press, 1988, 65.

13. "Bits of Race News from Here, There and Everywhere." *Oakland Tribune* (Calif.), May 2, 1915.

14. "Homer George Breaks Cross-Country Record, Atlanta to Knoxville." *Atlanta Constitution*, Apr. 14, 1917.

15. "Asa Candler, Jr., Praises Locomobile." *Atlanta Constitution*, Mar. 25, 1917.

CHAPTER 11. Build Your Own Empire

1. "Use of Electricity on Dairy Farms to Increase Production." *Electrical Review* 73, no. 36 (Dec. 28, 1918): 995.

2. "Mr. Patton Wins at Madison Square." *Charlotte News* (N.C.), Jan. 5, 1913.

3. "Division Manager Praises Local Work." *Asheville Citizen-Times* (N.C.), Aug. 24, 1917.

4. "Use of Electricity on Dairy Farms to Increase Production."

5. "Napp [*sic*] Rucker Lands in Town and Hikes Out for Speedway." *Atlanta Georgian and News*, Oct. 11, 1910.

6. "Auto Races Begin on Atlanta Track." *Lincoln Star* (Neb.), Nov. 3, 1910.

7. "C[.] Frank Visits Local Speedway." *Atlanta Constitution*, Oct. 26, 1910.

8. "Candler Wanted It." *Atlanta Georgian and News*, Sept. 16, 1911.

9. "Candler Agrees to Finance Club." *Atlanta Constitution*, Feb. 27, 1915.

10. "Charlie Frank Gets Atlanta B.B. Franchise." *Town Talk* (Alexandria, La.), Nov. 3, 1915.

11. Karmik, T. "An Almost Complete Surrender." *Baseball History Daily*, Sept. 23, 2013. https://baseballhistorydaily.com/2013/09/23/an-almost-complete-surrender/, accessed Oct. 25, 2020.

12. "Candler's Car Strikes Man in Peachtree Road." *Atlanta Georgian and News*, July 18, 1911.

13. "Commission Postals Keep on Stacking Up." *Atlanta Georgian and News*, July 18, 1911.

14. "Police Close on Auto Speeders." *Atlanta Constitution*, May 24, 1912.

15. "Candler Is Charged with Pointing Pistol." *Atlanta Constitution*, Sept. 14, 1913.

16. "$50,000 Pledge to Get University." *Atlanta Constitution*, Aug. 1, 1914.

17. Candler, *Asa Griggs Candler*, 207.

18. Callanwolde Fine Arts Center. "History." 2018. https://callanwolde.org/about-callanwolde/history/, accessed Oct. 25, 2020.

19. Burns, R. "The Second Burning of Atlanta." *Atlanta Magazine*, Feb. 16, 2017.

https://www.atlantamagazine.com/great-reads/second-burning-atlanta/, accessed Oct. 25, 2020.

20. Allen, Frederick, and Tim Allen. *Secret Formula: How Brilliant Marketing and Relentless Salesmanship Made Coca-Cola the Best-Known Product in the World.* New York: HarperBusiness, 1994.

21. "To Make Ansley Largest Hotel in Southland." *Atlanta Constitution*, Mar. 30, 1919.

22. "Dinklers Close Lease on Ansley." *Atlanta Constitution*, Mar. 8, 1921.

23. Roberts and Graham, *Real Ones*, 170.

24. "Big Holstein Sale at Candler Farm on Thursday Last." *Atlanta Constitution*, Jan. 11, 1920.

25. Matthews, Antoinette Johnson. "Oakdale Road, Atlanta, Ga.," in *DeKalb County: Its History & Its People.* Atlanta, Ga.: Atlanta Historical Society, 1972.

CHAPTER 12. A New Cycle Begins

1. "Palatial Floating College Will Be Reconditioned Here." *Baltimore Sun*, Feb. 20, 1923.

2. "Social Items." *Atlanta Constitution*, July 10, 1920.

3. "Atlanta Has Her Navy if Switzerland Hasn't." *Atlanta Constitution*, Oct. 10, 1920.

4. "Forty Acres of Fairyland." *Atlanta Constitution*, Aug. 14, 1921.

5. Newton, Louie D. "Good Morning." *Atlanta Constitution*, May 25, 1943.

6. "Young Millionaire Fights Woman's Charges as Did Wealthy Father Who Foiled Plotters." *Buffalo Times* (N.Y.), Aug. 23, 1922.

7. "Jilted Beauty Says Candler Vowed His Love." *Washington Times*, Oct. 15, 1922.

8. "School on Ocean Wave Is Latest." *Evening Journal* (Wilmington, Del.), Nov. 27, 1922.

9. "Asa Candler, Jr., Will Head Novel Plan to Aid Boys." *Times* (Shreveport, La.), Nov. 8, 1922; "Transport Logan May Be Floating School." *Philadelphia Inquirer*, Nov. 10, 1922.

10. "Candler to Leave as Ex-Fiancee Sues." *Baltimore Sun*, Nov. 9, 1922.

11. "Manitoba: Atlantic Transport Line." 1998. http://www.titanicinquiry.org/ships /manitoba.php, accessed Oct. 25, 2020.

12. "Obituary, Col. E. T. Winston." *Daily Arkansas Gazette*, Feb. 17, 1923.

13. Auburn University Libraries, Auburn Special Collections. Zebulon Vance Judd Papers, 1876–1960.

14. *School Life* 8, no. 8 (Apr. 1923): 192. Department of the Interior, Bureau of Education.

15. "Asa Candler, Jr., Will Head Novel Plan."

16. "School on Ocean Wave."

17. "Palatial Floating College"; "School on Ocean Wave"; *School Life* (Apr. 1923): 192.

18. "School on Ocean Wave."

19. "Candler Floating School." Candler Floating School Company flyer, 1923. In possession of author.

20. "Palatial Floating College."

21. "Obituary, Col. E. T. Winston."

22. "Palatial Floating College."

23. "Candler Floating School Postpones Maiden Voyage until September 1924." *Atlanta Constitution*, Apr. 3, 1923; "Ship 'College' Will Float around World to Visualize Studies for 400 Students." *Journal Times* (Racine, Wisc.), Apr. 14, 1923.

24. "Manitoba: Atlantic Transport Line."

25. "Candler Wins Quick Verdict over Widow." *Gadsden Daily Times-News* (Ala.), Feb. 6, 1924.

26. "Japanese Garden Is Setting for Miss Candler's Debut." *Atlanta Constitution*, Jan. 11, 1923.

27. Roberts and Graham, *Real Ones*, 306.

28. "Perilous Accidents to the Two Candler Brides That Set Atlanta to Talking." *St. Louis Post-Dispatch*, July 13, 1924.

29. "Graphics [*sic*] Films Formed." *Film Daily* 27, no. 28 (Jan.–June 1924): 9. https://lantern.mediahist.org/catalog/filmdaily2728newy_0249, accessed Nov. 1, 2020.

30. "Film Firm's Strickland Dies at 56." *Atlanta Constitution*, Aug. 18, 1954; Kessler, K. "History—Nassau Street Sessions." 2019. Nassau Street Sessions. http://www.nassaustreetsessions.com/history/, accessed Nov. 1, 2020.

31. Krows, A. E. "Educational Screen Combined with Visual Instruction News." *Motion Pictures—Not for Theaters* 15, no. 6 (June 1936): 167. https://issuu.com/nontheatrical/docs/motion_pictures_not_for_theaters, accessed Nov. 1, 2020; "Regional News from Correspondents: Atlanta." *Motion Picture News* 36, no. 1 (July 8, 1927): 63. https://archive.org/details/motion36moti/page/n175/mode/2up, accessed Nov. 1, 2020.

32. "Graphic Films Corporation." Advertisement. *City Builder* (Apr. 1925): 2. http://album.atlantahistorycenter.com/cdm/ref/collection/ACBuilder/id/6545, accessed Nov. 1, 2020.

33. "Diversified Farming in Colquitt Shown." *Atlanta Constitution*, Feb. 5, 1925; "Community Chest in Session Tonight." *Atlanta Constitution*, May 17, 1926; "Salmon Canning Industry Shown in Novel Movie Film." *Atlanta Constitution*, May 2, 1926; "Romance of Big Newspaper Will Be Shown at Howard." *Atlanta Constitution*, Aug. 7, 1926.

34. "Regional News from Correspondents: Atlanta." *Motion Picture News* 36, no. 1 (July 8, 1927): 63. https://archive.org/details/motion36moti/page/n175/mode/2up, accessed Nov. 1, 2020.

35. "Visit of Straus Revives Rumors of Great Store." *Atlanta Constitution*, Oct. 18, 1924.

36. "City and State Welcome Head of Macy Firm." *Atlanta Constitution*, Mar. 13, 1925.

37. "Strauss [*sic*] Impressed with Store Progress." *Atlanta Constitution*, Feb. 23, 1927.

38. Atlanta Preservation Center. "Davidson-Paxon [*sic*] / Macy's Department Store." 2011. http://www.atlantapreservationcenter.com/place_detail?id=50, accessed Nov. 1, 2020.

39. Application, National Register of Historic Places. 1982. https://npgallery.nps.gov/NRHP/AssetDetail/98a092c5-61a1-416a-bfaa-04d483b5fed8, accessed Nov. 2, 2020.

40. "Atlanta Urban Design Commission Nomination Resolution: Briarcliff Plaza Landmark District." 2017. https://www.atlantaga.gov/home/showdocument?id=28896, accessed Nov. 1, 2020.

41. "Candler Family Shows Faith in Atlanta by Buying Central Property: Group Owns More than $30,000,000 in Local Realty." *Atlanta Constitution*, Nov. 1, 1925.

42. "Prominent Shriners Named on New Mosque Committee." *Atlanta Constitution*, Sept. 11, 1925.

43. "$1,000,000 Drive for Great Shrine Mosque over Top." *Atlanta Constitution*, Oct. 17, 1925.

44. Ibid.

45. "Shriners from Atlanta Are Due This Morning." *Atlanta Constitution*, May 31, 1926.

46. "Cross Section of Life in Gate City of South." *Atlanta Constitution*, Apr. 30, 1932.

47. Sparks, Andrew. "Air Castle of the Jet Age." *Atlanta Journal-Constitution Magazine*, Apr. 27, 1958, 8. http://www.atlantatimemachine.com/misc/airport24.htm, accessed Nov. 1, 2020.

48. Garrett, Franklin M. *Atlanta and Environs: A Chronicle of Its People and Events, 1880s–1930s*. Athens: University of Georgia Press, 2011.

49. "$400,000 Enlargement Program under Way on White Provisions' Properties Here." *Atlanta Constitution*, Nov. 5, 1922.

50. "Stockyards in Atlanta Sold to White, Candler." *Star Tribune* (Minneapolis, Minn.), Nov. 11, 1923.

51. "Great Mule Mart Plans in Doubt." *Atlanta Constitution*, July 31, 1924.

52. Ibid.

53. "White on Stand in Own Defense." *Atlanta Constitution*, Aug. 6, 1926.

54. "White Indicted for Embezzlement." *Atlanta Constitution*, Mar. 3, 1926.

55. "Candler on Stand at White Trial." *Atlanta Constitution*, Aug. 3, 1926.

56. "White Found 'Not Guilty' on Embezzlement Charge." *Atlanta Constitution*, Aug. 7, 1926.

57. "Work of a Pioneer." *Atlanta Constitution*, Oct. 26, 1926.

58. "Livestock Trade Growth Bringing Wealth to Georgia." *Atlanta Constitution*, Jan. 29, 1928.

59. "Candler Buys Stock Yards for $500,000." *Atlanta Constitution*, May 11, 1928.

60. "Asa Candler, Jr., Winner in Fight over Stockyards." *Atlanta Constitution*, Mar. 15, 1929.

61. "Asa Candler Buys 50-Year Leasehold in Fulton Hotel." *Atlanta Constitution*, May 4, 1930.

CHAPTER 13. Buddie the Phoenix: The Great Sell-Off

1. "Coca-Cola Man Has No Time For Reporters." *Honolulu Star-Bulletin*, Nov. 11, 1927.

2. "Smuggled Pearls Are Surrendered by Asa G. Candler, Jr." *Weekly Town Talk* (Alexandria, La.), Feb. 14, 1925.

3. Roberts and Graham, *Real Ones*, 193.

4. "Storm and Sea Rescue Recounted." *Los Angeles Times*, Oct. 31, 1927.

5. "Coca-Cola Man Has No Time for Reporters."

6. "Candler Yacht Is Moored Here." *Tampa Times*, Mar. 5, 1928.

7. "Candler Yacht Gives Aid in Harbor Fire." *Tampa Tribune*, Mar. 29, 1928.

8. "Liquor Is Seized Aboard Yacht of Asa Candler, Jr." *Miami News-Record*, Apr. 1, 1928.

9. Louis, Bertin M. *My Soul Is in Haiti: Protestantism in the Haitian Diaspora of the Bahamas.* New York: New York University Press, 2016, 54.

10. "Three Ships Leave on Cruises Today." *New York Times*, Jan. 22, 1929.

CHAPTER 14. Airplanes and the Dark Arts

1. "Love Affair of Filipino and American Ends in Two Deaths." *Albuquerque Journal*, Jan. 19, 1931.

2. "Aero Club Plans Change in Policy." *Atlanta Constitution*, Aug. 3, 1919.

3. "Asa G. Candler, Jr., Purchases Plane to Expedite Visits to Multiple Interests." *Atlanta Constitution*, Oct. 23, 1929.

4. Hinton, G. "Air Views." *Atlanta Constitution*, Nov. 26, 1931.

5. "Aviation Body to Discuss Airport Fire Hazard Today." *Atlanta Constitution*, Mar. 6, 1930.

6. "Airport Damaged by $140,000 Fire." *Atlanta Constitution*, Mar. 5, 1930.

7. "Lockheed Vega Model 5B NC49M." 2006. https://dmairfield.org/, accessed Nov. 1, 2020.

8. "Plane and Auto Are Graduation Gifts to Two Daughters of Asa Candler, Jr." *Atlanta Constitution*, June 5, 1930.

9. "New York Full of Wizards Big and Small." *Cumberland Evening Times* (Md.), May 16, 1930.

10. Roberts and Graham, *Real Ones*, 200.

11. Soper, *These Found the Way*, 58.

12. Cox, J. "Houdini and Zukor." *Wild about Harry*. Feb. 1, 2012. https://www .wildabouthoudini.com/2012/02/houdini-and-zukor.html, accessed Nov. 1, 2020.

13. Smith, Rollin. *The Aeolian Pipe Organ and Its Music*. Villanova, Pa.: Organ Historical Society, 1998.

14. "California, Passenger and Crew Lists, 1882–1959." *Ancestry*. https://www .ancestry.com/search/collections/7949/, accessed Oct. 18, 2017.

15. "Mr. and Mrs. Asa Candler, Jr., Fly to St. Petersburg from Home in Atlanta, Ga., in Three Hours." *Evening Independent* (Massillon, Ohio), Jan. 11, 1930.

16. "School Boy Given Ovation by Magicians for Ability." *Akron Beacon Journal* (Ohio), June 9, 1928.

17. "Business Men Find Thrill in Magic." *Star Press* (Muncie, Ind.), July 14, 1929.

18. "New York Full of Wizards Big and Small."

19. Bill Schulert in discussion with the author, Aug. 2019.

20. David Ginn in discussion with the author, Aug. 2019.

21. "The Great Raymond Entertained at Asa Candler's Home on His Visit to Atlanta." *Seven Circles* 2, no. 2 (Nov. 1931): 26. http://askalexander.org/display/7466 /Seven+Circles+Vol+02/, accessed Nov. 2, 2020.

22. Ibid., 27.

23. Sachs, Bill. "Hocus Pocus." *Billboard* (May 5, 1951): 44.

24. Ibid.

25. "Filipino Butler and Girl Found Dead in Automobile on Asa Candler Estate." *Atlanta Constitution*, Jan. 19, 1931; "Stenographer and Butler Are Found Murdered in Car." *Orlando Sentinel* (Fla.), Jan. 19, 1931; "Atlanta Girl Found Dead." *Macon Telegraph Morning* (Ga.), Jan. 19, 1931; "Police Doubt Girl Entered Suicide Pact." *Orlando Evening Star*, Jan. 19, 1931; "Victim of Filipino Laid to Last Rest." *Atlanta Constitution*, Jan. 20, 1931; "Miss Gladys Frix Buried in Austell Cemetery Monday." *Marietta Journal* (Ga.), Jan. 22, 1931.

26. Roberts and Graham, *Real Ones*, 257.

27. U.S. Census, 1930. Georgia, DeKalb, Militia District 0531 ED 23. https://

familysearch.org/ark:/61903/3:1:33SQ-GR46-D4Y?mode=g, accessed Nov. 2, 2020.

28. "Love Affair of Filipino and American Ends in Two Deaths."

29. "Filipino Slew Atlanta Girl and Ended Life with Gun, Verdict of Coroner's Jury." *Atlanta Journal*, Jan. 19, 1931.

30. Hinnershitz, Stephanie. *A Different Shade of Justice: Asian American Civil Rights in the South*. Chapel Hill: University of North Carolina Press, 2017, 125.

31. Deneen, P. "Gladys Mildred Frix (1911–1931)." 2010. https://www.findagrave .com/memorial/48105809/gladys-mildred-frix, accessed Nov. 2, 2020.

32. "Application for Burial." West View Cemetery, Atlanta, Ga. Photocopies provided to author, 2019.

33. "New Plane Is Ready for Debut." *Los Angeles Times*, July 7, 1931.

34. "Lockheed Vega Model 5B NC49M."

35. "Two Planes Speed over U.S.: Try for New Records." *Belvidere Daily Republican* (Belvidere, Ill.), July 11, 1931.

36. "Coca-Cola King Escapes Injury in Plane Tilt." *Marshall News Messenger* (Tex.), July 12, 1931.

37. Hinton, G. "Air Views." *Atlanta Constitution*, Dec. 6, 1931.

38. "Aviator Describes Ferry Experience." *Atlanta Constitution*, Oct. 23, 1941.

39. Soper, *These Found the Way*, 57.

CHAPTER 15. Lions and Tigers and . . . Elephants?

1. Rogers, Ernest. *Peachtree Parade: Rollicking Recollections of Atlanta's Favorite Columnist*. Atlanta, Ga.: Tupper & Love, 1956, 171.

2. McKoy, R. "In the Eddies of the News Stream." *Atlanta Constitution*, Dec. 27, 1931.

3. "Asa Candler Buys Score of Animals for Private View." *Atlanta Constitution*, Mar. 2, 1932; "Rosie Leaves Sands for Atlanta's Zoo." *Palm Beach Post*, Apr. 25, 1932.

4. Ostrow, A. "Violinist to Zoo Keeper." *St. Louis Post-Dispatch*, Jan. 3, 1954.

5. Ibid.; "Names Make News." *Time Magazine* (Aug. 15, 1932). http://content.time. com/time/magazine/article/0,9171,744188,00.html, accessed Nov. 2, 2020; "Animals Arrive Today for Asa Candler Zoo." *Atlanta Constitution*, Apr. 20, 1932.

6. Rogers, *Peachtree Parade*, 171.

7. "Names Make News."

8. "Candler Zoo Is Opened; Admission Fee Charged." *Atlanta Constitution*, Sept. 3, 1932.

9. "New Crop of Short-Lived Clues Given." *Marshall News Messenger* (Tex.), Apr. 23, 1932.

10. Ostrow, "Violinist to Zoo Keeper."

11. "Beautiful Briarcliff Pool Is Open to Public." *Atlanta Journal*, June 11, 1933.

12. "Candler, in First Statement on Zoo, Denies Neighbors' Nuisance Charges." *Atlanta Constitution*, Aug. 12, 1932.

13. "Druid Hills Residents to Ask Asa G. Candler to Remove Zoo." *Atlanta Constitution*, Aug. 6, 1932.

14. "Crippled Children's Hospital Benefits from Opening of Candler Zoo Saturday." *Atlanta Constitution*, Aug. 11, 1932.

15. "The Zoo at Hearst Castle." 2013. https://hearstcastle.org/history-behind -hearst-castle/the-castle/the-zoo/, accessed Nov. 2, 2020.

16. "Atlanta Folk Protest Zoo in Candler's Back Yard." *Altoona Tribune* (Pa.), Aug. 15, 1932.

17. "High Court Upholds Baboon Case Verdict." *Atlanta Constitution*, May 30, 1935.

18. "Candler, in First Statement on Zoo, Denies Neighbors' Nuisance Charges."

19. "Druid Hills Residents to Ask Asa G. Candler to Remove Zoo."

20. "Candler Dismisses Curator of Zoo, Seeks to Sell Animal Collection." *Atlanta Constitution*, Sept. 21, 1933.

21. "Extortioner Trapped." *Index-Journal* (Greenwood, S.C.), Mar. 2, 1933.

22. "Cross Sections of Life in Gate City of South." *Atlanta Constitution*, Apr. 30, 1932.

23. "Asa Candler Zoo Sued for $25,000." *Atlanta Constitution*, Mar. 2, 1933.

24. "Asa G. Candler Sued for Attorney's Fees." *Atlanta Constitution*, Aug. 24, 1933.

25. "Wife of Asa Candler Sueing [*sic*] for $250,000 Additional from Estate." *Greenville News*, Aug. 16, 1933.

26. Ostrow, "Violinist to Zoo Keeper."

27. "Candler Zoo Is to Be Disposed by the Owner." *Middlesboro Daily News* (Ky.). Sept. 21, 1933.

28. "Candler Dismisses Curator of Zoo, Seeks to Sell Animal Collection."

29. "Asa Candler, Jr., Denies He Plans to Sell Zoo." *Atlanta Constitution*, Sept. 22, 1933.

30. "Coca, Lonely at Grant Park Home, Wimpers for Cola, Briarcliff Pal." *Atlanta Constitution*, Oct. 29, 1933.

31. "Sale of Lockheed by Asa G. Candler Reported at Field." *Atlanta Constitution*, Oct. 12, 1933.

32. "Candler's Injunction against Zoo Tax Voided." *Baltimore Sun*, Feb. 25, 1934; "Decatur Court Hears Candler Monkey Suit." *Atlanta Constitution*, Nov. 15, 1933.

33. "Candler Loses Suit on Zoo Equipment." *Atlanta Constitution*, July 18, 1934.

34. "Suit Asks $18,000 for Injury to Child." *Atlanta Constitution*, Mar. 29, 1935.

35. "Grant Park Zoo Fund Still $10,600 Short." *Atlanta Constitution*, Apr. 21, 1935.

36. "Rosie: The Circus Elephant." 2014. *Awesome Stories*. https://www. awesomestories.com/asset/view/ROSIE-the-CIRCUS-ELEPHANT-Water-for -Elephants, accessed Nov. 3, 2020.

37. Ostrow, "Violinist to Zoo Keeper."

38. "Asa Candler and Wife Hurt in Auto Accident." *Atlanta Constitution*, Aug. 23, 1935.

39. Soper, *These Found the Way*.

40. St. Andrews Bay Yacht Club. "Our History." 2015. https://stabyc.com/About-Us/History-(1).aspx, accessed Nov. 3, 2020.

41. "9 Gulf Crews in Yacht Race." *Pensacola News Journal*, May 26, 1937.

42. "Pensacola Wins First Place in Candler Regatta." *Pensacola News Journal*, June 1, 1936.

CHAPTER 16. Laundry and the Eternal

1. Soper, *These Found the Way*, 56.

2. "Georgia—South's Stepping Stone." *Motor Age* 16, no. 19 (Nov. 4, 1909): 21.

3. Clemmons, Jeff. *Atlanta's Historic Westview Cemetery*. Charleston, S.C.: History Press, 2018.

4. Ibid.

5. "Investment Company Acquires Hotel Here." *Atlanta Constitution*, Dec. 13, 1935.

6. "William Candler, Atlanta Hotel Man, Is Killed as Auto Strikes Cow on Highway near Valdosta." *Atlanta Constitution*, Oct. 3, 1936.

7. Soper, *These Found the Way*, 55–56.

8. Ibid., 57.

9. "Briarcliff, Inc. Buys Another Apartment." *Atlanta Constitution*, Sept. 3, 1939.

10. "Some of the 140 Pantex Laundry Presses at Briarcliff Laundry." Pantex Pressing Machine, Inc., postcard. In possession of author.

11. "Laundry Asked to Put $35,000 in Trust Fund." *Atlanta Constitution*, July 29, 1943.

12. "Candler Dedicates New Yacht Basin." *Atlanta Constitution*, Nov. 3, 1939.

13. Soper, *These Found the Way*, 60–62.

14. West View Abbey, Inc. "Announcing West View Abbey." *Atlanta Constitution*, Feb. 15, 1942.

15. "Insurance Law Violation Charged to Cemetery Group." *Atlanta Constitution*, June 16, 1942.

16. Clemmons, *Atlanta's Historic Westview Cemetery*.

17. "Georgia Ham from Asa Candler Wings Its Way to Churchill." *Atlanta Constitution*, Mar. 25, 1943.

18. Newton, L. D. "Good Morning." *Atlanta Constitution*, Dec. 8, 1937.

19. Brumfield, B. B. "Journalettes." *McComb Daily Journal* (Miss.), Mar. 29, 1943.

20. Worden, M., and Rosallini, G. "The Dry Drunk Syndrome: A Toximolecular Interpretation." 2007. http://pdfs.semanticscholar.org/bd5f/645676fddc90b6d25374945a6d4de2fe1a2.pdf, accessed Jan. 9, 2021.

21. "Dear Buddy [sic]." *Atlanta Constitution*, June 20, 1943.

CHAPTER 17. Buddie Candler on Trial

1. "Briarcliff Jury Hears Insurers." *Atlanta Constitution*, Apr. 13, 1944.
2. *Briarcliff Inc. v. Kelley*, 198 Ga. 390, 31 S.E.2d 586 (Ga. 1944).
3. "Fire Insurance of Briarcliff Only $1,000." *Atlanta Constitution*, July 21, 1943.
4. "Laundry Asked to Put $35,000 in Trust Fund." *Atlanta Constitution*, July 29, 1943.
5. "Candlers Involved in Laundry Case." *Atlanta Constitution*, Aug. 21, 1943.
6. "Laundry Suit Testimony Aimed at Candler Status." *Atlanta Constitution*, Dec. 15, 1943.
7. "Records Submitted in Laundry Fire." *Atlanta Constitution*, Dec. 17, 1943.
8. "Fraud Indictments Name Asa Candler, Jr., 2 Sons." *Atlanta Constitution*, Feb. 2, 1944.
9. Ibid.
10. "Pulse of the Public." *Atlanta Constitution*, June 24, 1943.
11. "Asa Candler and Aids [*sic*] Indicted." *Greenville News* (S.C.), Feb. 2, 1944.
12. "Candlers Plan Soldier Memorial Chapel, Cemetery in West View." *Atlanta Constitution*, Mar. 21, 1944.
13. "Briarcliff Jury Hears Insurers."
14. "Young Candler Defines Job." *Atlanta Constitution*, Apr. 20, 1944.
15. "Candler Freed in Fraud Case." *Miami News*, Apr. 21, 1944.
16. "3 Candlers Acquitted." *New York Times*, Apr. 22, 1944.
17. "All 3 Candlers Acquitted of Fraud Charges." *Atlanta Constitution*, Apr. 22, 1944.
18. *Briarcliff Inc. v. Kelley*, 586.
19. "Fire Destroys Building." *Atlanta Constitution*, June 18, 1944.

CHAPTER 18. The Long, Slow Slide

1. "Candler Promises to Make West View Beauty Spot." *Atlanta Constitution*, Nov. 24, 1949.
2. Clemmons, *Atlanta's Historic Westview Cemetery*.
3. Abrams, *Formula for Fortune*.
4. Troy, J. "All in the Game." *Atlanta Constitution*, Jan. 31, 1946.
5. "Candler's Thunderbolt Yacht Basin Offered for Sale at Savannah." *Atlanta Constitution*, July 12, 1946.
6. "Ga. Legion to Get New Headquarters." *Clarion-Ledger* (Jackson, Miss.), July 25, 1946.
7. "Atlanta Hotel Evicts Eleven Women Guests." *Miami News*, July 3, 1946.
8. Harris, P. "Things Were Different in Biblical Days." *Miami News*, July 14, 1946; O'Donnell, R. "Top o' the Morning." *Tennessean* (Nashville), Oct. 30, 1946.

9. "Candler Bags Elk, Moose." *Jackson Hole Courier* (Wyo.), Sept. 19, 1946; Roberts and Graham, *Real Ones*, 220.

10. "Baptist Leader Calls for World Christian Rule." *Town Talk* (Alexandria, La.), Nov. 22, 1946.

11. Edgar Chambers IV in discussion with the author, May 2018; Roberts and Graham, *Real Ones*, 320–321.

12. "Coca-Cola Co-Founder, Asa Candler, Jr., Dies." *Battle Creek Enquirer* (Mich.), Jan. 12, 1953.

13. "Hospital Site, Landmark Sold." *Atlanta Constitution*, June 24, 1949.

14. Soper, *These Found the Way*, 61.

15. "Staff, Students Restore Chapel Organ; Fully Functional First Time in 29 Years." 2018. https://www.charlestonsouthern.edu, accessed Nov. 1, 2020.

16. Clemmons, *Atlanta's Historic Westview Cemetery*; and Edgar Chambers IV interview, June 6, 2018.

17. "Lot Owners Say Rights Violated." *Atlanta Constitution*, July 14, 1949.

18. Soper, *These Found the Way*.

19. "Candler Promises to Make West View Beauty Spot." *Atlanta Constitution*, Nov. 24, 1949.

20. "West View Books Denied Auditors, Counsel Charges." *Atlanta Constitution*, Nov. 26, 1949.

21. Clemmons, *Atlanta's Historic Westview Cemetery*, 114.

22. Sibley, C. "Atlanta's Just Wild about Elephants." *Atlanta Constitution,* Mar. 10, 1950.

23. Sibley, C. "Coca II Gets Heroine's Welcome in Atlanta." *Atlanta Constitution*, Apr. 9, 1950.

24. "Candler Reported Slightly Better." *Atlanta Constitution*, June 24, 1950.

25. "Asa Candler's Right to Sell Is Affirmed." *Atlanta Constitution*, Feb. 15, 1951.

26. *West View Corporation v. Alston et al.* 208 Ga. 122, 65 S.E.2d 406 (Ga. 1951).

27. Clemmons, *Atlanta's Historic Westview Cemetery*; "West View's New Owners Plan Improvements." *Atlanta Constitution*, Jan. 10, 1951.

28. "Kin of Coca-Cola Founder Claimed." *Daily Times* (New Philadelphia, Ohio), Jan. 12, 1953; Abrams, *Formula for Fortune*, 235.

29. "Candler Will Said to Top $2 Million." *Atlanta Constitution*, Jan. 17, 1953.

30. "Asa Candler, Jr., Coca-Cola Heir, Developer, Dies." *Atlanta Constitution*, Jan. 12, 1953.

31. Edgar Chambers IV in discussion with the author, May 2018.

32. McNeel Marble-Granite Catalog. 1932. HathiTrust Digital Library. https://hdl .handle.net/2027/nnc2.ark:/13960/t9h51cr2d, accessed Sept. 4, 2022.

CHAPTER 19. Buddie's Best Buds

1. Herman Talmadge quoted in "Asa Candler Jr., Coca-Cola Heir, Developer, Dies." *Atlanta Constitution*, Jan. 12, 1953.

2. "Man Who Invaded Owens Home Held as Blackmailer." *Atlanta Constitution*, Sept. 18, 1915.

3. Ibid.

4. "Burnett Is Freed, Then Rearrested on Drunk Charge." *Atlanta Constitution*, Sept. 30, 1915.

5. "Chemicals Used in Drycleaning Operations." Wisconsin Department of Natural Resources. 2002. https://dnr.wi.gov/topic/SmallBusiness/documents /drycleaning/ChemicalsUsedInDrycleaningOperations.pdf, accessed Nov. 4, 2020.

6. "Stoddard Solvent." Agency for Toxic Substances and Disease Registry. U.S. Department of Health and Human Services. https://www.atsdr.cdc.gov/substances /toxsubstance.asp?toxid=73, accessed Nov. 4, 2020.

7. "Mrs. Candler Freed by Court." *Atlanta Constitution*, Mar. 4, 1924.

8. Ibid.

9. "Mrs. Candler Is Freed; Sleuth's Work Is Bared by Chief of Police." *Houston Post*, Mar. 4, 1924.

10. "Mrs. Asa Candler and Companions Face Trial Today." *Atlanta Constitution*, Mar. 3, 1924.

11. "Police Committee Suspends Chief Beavers on Charge of Violating Rules of Department." *Atlanta Constitution*, Mar. 26, 1924.

12. "Trial of Beavers Again Postponed." *Atlanta Constitution*, Oct. 17, 1917.

13. "Police Chief Beavers Fired from Department." *Atlanta Constitution*, Apr. 12, 1924.

14. "Mayor Surprised He Was Not Sued by Chief Beavers." *Atlanta Constitution*, June 10, 1924.

15. "Beavers' Return to Chief's Post to Be Unopposed." *Atlanta Constitution*, May 16, 1926.

16. Roberts and Graham, *Real Ones*, 237.

17. "Georgia Death Index, 1933–1998," s.v. Landers Anderson (1887–1954). FamilySearch.org.

18. U.S. Census, 1910. Atlanta, Ward 9 ED 112. https://www.familysearch.org /ark:/61903/3:1:33SQ-GRJZ-WZB?i=13&cc=1727033, accessed Nov. 2, 2020.

19. U.S. Census, 1920. Georgia, DeKalb, Decatur ED 11. https://www.familysearch. org/ark:/61903/3:1:33SQ-GR6H-XB1?cc=1488411, accessed Nov. 2, 2020.

20. U.S. Census, 1930. Georgia, DeKalb, Militia District 0531 ED 23. https:// familysearch.org/ark:/61903/3:1:33SQ-GR46-D4Y?mode=g, accessed Nov. 2, 2020.

21. U.S. Census, 1940. Georgia, DeKalb, Militia District 531, Emory, Tract DC-4
. https://www.familysearch.org/ark:/61903/3:1:3QS7–89M1-WX2J?i=15, accessed
Nov. 2, 2020.

22. Roberts and Graham, *Real Ones*, 238.

23. "Lula Mae Ware: Family-Placed Death Notice." 2012. https://www.legacy.com
/obituaries/atlanta/obituary.aspx?n=lula-mae-ware&pid=159877340&fhid=5031,
accessed Oct. 25, 2020.

24. Edgar Chambers IV in discussion with the author, May 2018.

25. U.S. Census, 1950. Center Hill, Fulton, Georgia. https://www.ancestry.com
/sharing/30192284?h=572551, accessed Aug. 23, 2022.

26. "Obituary: Lander Anderson." *Atlanta Constitution*, Sept. 11, 1954.

27. "Candler Will Said to Top $2 Million." *Atlanta Constitution*, Jan. 17, 1953.

CHAPTER 20. What's Next for Briarcliff Mansion?

1. "Forty Acres of Fairyland." *Atlanta Constitution*, Aug. 14, 1921.

2. David C. Payne in discussion with the author, June 2022.